CLASS AND HEALTH: research and longitudinal data, ed. by Richard G. Wilkinson. Tavistock/Methuen, 1987 (c1986). 223p bibl indexes 86-5972. 39.95 ISBN 0-422-60360-0. RA 418. CIP

The effects of socioeconomic station, studied in Great Britain as class, are not easily discerned as far as health or illness are concerned. In the US such matters are studied with great difficulty because of the relative lack of distinction between socioeconomic groups. For this reason, studies from Britain may provide clues to various factors applicable to other populations. Such works are often dry or arcane, laden with statistical data and interpretations. This little volume is a combination of both workshop and independent papers. The thesis of the editors is that a disparity in health outcome between social classes is widening despite secular changes in causes of death and overall improvement in health and working conditions. The advantage of British studies is their long-term nature and intergenerational comparisons. This feature somewhat overcomes the two fundamental problems of confounding variables and ascertainment, which this work effectively addresses. Extremely well referenced, the volume also includes a comprehensive listing of longitudinal studies in Great Britain on health matters from many different aspects. The focus of the book limits its audience to researchers and health policymakers. Upper-division and graduate collections.—*D.R. Shanklin, University of Chicago*

CLASS *and* HEALTH

CLASS *and* HEALTH

RESEARCH and LONGITUDINAL DATA

Edited by

Richard G. Wilkinson

for the
Economic and Social
Research Council

TAVISTOCK PUBLICATIONS
London and New York

First published in 1986 by
Tavistock Publications Ltd
11 New Fetter Lane, London EC4P 4EE

Published in the USA by
Tavistock Publications
in association with Methuen, Inc.
29 West 35th Street, New York, NY 10001

Typeset by Keyset Composition, Colchester, Essex
Printed in Great Britain at the University Press, Cambridge

British Library Cataloguing in Publication Data

Class and health: research and longitudinal
data.
1. Social medicine
I. Wilkinson, Richard G.
362.1'042 RA418
ISBN 0-422-60360-0

Library of Congress Cataloging in Publication Data

Class and health.
Includes bibliographies and index.
1. Social medicine—Great Britain. 2. Mortality—
Great Britain. 3. Social classes—Great Britain.
4. Social medicine—Great Britain—Longitudinal
studies. 5. Mortality—Great Britain—Longitudinal
studies. 6. Social classes—Great Britain—Longitudinal
studies. I. Wilkinson, Richard G. [DNLM: 1. Health
Services Accessibility—Great Britain. 2. Longitudinal
Studies—Great Britain. 3. Mortality—Great Britain.
4. Socioeconomic Factors—Great Britain.
WA 900 Fal C57]
RA 418.3.G7C56 1986   362.1'0941   86-5972
ISBN 0-422-60360-0

Contents

List of contributors

M. BLAXTER is a Research Fellow in the School of Economic and Social Studies at the University of East Anglia.

A. J. FOX is Professor of Social Statistics and Director of the Social Statistics Research Unit at City University, London.

P. O. GOLDBLATT is a Senior Research Fellow in the Social Statistics Research Unit at City University, London.

D. R. JONES is a Senior Lecturer in Epidemiology at the Department of Clinical Epidemiology and Social Medicine, St George's Hospital Medical School, London.

J. Le GRAND is a Senior Research Fellow at the Suntory Toyota International Centre for Economics and Related Disciplines at the London School of Economics.

M. G. MARMOT is Professor of Community Medicine at University College and Middlesex Hospital Medical School, London.

K. A. MOSER is a Research Fellow in the Social Statistics Research Unit at City University, London.

M. E. J. WADSWORTH is Director of the Medical Research Council National Survey of Health and Development, in the Department of Epidemiology and Community Health at University College and Middlesex Hospital Medical School, London.

R. G. WILKINSON is a Research Fellow in the Centre for Medical Research at the University of Sussex.

Preface

The initiative for the publication of this book came from an ESRC committee on inequalities in health, chaired by Professor Raymond Illsley. The plan was to publish some of the papers given at a small, ESRC-funded workshop set up to identify the main issues for future research in the field; however, as things have turned out, only four of the papers presented here were first prepared for that workshop. The book has developed into an attempt to indicate some of the key areas of research undertaken since the publication of the Black Report on inequalities in health and then to look briefly at some of the opportunities for further research.

When the Black Report was written, there were a number of crucial issues on which evidence was almost entirely lacking. Little was known either of the soundness of the main measures of class differences in health or of the causes of those differences. As a result, many of the report's policy recommendations were based largely on surmise and, inevitably, this weakness was exploited by the report's opponents. Since then, however, the picture has become a good deal clearer in several important respects. Research has begun to fill in a few of the gaps in our knowledge. In many ways, what emerges from such research bears out the basic soundness of the Black Report. It seems the authors were largely correct in their understanding of the problem and in their recognition of its failure to go away on its own.

With the benefit of a more thorough analysis of previous figures behind us, we can now approach the 1981 figures of class differences in mortality with a little less uncertainty. What they tell us about trends in inequalities must surely gain urgent attention. The tendency for class differences in death rates to widen during previous periods of prosperity means that the most recent widening cannot be blamed on the economic recession alone. It would seem that the trends in mortality differentials raise fundamental questions about the nature of modern social development.

I am grateful to all contributors to this volume for their patience, both with me and with each other, which has at last brought this work to fruition. Many deadlines have passed and several papers have had to be revised since they were originally submitted. In particular I would like to thank Mildred Blaxter, whose painstaking review of British longitudinal studies not only met the first deadline but has since been brought right up to date and will serve as a valuable resource for researchers for many years to come.

Richard G. Wilkinson

CLASS *and* HEALTH

ONE

Socio-economic differences in mortality: interpreting the data on their size and trends

R. G. Wilkinson

Prior to the 1980s, it was widely assumed that Britain was becoming a more egalitarian society. The predominant impression was that class divisions and socio-economic inequalities were becoming less important. Although long-term changes in income distribution have been comparatively small, it seemed reasonable to assume that this was compensated for by the growth of welfare services and the increasing volume of protective and regulatory legislation.

In 1980, however, the Black Report—dealing with class differences in health—seemed to cast serious doubt on this picture. Not only did it draw attention to very large differences in death rates between occupational classes but it also suggested that these differences were not declining (DHSS 1980). The crucial figures are reproduced in *Table 1.1*. They show that mortality differentials, as measured by age-standardized death rates for occupational classes, have increased since the 1930s. What these inequalities amount to can be summed up in terms of differences in life-expectancy. If the 1971 age-specific death rates for classes I (professional occupations) and V (unskilled manual occupations) were applied throughout the lives of a cohort, they would produce a difference in life-expectancy at birth of just over seven years (Registrar General 1978). This amounts to a lower-class disadvantage of about 10 per cent of life.

The figures in *Table 1.1* provided the core of the Black Report: indeed, as the best record we have of the changing social distribution of health in British society, they may be seen as its rationale. The issue of the size and trends in class differences in mortality that these figures raise is clearly crucial, not only to health but to our understanding of the direction of modern social development. The problems of measurement are complicated, however, and the different interpretations of the data are

Table 1.1 *Mortality by social class 1931–81 (Men, 15–64 years, England and Wales)*

Class	1931	1951	1961*	1971*	1981**
I professional	90	86	76 (75)	77 (75)	66
II managerial	94	92	81	81	76
III skilled manual and non-manual	97	101	100	104	103
IV semi-skilled	102	104	103	114	116
V unskilled	111	118	143 (127)	137 (121)	166

*To facilitate comparisons, figures shown in parentheses have been adjusted to the classification of occupations used in 1951. ** Men, 20–64 years, Great Britain.
Note: Figures are SMRs—which express age-adjusted mortality rates as a percentage of the national average at each date.
Source: DHSS (1980), Table 3.1.

controversial and have far-reaching implications. This chapter provides a discussion of the issues and reviews what recent research, including some of that presented in subsequent chapters of this volume, can tell us about how we should interpret the key figures in *Table 1.1*. The issues involved can only be disentangled by a careful assessment of the evidence.

The real size and trends in class differences in mortality are important not only because health matters in itself but also because health serves as a barometer of the social and economic conditions in which people live. Though we can quantify changes in class access to housing, education, jobs, and services, and can also describe some of the wider but perhaps less tangible changes in the social and physical environment in which people live, we do not know what all these changes add up to in human terms. There is no unified summary of changing class differentials in the quality of life and human welfare. Familiar summary measures of changes in the standard of living, such as indices of real income, suffer from a number of important weaknesses. Economic indicators are largely blind to the qualitative changes in the material and social environment, which are so crucial to human welfare. Health, on the other hand, is not only sensitive to qualitative changes in material life but the accumulating research evidence on stress, boredom, inactivity, depression, and lack of close social contact shows that it is also sensitive to many psychosocial aspects of the quality of life.

To point out the value of health as a social indicator does not detract from its own importance; rather, to do so serves as a reminder that insofar as the shortening of life is associated with poor social and economic circumstances, class differences in health represent a double injustice: life is short where its quality is poor. While we may focus principally on the shortening of life as a health issue, those who live on low incomes and in poor housing are no doubt more concerned with these problems for more immediate reasons than their effects on life-expectancy.

As a record of the social distribution of health in society, there are a number of ways in which the figures in *Table 1.1* may be affected by problems of measurement. An unwary acceptance of the picture they present of the size and trends in social inequalities in health may be unnecessarily alarmist; but if, after looking at the evidence, it appears that health differences really have failed to narrow, we would surely need to reassess the belief that the burden of socio-economic differentials has narrowed. Expectations of growing equality have understandably led several analysts to infer that problems of measurement have resulted in an exaggeration of the size of class differences in mortality and a masking of an assumed diminution of differentials. I shall try here to approach the evidence more even-handedly, assuming that problems in the data are as likely to have under- as overestimated the size of the differentials and their apparent resistance to narrowing during most of this century.

What, then, does the evidence tell us about the interpretation of the figures in *Table 1.1*? A potential weakness of these figures that has always been recognized comes from the fact that they depend on dividing the number of deaths in occupations stated on death certificates by the number of people in each occupation as recorded at census. Inaccurate occupational descriptions at either point will give rise to a considerable but usually random mismatch. More systematic biases may, however, creep in from sources such as a respectful desire among the next of kin (who are the informants) to 'promote the dead'.

Most of these problems were dealt with in the first publication (Fox and Goldblatt 1982) from the OPCS Longitudinal Study (LS). By following a 1 per cent sample of people identified at the 1971 census, the LS enabled deaths to be classified according to the occupations given at census. Using truly comparable numerators and denominators in the calculation of death rates, the results show 1971 mortality differentials much like those in *Table 1.1*. Part of the 1981 differential may, however, be spurious.

In chapter 2 of this volume, Marmot provides completely independent evidence of class differences in death rates among a cohort of civil servants classified by their employment grades. Using a different classification, he found the mortality gradient among civil servants (shown in his *Table 2.1*) is considerably steeper than that between the Registrar General's social classes, recorded in *Table 1.1*. As Marmot points out, there is a more than threefold difference in mortality between the lowest and highest grades in the civil service. As with the LS, the data on civil servants do not suffer from the problems of relating occupations on death certificates to separately determined population numbers in those occupations. The employment grade of everyone in the study was established at one point in time and individual deaths were related to the employment grade originally stated for that individual. As the study is of a well-defined group of employees and was carried out with the co-operation of the employer, it is likely that the occupational information is very accurate. It will, therefore, be free both of biases and of the fudging of differences that results simply from random occupational misclassification.

A more difficult question about the way we should interpret the observed class differences in health concerns the possible contribution of social mobility. As early as 1955, Illsley published evidence suggesting that social mobility discriminated in favour of the healthy and against the unhealthy (Illsley 1955). More recently, Stern has expressed this possibility in terms of a theoretical model, showing how, under various assumptions, social class differences in health could occur simply as a result of the healthy moving up and the unhealthy moving down the social scale (Stern 1983). This is an important issue because it suggests that to some extent inequalities in health are not attributable to structural socio-economic inequalities. Instead of saying that people are less healthy because they are in lower classes, it suggests that they are in lower classes because they are less healthy.

To analyse this possibility, we must start off by distinguishing between two different ways in which social mobility could be selective in relation to health. A person's chances of upward or downward mobility could be influenced either directly by their current, or manifest, health status, or indirectly through selection according to factors associated with health, such as height or education. In the first case, long-term illness or disability during any period in a person's working life may affect their job prospects. Among young people, it may restrict initial job choices, while later in life it may force people to move to less demanding and perhaps lower-status jobs. The mobility chances of those who suffer from chronic illnesses or disabilities throughout their lives would be most affected. An important factor that reduces the size of this effect on the recorded class differences in death rates is that the social class classification is based on economic activity. People who are not economically active are excluded from the classification (except in special tabulations which may classify wives by husbands', or children by fathers', occupations). What may be more important to the class differences in health, as they are recorded, is the impact of the much greater burden of illness later in life. Social class at death—based on a person's last full-time occupation as stated on the death certificate—may be substantially affected by the downward mobility of those who are forced by illness to take up less demanding jobs later in life.

A paper by Fox, Goldblatt, and Jones (published here as chapter 3) examines this possibility using more data from the LS. By classifying deaths during the period 1976–81 according to the person's social class at the 1971 census, the authors have been able to cut out the effect of mobility during the last 5–10 years of life, when the impact of ill health would be at its maximum. After comparing the size of class differentials in death rates produced by this method with the 1971 figures reproduced in *Table 1.1*, the study concludes that social mobility later in life contributes very little to the disparity in death rates between classes. This does not necessarily mean that there is no deterioration in the job prospects of those who do contract chronic illness towards the end of their working lives; it means that the proportion of people affected is too small to have a major influence on the overall figures.

This result is supported by data from other studies. Marmot's civil servants in chapter 2 show that the mortality gradient is maintained even ten years after the original classification by employment grade. American data from the Veterans' Administration show the same pattern: during a 23-year follow-up of some 85,000 veterans discharged from the US army in 1946, the mortality differentials by military rank showed 'little if any change' (Seltzer and Jablon 1977: 563).

Wadsworth's paper (chapter 4), based on the cohort of British births born in one week in 1946, tackles the problem of social mobility in relation to illness at younger ages. Instead of trying to see whether social mobility makes a significant contribution to the overall class differentials in health, he assesses the effects of childhood illness on people's subsequent chances of mobility. *Table 4.14* shows that serious illness in childhood is indeed related to subsequent downward mobility. Compared to those who were stationary or who moved up, an additional 8 or 9 per cent of boys who become downwardly mobile from the non-manual social classes had been seriously ill as children. Compared to other boys from manual social classes, an additional 11 per cent or so of those not working at the age of twenty-six had been seriously ill in childhood. (Corresponding figures for girls are not available because only a very small proportion of them were employed and could be classified by their own employment when con- tacted at twenty-six years old.) No doubt some of the boys who were seriously ill in childhood and were not working at twenty-six (in 1972) had permanent disabilities, which would have prevented them from ever becoming economically active and so would have excluded them from classification in the Registrar General's occupational classes. Ignoring these, it is possible to make a rough calculation of the contribution that this amount of illness-related downward mobility might make to the overall class differentials in health. To do so, it is necessary to know how predictive childhood illness is of poor health in adult life. *Table 4.8* shows that for boys and girls together, the risks of being seriously ill in their early twenties rose from 11 per cent to 25 per cent if they had been seriously ill as children. Applying this increase in risk to the total numbers ill in child- hood suggests that some 15 per cent of all serious illness in the early twenties is associated with previous childhood illness. This figure must then be coupled with the illness-related 8 or 9 per cent increase in downward mobility from (or within) non-manual classes and the 11 per cent increase in those remaining out of work among manual classes found in *Table 4.14*. To put the arithmetic in a nutshell: the proportion of adult illness which is associated with childhood illness, multiplied by the effect of childhood illness on mobility, gives the effect of the interaction between childhood illness and mobility on the social distribution of adult illness. The result of this calculation suggests that in this population only about 1.5 per cent of those seriously ill in their early twenties have suffered downward mobility as a result of previous childhood illness. Thus, as with the data on selective mobility later in life, this study provides no evidence for thinking that the class distribution of health is noticeably altered by the influence which childhood illness clearly can have on the direction of social mobility in early adulthood.

Having looked at evidence related to the effect of manifest illness on social mobility, we can now turn to the second way in which social mobility might discriminate between the healthy and the unhealthy. Instead of being affected directly by actual episodes of illness, social mobility might select for characteristics associated with a person's health potential.

Except for diseases in which a genetic component has been identified, the idea that people possess different health potentials, independent of later environmental influences, still needs to be clarified. To the extent that it is a physological but not a genetic concept, such a potential could presumably be determined by early environment. It could also include a behavioural component, perhaps related to such things as dietary habits and smoking, insofar as these are unaffected by social mobility. Fundamentally, however, it must include all those character-istics, whether embodied physiologically or behaviourally, that people take with them and that, to some extent, affect their health, independent of changes in their later socio-economic environment.
environment.

Evidence that social mobility may be selecting for factors that are usually closely related to health appears in Marmot's paper (chapter 2). He notes that the heights of civil servants are more closely related to his data on their achieved employment grade than to their class of origin. However, much the most important evidence that social mobility may be selective in relation to a prior health potential is provided by Illsley's work on perinatal mortality and the social mobility of mothers in Aberdeen. Instead of looking at the effects of prior episodes of illness on social mobility, Illsley related health status to prior mobility (Illsley 1955, 1980, 1983, 1986). Using figures from the Aberdeen Maternity and Neonatal

Data Bank, he was able to look at the social mobility of mothers by comparing the social class of their fathers to that of their husbands. *Table 1.2* shows the relationship between perinatal mortality rates and the social mobility of mothers. It can be seen that the mortality rates associated with these first births are more closely related to the class mothers marry into than to the class they came from. In effect, the health status (as measured by reproductive performance) of mothers who were upwardly mobile from any given class, is better than that of those who were downwardly mobile from the same class.

In itself, this is exactly the pattern one would expect if perinatal mortality were determined almost entirely by the environment during pregnancy

Table 1.2 *Social mobility and perinatal mortality: indices of perinatal mortality rates (births in Aberdeen 1951–80. Mothers classified by their fathers' and husbands' occupation)*

social class of fathers	social class of husbands			
	I–IIINM	IIIM	IV & V	all classes
I–IIINM	73	74	129	81
IIIM	80	107	119	109
IV & V	71	108	138	111
all classes	75	101	129	100

Note: mean = 100 = 24 deaths per 1000 births.
Source: Aberdeen Maternity and Neonatal Data Bank, calculated from Illsley (1983).

and so by class at marriage. Taken in isolation, the pattern of perinatal mortality rates shown in this table can be explained without reference to selective mobility. There is, of course, no lack of evidence that the outcome of pregnancy is affected by the environment during pregnancy. Among some of the better-known risk factors are the effects of smoking on birth-weight, the effects of stress on premature labour (Newton *et al.* 1979) and the effects of vitamin intake on birth defects (Smithells *et al.* 1983). Indeed, almost all non-genetic malformations result from environmental influences in early pregnancy and these make a very considerable contribution to perinatal mortality.

Illsley rejects this interpretation because additional data collected on mother's heights and school-leaving age show that these factors are related to social mobility in rather the same way that perinatal mortality is. Mothers who married upwards were taller, better educated, and probably better fed than other women in their class of origin. Similarly, those who married downwards fared worse than those in their class of origin, on each count. This is important because, in contrast to perinatal mortality rates, a woman's height and school-leaving age are unambiguously determined before marriage.

Essentially, the evidence that social mobility is selective for health rests on the similarity between the mobility data for perinatal mortality on the one hand and height and education on the other. Illsley believes that the similarity arises because in many respects the family background of mothers who became socially mobile was already typical of the class into which they were eventually to marry. In his words, 'change of class at marriage appears seldom to involve a substantial change in living standards' (Illsley 1955:1523). If the environment is relatively constant, then perhaps it does not matter whether perinatal risks are determined during pregnancy or earlier in a mother's life.

There can be little doubt that the Aberdeen data provide evidence that social mobility is selective for characteristics closely related to health. What we need to know is, how many of the class differentials in perinatal mortality are the result of selection? Unfortunately, Illsley does not tackle this question: the reader is left with the unlikely impression that class differences in perinatal mortality are entirely due to selection. Our best guide to the extent of health selection is the data on height, perhaps supported by the data on school-leaving age. Although there is also some supplementary information from special surveys on the IQ scores and nutrition of Aberdeen mothers during pregnancy, these factors are less clear indicators of the pre-mobility environment than height. In addition, survey numbers are too small to allow us to look at mobility flows in detail and the data are now over thirty years out of date. In contrast, the fact that height is more closely related to the class into which women marry than to their class of origin is very good evidence that social mobility is selective. Height is not only unambiguously determined before marriage but is also likely to serve as a proxy for nutritional status and is known to be an indicator of reproductive performance. When comparing the proportion of mothers over 5 ft 4 ins tall in social classes I and II (combined) with IV and V (combined), Illsley found a difference of 15.2 per cent when classified by class of upbringing. This increased to 18.3 per cent when classified by class of marriage (Illsley 1986). In other words, the height differential increases by some 20 per cent when classifying by class at marriage. The differential in school-leaving age increased similarly by 24 per cent. In contrast, the differential in perinatal mortality rates increased by some 116 per cent. However, as we saw in *Table 1.2*, the perinatal mortality rates of the different mobility streams can be explained just as well without reference to selection. The Aberdeen data on heights are not only the primary evidence that health selection is involved but are also the best guide as to the extent of its involvement. We can then only assume that selective mobility adds the same 20 per cent to the pre-mobility perinatal mortality differential as it adds to the height differential. Mortality differentials are, however, normally shown classified by class of marriage. As on this basis the observed perinatal mortality differential more than doubles, expressed as a percentage of this larger differential, the selective contribution is more than halved, to just under 10 per cent.

The same point about the size of the selective contribution to class differences in perinatal mortality can be made in another way. From the previous paragraph we can see that the ratio of the proportion of women under a given height (5 ft 4 ins) to the perinatal death rate changes according to whether one classifies by class of origin or class at marriage. This means that different processes are involved in the production of the differentials in each of the factors. To suggest, on the basis of the height data, that the perinatal mortality differences between classes at marriage are primarily the result of selection implies that the real risk of perinatal death associated with mother's height changes according to whether you classify by class of origin or class at marriage.

Before leaving the issue of selection, one difficulty which affects almost all data on intergenerational mobility should be mentioned. It is likely to affect the Aberdeen data as well as Marmot's finding that the heights of civil servants were more closely related to their achieved employment grade than to their class of upbringing. Because social mobility is measured by comparing the class of two different people's occupations (intergenerational mobility) or of one person's occupation at two different points in time (intragenerational mobility), inaccurate or inadequate occupational information resulting in misclassification will tend to exaggerate the scale of mobility. In a paper entitled *Social Class and Occupational Mobility Shortly Before Men Become Fathers*, Fox has illustrated the size of the problem that misclassification can cause in a large data set (Fox 1984). Of men registered as social class III (manual) at the 1971 census who had a baby in the same year, 10 per cent appeared from the birth records to have changed their social class. While one might expect some job-changing as men become fathers, it seems likely that most of this apparent mobility represents a reclassification of the same jobs. If 10 per cent can appear to change not only their jobs but also their class within a year, largely as a result of misclassification, it is clear that misclassification will sometimes make a substantial contribution to the impression of social mobility.

In studies of intergenerational mobility, the usual practice is to ask informants about their own and their fathers' occupations. Although it is often possible to check on the accuracy of occupational classifications in a small subsample of a population, it may be very difficult to do so in studies of intergenerational mobility, where the informant may be the only source of information on his or her parent's occupation. Inevitably, the information on a person's own occupation tends to be more accurate than that on his or her father's occupation. If the informants are classified more

accurately than their fathers, the distinctions between classes will be less
fudged. This effect alone, without any social mobility, would lead to
greater class differences in the younger generation. The Aberdeen women
were asked what their husbands' current occupations were and what their
fathers' occupations had been some ten or fifteen years earlier, when the
informants were still at school. The likely difference in the accuracy of the
information given is particularly important when we bear in mind that the
social class classification depends not only on someone's trade or skill but
also on factors that often require more detailed knowledge of their
working situation, such as whether they are supervised, unsupervised, or
supervise others. This means that the 20 per cent increase in the height
differential of mothers when classified by their husbands' rather than
their fathers' occupations may well be an overestimate of the selective
element in social mobility.

That the heights of civil servants should be more closely related to their
achieved employment grade than to their fathers' social class may reflect
differences in the two classifications as well as in the accuracy of the
information provided. Employment grade within the Civil Service provides a much clearer socio-economic ordering of the population than do
the Registrar General's occupational classes. We shall look briefly at
evidence on the economic heterogeneity of occupational classes below, but
in terms of factors such as incomes and education there can be little doubt
that the categories of employment grade achieve a much better sorting
than do occupational classes. In addition, the information on civil
servants' employment grade is likely to be almost 100 per cent accurate.
The same cannot be said of the classification of fathers' occupations. This
is why the mortality differentials found in this study are so much greater
than those shown in *Table 1.1*. It seems possible then that at least part of
the fit between the data on civil servants' heights and achieved employment grade is artefactual.

We can sum up the evidence on selective social mobility by saying that
although there is evidence that social mobility is affected by ill-health
and/or health potential, its contribution to observed class differences in
health is probably always small in relation to the overall size of the
mortality differentials. At older ages, the contribution may become almost
insignificant.

What does this tell us about the size of the class differences in
health that may legitimately be attributed to socio-economic inequalities in society? Selective social mobility has a small inflationary
effect on the size of differentials but we have to set against this the failure
of the Registrar General's occupational classification to provide a clear
rank ordering of the population in terms of socio-economic circumstances.
If we take income as a reasonable indicator of people's standard of living,

Table 1.3 *Gross weekly income by social class*

social class	median income (1971)	percentage of s.c. V
I	£44.14	200
II	£34.02	154
IIIN	£24.12	109
IIIM	£27.05	122
IV	£22.46	102
V	£22.09	100

Source: Registrar General (1978), page 151.

Table 1.4 *Distribution of earnings* within *occupations (1971 gross weekly earnings of full-time men)*

lowest 10% earned less than £19.7
lowest 25% earned less than £24.0
median £29.8
highest 25% earned more than £37.8
highest 10% earned more than £48.0

Note: The figures are averages across all occupations of percentile points taken within each occupation.
Source: Department of Employment (1971), Table 57.

it is clear that there are neither the differences between classes nor the homogeneity within classes that we might expect to find. As *Table 1.3* shows, in 1971 only classes I and II were clearly distinguished from others in terms of their median income. Not only was there no clear gradient across the other four classes but the differences were inconsequential. An impression of the degree of income variation within each class may be gained from *Table 1.4*, which gives an impression of the income distribution *within* occupations. Although the occupational classification on which this table is based is not the same as that used to allocate occupations to the Registrar General's classes, the variation of earnings within occupations suggests that any purely occupationally based class classification may be a poor guide to the standard of living.

If the variation in incomes, and perhaps by inference in the standard of living, is as great or greater within as between classes, serious problems arise about the uses to which this classification is put. In a great many research reports, occupational class is used as a control for the effects of different socio-economic circumstances. As a result, the researchers almost certainly underestimate the effects of socio-economic factors on the measures they are concerned with and are in danger of attributing them to other variables. In terms of the analysis of health differences, any failure of classification by occupational class to produce a neat ordering of the population in terms of fundamental socio-economic standards will mean that such a classification understates the true impact of socio-economic inequalities on health. This is confirmed once again by the comparison of the mortality differentials shown by the Registrar General's social classes and those produced by the more homogeneous classification of civil servants. In *Table 1.1*, the 1971 mortality in class V is almost 80 per cent higher than it is in class I; among the civil servants, however, the lowest grade has a mortality rate over three times as high as that of the administrators.

Crude though these comparisons are, they confirm that the health differences associated with socio-economic disparities are understated by the heterogeneous nature of the occupational class classification by very much more than they are overstated by selective social mobility. In other words, the true health costs of socio-economic inequalities are likely to be considerably greater than the well-known figures in *Table 1.1* suggest.

We can now move on from the question of the overall size of socio-economic differences in mortality to discuss the problems in interpreting the apparent *trends* in the size of class differences in mortality during recent decades. There are three key issues here: first, possible changes in the contribution of selective mobility over time; second, the shift in the population distribution away from class V and towards class I; third, the effects of successive revisions in the classification of occupations and their allocation to classes.

If the rate of social mobility increased, it would be reasonable to suppose that the contribution of selection to observed class differences in health would also have increased. Good evidence on the changing rate of mobility is scarce. To compare mobility rates at different points in time, it is necessary to use the same class classification at both points and to classify people at the same point in their respective careers. Virtually the only data which satisfy these conditions come from the Oxford Social Mobility Study. The study allows the mobility of different cohorts to be compared, contrasting each person's occupational class ten years after they entered the labour force with that of his or her father. The oldest cohort in the study was composed of people born in the years 1908–17, who would almost all have completed their first ten years in the labour force between 1932 and the early 1940s: some 45 per cent of this cohort were mobile in relation to their fathers' occupational class (Heath 1981: Tables 3.1 and 3.2). The proportion slowly increases for later cohorts until it reaches 51 per cent of those born in the years 1938–47, who would have been in the labour force for ten years somewhere between 1963 and 1972, when the survey was conducted. Earlier but less dependable figures from the Glass study (discussed by Heath 1981) suggest that the gentle rise in mobility recorded in the period covered by the Oxford study was preceded by a slight decline during the early years of the present century. For the period from about 1940 to 1970 the Oxford figures suggest that there was a rise of only about 6 per cent in the proportion of the population who were mobile. Whatever one's beliefs as to the selectivity of this mobility, such a small increase in mobility would clearly make only a trivial selective addition to the observed class differences in mortality. There is, then, no reason to think that social mobility has adversely affected the trends in the size of class differences in mortality.

The question of the upward shift in the class distribution of the population is quite separate from the issue of the rate of mobility. Both high and low rates of mobility are consistent with either a stable or a shifting class distribution of the population. While from the health point of view we are interested in the way the rate of mobility might affect the size of the selection effect, the upward shift in the population affects the proportion of the population covered by comparisons of class differences. During much of this century, net upward mobility has decreased the proportion of the population in classes IV and V and increased the proportion in classes I and II. This means that in making comparisons of the difference in death rates between these classes at different points in time, one is not comparing like with like. In 1931, classes I and II combined contained 14 per cent of the economically active male population (DHSS 1980). In 1971, this had risen to 23 per cent. During the same period the proportion in classes IV and V fell from 38 to 26 per cent.

In which direction will this upward shift in the class distribution of the population have distorted our view of changing class differences in mortality rates? It is worth noting that, despite the shift, it is still perfectly legitimate to compare changes in the death rates of particular occupations—say, building labourers—with average death rates for the population at different points in time, even if building labourers are a smaller proportion of the population than they once were. The point about the changing class distribution of the population, however, is usually made with an eye to the extent of inequality over the population as a whole. Given that we are unable to compare changing mortality differentials between constant proportions of the population at the top and bottom of the social scale, what are we to make of increasing mortality differentials as measured between changing proportions? An increase in the proportion of the population in classes I and II would, other things being equal, cause an apparent narrowing of mortality differentials, while a decrease in the proportion in classes IV and V would cause an apparent widening. The Black Report (DHSS 1980) gives figures for the changing distribution of the economically-active male population on a number of different bases. Taking figures of the class classifications used to derive the mortality rates in *Table 1.1*, the Report shows that between 1951 and 1971 the proportion of men in classes I and II increased by almost 6 per cent, while the proportion in classes IV and V decreased by almost 3 per cent (see *Table 1.5*). In itself, the fact that the upper classes increased a little faster than the lower classes decreased might lead one to expect that the apparent widening of mortality differences over that period was more likely to underestimate than overestimate the real divergence.

Fortunately, Koskinen has recently tackled this problem in an important new analysis using an 'index of dissimilarity' (Koskinen 1985). This index is calculated by simply halving the total, summed over all

Table 1.5 *Changing mortality ratios and the class distribution of the population (men, England and Wales)*

social class	1951	1961	1971
I & II SMR	91	80	80
% popn	18%	19%	23%
IV & V SMR	110	115	121
% popn	29%	29%	26%
Difference in SMRs	19	35	41

Note: Social class SMRs have been combined by weighting according to the proportion of the population in each class.
Source: DHSS (1980), Tables 3.1 and 3.16.

classes, of the absolute difference between the proportion of observed and the proportion of expected deaths in each class. This gave him the proportion of all deaths that would have to be redistributed between classes in order to yield the same age-standardized mortality in each class. He shows that this proportion doubled among men between 1931 and 1971 and doubled among married women between 1951 and 1971. Since 1951, class differences seem to have widened in absolute as well as relative terms. In an analysis by separate causes, Koskinen shows that an increasing lower-class disadvantage appears in a wide range of different diseases. The overall picture he provides of widening inequality is confirmed by Pamuk, using a different method for calculating the effects of the changing class distribution of the population (Pamuk 1985). (Her index was based on the slope of a regression equation, which related death rates for each class to the mid-point of each class's position in a cumulative frequency distribution of the total population, arranged in ascending class order.)

The remaining problem, which must briefly be mentioned, is the effect of revisions in the occupational classification and the allocation of occupations to classes. This problem was discussed in the 1971 occupational mortality tables (Registrar General 1978: 178–79), with charts that show that the trends in age-specific mortality in each class are generally similar to the trends in groups of representative occupations that have been analysed regularly in each class. Pamuk developed this kind of analysis much further, taking 143 occupations that she could trace consistently in the five occupational mortality reports 1921–71. She showed that the use of different class classifications had very little impact on the picture of trends in mortality differentials, even after allowing for the expansion and contraction of the numbers of people in the selected occupations (Pamuk 1985).

The trends identified by Koskinen and Pamuk inspire confidence not only because of the strength of their methods but also because of the similarity in their results. Both agree that male mortality differentials decreased between 1921 and 1931 and increased both absolutely and relatively in both decades 1951–71. The earliest figures for married women are for 1931 and show a decline in differentials between then and 1951. Between 1951 and 1971, Koskinen finds an absolute increase in mortality differentials whereas Pamuk finds only a relative increase. Pamuk also analyses trends in infant mortality and shows that while the rapid decline in infant death rates has produced an absolute decline in differentials, there has been a continuous relative increase since 1931. More recent work suggests that these trends continued to 1981 (McDowell and Marmot, forthcoming).

The period when we can be most confident of trends in mortality differentials is from 1951 onwards. During the decade 1951–61, there was (as *Table 1.5* shows) no appreciable shift in the class distribution of the population. The increase in mortality differentials between classes I and II combined and classes IV and V combined (covering almost 50 per cent of the population) was very substantial indeed. Most of the occupations reclassified between those dates involved movements between classes IV and V and so are taken care of by combining the two classes.

Some of the reasons why differentials widened during this decade are not hard to find. Two factors stand out particularly clearly: the first is the gradual downward shift in the class distribution of tobacco consumption (Todd 1976); the second factor is diet. War-time food-rationing resulted in a comparatively egalitarian distribution of many different foodstuffs. It was only after the ending of food-rationing in the early 1950s that the modern inequalities in food consumption grew up. These two factors had a very pronounced effect on the social distribution of heart disease (Marmot *et al.* 1978), stroke and lung cancer in both sexes: where previously there had been higher death rates in upper classes, the gradient was reversed; where there had been no clear gradient, lower-class rates dramatically increased compared to upper classes. The 1950s also saw a change in the social distribution of sugar consumption, which may well have been part of a longer-term pattern involving other refined foods. In the early decades of the century, it is likely that most refined foods were consumed more by the upper classes. As price differentials changed in the post-war era, refined foods were consumed increasingly by the less well off. The importance of these changes is also reflected in the change in the class distribution of obesity, which probably accompanied the change in the social distribution of heart disease (Wilkinson 1976).

The evidence reviewed in the preceding pages provides no support to the assumption that *Table 1.1* gives an unnecessarily alarmist view of the size and the trends in socio-economic inequalities in health. The main points can be summarized as follows. On the current size of mortality differentials:

1 The evidence suggests that illness in neither childhood nor later life has enough impact on social mobility to make more than a marginal difference to mortality differentials.
2 There is almost certainly a selective-mobility factor operating in early adulthood, which at least contributes to differentials in reproductive performance. It is probably responsible for less than 10 per cent of the differential in perinatal mortality between classes I and II and classes IV and V.
3 The positive contribution of selection to observed class differences is heavily outweighed by the negative effect of the socio-economic heterogeneity of classes. This means that the well-known figures on social-class differences in mortality are likely to understate the mortality differentials attributable to socio-economic inequalities.

On trends in mortality differentials:

1 The lack of any dramatic increase in rates of social mobility suggests that selection is not responsible for widening mortality differentials.
2 The changing distribution of the population between classes makes direct comparisons difficult but analytical methods that take population distribution into account suggest that mortality differentials have increased.
3 The revisions in the occupational classification and the allocation of occupations to classes have been shown to have little effect on our picture of trends in differentials.
4 Koskinen's and Pamuk's work makes it hard to doubt that mortality differentials between classes have increased, at least relatively for women and babies, and absolutely for men between 1951 and 1971. Even allowing for numerator biases, this trend probably continued through 1981.

The fact that social-class differences in mortality increased so soon after the introduction of the National Health Service in 1948 does not detract from the essentially progressive nature of that move. To use an analogy, the introduction of more egalitarian medical treatment for wounded troops would not be expected to make much difference to the ratio of officers to men killed in battle. Although modern medical services are invaluable in the treatment of many common ailments, they are less successful in the treatment of some of the major life-threatening cancers and degenerative diseases that account for such a large proportion of deaths. For conditions such as heart disease or stroke, where people are often unaware of symptoms before sudden death, the scope for curative medicine is particularly limited. However, the data available on class differences in the uptake of medical care per episode of illness make it clear that, even with the NHS, considerable class differences in treatment have not been eliminated (OPCS). Differential access to medical care that is effective in reducing case-fatality rates will obviously increase class differences in mortality.

Given that the NHS narrowed but did not eliminate class differences in access to medical care, it is possible that the beneficial effects of improved access were outweighed by the post-war improvements in the effectiveness of medical care associated with the development of new drugs. More effective medical care would have meant that the remaining differences in access had a greater impact on class differences in mortality. Some slight confirmation that this may indeed have happened is provided by Koskinen's finding that inequalities have increased slightly faster among those causes of death that are amenable to medical care than among those that are not (Koskinen 1985).

It is interesting to note that the increase in class differences in death rates has taken place against a background of decreases in variations in the age of death among individuals at large—regardless of their socio-economic position. Le Grand has recently used gini coefficients to measure inequalities in the age of death between individuals. These coefficients provide what might be called a 'pure' measure of inequalities in longevity, as distinct from a measure of the social distribution of those inequalities. Gini coefficients calculated for different dates this century show that variations in the age of death have decreased despite the increased disparities in mortality by class (Le Grand 1985). What the gini coefficients show is, however, almost certainly a reflection of the changing importance of different causes of death. Each disease and cause of death is associated with a particular age-distribution of deaths. Infectious diseases, which cause a large number of deaths at younger ages, have given way to the modern predominance of cancers and degenerative diseases, which take their toll almost exclusively in later life. This change has long been recognized as the explanation for the dramatic improvement in survival rates at younger ages, which contrasts so sharply with the very minor increases in survival later in life. It is this picture of more rapid improvements in survival at younger ages that the gini coefficients express as a narrowing of variations in age of death.

Current interest in the problem of class differences in health is primarily a concern for the social distribution of health rather than for the range of purely individual differences. The difference between the two is fundamental. The change in the social distribution of heart disease, for instance, may have had no effect on gini coefficients of the variation in the population's age of death, yet such a change in social distribution is not only an indicator of the increasing burden of socio-economic disadvantage but may also provide important clues to the causes of heart disease (Marmot *et al.* 1978).

Ultimately, the search for better measures of the socio-economic distribution of health should not be separated from the need to define the principal socio-economic factors that affect health. If we are to develop measures of the social distribution of health that show how much people's position in society causally affects their health, then we must know what effect each component of the ranking system has on health. From this point of view, the problem with occupational classes is their arbitrariness; because the ranking system has no objective criteria (not even the manual/non-manual division is clearly defined), it is impossible to measure any causal effects of its components on health. Paradoxically, it is this irreducibility of occupational class that ensures its status as a privileged ranking system. If we could define its components in terms of factors such as income, wealth, education, housing tenure—i.e., if we knew what it meant—it would lose its special status. Class often serves simply as an undefined proxy for the effects of unknown socio-economic differences. There would be no harm in that if the class differences in health (or whatever) captured the full range of socio-economic inequalities and were taken as an indication of how much we do *not* understand; however, explanations in terms of class are more often used to give a spurious impression of understanding, which we might be better off without. We might then get down to the real task of identifying the mortality risks attributable to the separate aspects of the socio-economic differentiation of the population. Measures of their independent and interactive effects would then enable us to state the mortality differentials attributable to specific combinations of factors. This approach obviously requires similar research methods to the attempts to define 'composite measures of disadvantage' that Blaxter discusses in her review of longitudinal studies (chapter 8). Scoring the relative risks associated with factors such as low income, large or single-parent families, housing tenure, unemployment, educational attainment, etc., has the additional advantage of not leaving out the economically inactive or treating them as appendages to others.

It is now possible to say, without risk of serious challenge, that the differences in life-expectancy associated with socio-economic position are larger than the figures of class differences in mortality suggest and that these differences have been increasing since 1951. It is still too early to say what this knowledge will do to our ideas of social progress and the comforting impression most of us have had of a long-term tendency towards declining social inequalities. That health inequalities should have grown particularly swiftly during the two decades of unparalleled post-war economic growth is especially hard to understand. Although the trends are now clear, it cannot be said that we understand them. Perhaps their most important message is that we cannot assume, as it was once tempting to do, that social progress rides piggy-back on economic growth. Human aspirations, in terms of increasing social equality, are not automatic; they must be won, and to win them will no doubt require a new political agenda.

Health inequalities are, of course, not the only important area in which popular perceptions of progress during the twentieth century can be shown to be false. We have already seen that the evidence suggests that there have not been any major increases in social mobility during much of this century. Data on income distribution also present a remarkably static picture and unemployment continues at record levels. These factors are not unrelated to one another. Evidence presented by Moser, Fox, and Jones (chapter 5) suggests that unemployment is associated with a very considerable increase in mortality rates. Whether this is a result of having to live on a reduced income or of other psychosocial problems associated with unemployment is not clear. That low income does lead to an increase in mortality is strongly suggested by the data discussed in chapter 6. The data also suggest that income distribution in developed societies has an important effect on overall life-expectancy. The argument would seem to have relevance not only to wage bargaining but also to the levels at which pensions and social security payments should be fixed.

© 1986 R. G. Wilkinson

REFERENCES

Department of Employment (1971) *New Earnings Survey*. London: HMSO.
Department of Health and Social Security (1980) *Inequalities in Health* (Black Report). Report of a research working group chaired by Sir Douglas Black. London: DHSS.

Fox, A. J. (1984) *Social Class and Occupational Mobility Shortly Before Men Become Fathers*. OPCS Series LS No. 2. London: HMSO.

Fox, A. J. and Goldblatt, P. O. (1982) *Socio-demographic Mortality Differentials: Longitudinal Study 1971–75*. OPCS Series LS No. 1. London: HMSO.

Heath, A. (1981) *Social Mobility*. London: Fontana.

Illsley, R. (1955) Social Class Selection and Class Differences in Relation to Stillbirths and Infant Deaths. *British Medical Journal* 2: 1520–524.

—— (1980) *Professional or Public Health: Sociology in Health and Medicine*. London: Nuffield Provincial Hospitals Trust.

—— (1983) *Social Mobility, Selection and the Production of Inequalities*. Paper presented at ESRC Conference on Research Priorities in Inequalities in Health. (Unpublished.)

—— (1986) Occupational Class, Selection and the Production of Inequalities. *Quarterly Journal of Social Affairs* 2(2): 151–65.

Koskinen, S. (1985) *Time Trends in Cause-specific Mortality by Occupational Class in England and Wales*. Paper presented at the IUSSP 20th General Conference, held in Florence. (Unpublished.)

Le Grand, J. (1985) *Inequalities in Health: The Human Capital Approach*. LSE Welfare State Programme Discussion Paper No. 1. London: London School of Economics and Political Science.

McDowell, M. and Marmot, M. G. (forthcoming).

Marmot, M. G., Adelstein, A. M., Robinson, N., and Rose, G. A. (1978) Changing Social Class Distribution of Heart Disease. *British Medical Journal* 2: 1109–112.

Newton, R. W., Webster, P. A. C., Binu, P. S., Maskrey, N., and Phillips, A. B. (1979) Psychosocial Stress in Pregnancy and Its Relation to the Onset of Premature Labour. *British Medical Journal* 2 (6187): 411–13.

OPCS (annual publication) *General Household Survey*. London: HMSO.

Pamuk, E. R. (1985) Social Class Inequality in Mortality from 1921 to 1972 in England and Wales. *Population Studies* 39: 17–31.

Registrar General (1978) *Occupational Mortality Tables, 1970–72 Decennial Supplement*. OPCS Series DS No. 1. London: HMSO.

Seltzer, C. C. and Jablon, S. (1977) Army Rank and Subsequent Mortality by Cause: 23-year Follow-up. *American Journal of Epidemiology* 105 (6): 559–66.

Smithells, R. W., Seller, M. J., *et al*. (1983) Further Experience of Vitamin Supplementation for Prevention of Neural Tube Defect Recurrences. *Lancet* i: 1027–031.

Stern, J. (1983) Social Mobility and the Interpretation of Social Class Mortality Differentials. *Journal of Social Policy* 12: 27–49.

Todd, G. F. (1976) *Social Class Variations in Cigarette Smoking and in Mortality from Associated Diseases*. Occasional Paper 2. London: Tobacco Research Council.

Wilkinson, R. G. (1976) *Socio-economic Factors in Mortality Differentials*. M.Med. Sci. thesis, University of Nottingham. (Unpublished.)

TWO

Social inequalities in mortality: the social environment

M. G. Marmot

The social environment affects health and disease in so many ways that it is impossible to deal with this subject in its entirety. In a recent review of this topic, Jerry Morris and I alluded (i) to the influence of politics, the economy and of culture; (ii) to the evidence that the social environment affects health and disease at various stages throughout the life cycle; and (iii) to the possibility that the social environment may exert its effect in different ways—via 'physical' pathways, such as poor nutrition or exposure to pathogens; or via *psycho*social pathways affecting the neuro-humoral system directly ('stress'); via an influence on medical care, broadly defined (Marmot and Morris 1984). In our sixty-page review we were, of necessity, superficial and not comprehensive. The present constraints dictate an even more restricted focus.

I shall concentrate on social inequalities in mortality in middle age, in order to pose two questions:

1 Are the general social class differences in mortality more likely to have a general explanation or to be the result of the combined effect of a number of specific factors?
2 What role might *psycho*social factors play in causing social differences in mortality?

In wrestling with these questions, I shall use data from our studies of civil servants. In addition, to argue the case for cultural as well as social structural influences on mortality, I will show one example from mortality studies of immigrants to England and Wales (Marmot, Adelstein, and Bulusu 1983).

INEQUALITIES IN DEATH — SPECIFIC EXPLANATIONS OF A GENERAL PATTERN?[1]

Background

Inequalities in Health (the Black Report; DHSS 1980) documented social class differences in mortality, across a wide range of diseases, that persist despite general improvements in mortality (Morris 1979). For these social class differences, the Report suggested that specific features of the socio-economic environment—such as smoking or accidents at work—might provide part, if by no means all, of the explanation. Other, more general social influences must be operating to explain this general pattern of lower class—higher mortality. Other authors, too, have suggested social class differences in general susceptibility to a variety of diseases, rather than a clustering of specific causes (Syme and Berkman 1976).

Two problems limit the exploration of this question in routinely published data on mortality by social class (Registrar General 1978; Fox and Goldblatt 1982): the crudity of the social classification based on a relatively arbitrary grouping together of diverse occupations; and the lack of data on other risk factors for disease. The Whitehall study of civil servants provides some opportunity to address these problems by studying mortality rates of men in different grades of employment in one occupation—office-based civil servants. We have shown that after seven and a half years of follow-up, there was a clear inverse association between grade of employment and mortality from coronary heart disease (lower grade—higher mortality) (Marmot *et al.* 1978a; Rose and Marmot 1981). Now, after ten years of follow-up, we can extend these observations to diseases other than coronary disease and ask how much of the differences in mortality can be explained by known risk factors.

Mortality differences by grade of employment

17,530 civil servants, working in London, were examined in 1967–69 and their records in the Central Registry of the National Health Service were identified and flagged. *Table 2.1* shows that in each of three age-groups, the lower the grade of employment the higher is the mortality from all causes, from coronary heart disease which accounts for 43 per cent of deaths, and from causes other than CHD. The cumulative probability of

---

[1]This section of the paper (pp. 22–9) has been published separately (Marmot, Shipley, and Rose 1984).

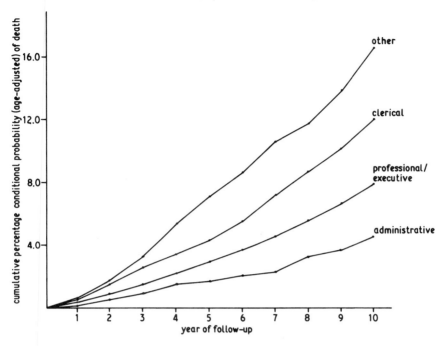

Figure 2.1 Whitehall study: all-cause mortality among total population by year of follow-up

death from all causes is shown in *Figure 2.1*. There is a gradient in mortality from the administrators (highest grade) to the 'others' (lowest).

Table 2.2 shows age-adjusted mortality by grade for all the major causes of death (92 per cent of all deaths). In calculating relative mortality, the professional and executive grade were assigned a risk of 1, as they are the largest group, and the other grades were compared with them. The consistency of the gradient is remarkable. For every cause of death (except genito-urinary diseases—18 deaths) the two lower grades have higher mortality risks than the two higher grades. For nearly every cause, there is a step-wise relationship between grade and mortality. The magnitude of the relative difference between the grades appears similar for the different causes, although the confidence intervals around these estimates do not allow a firm conclusion. With this caution in mind, it is interesting to note that the steepest gradients in risk are for lung cancer, chronic bronchitis and other respiratory disease: all strongly smoking-related. There were marked differences between the grades in prevalence of smoking at entry: of the administrators, 29 per cent were current smokers; of the

Table 2.1 *Mortality in ten years (and number of deaths) by Civil Service grade and age from all causes, coronary heart disease, and other causes*

cause of death by age-group	ten-year mortality percentage (number of deaths)			
	administrators	professionals and executives	clerical	other
CHD				
40–49	(0)	1.4 (78)	2.3 (18)	5.0 (14)
50–59	3.3 (14)	4.5 (242)	6.2 (84)	7.2 (58)
60–64	4.2 (3)	7.2 (79)	9.4 (58)	10.4 (56)
age-adjusted rate	2.2 (17)	3.6 (399)	4.9 (160)	6.6 (128)
other causes				
40–49	2.1 (10)	2.3 (133)	1.4 (11)	4.6 (13)
50–59	3.1 (13)	4.7 (251)	9.8 (132)	12.0 (97)
60–64	1.4 (1)	10.0 (109)	14.5 (90)	16.3 (88)
age-adjusted rate	2.6 (24)	4.4 (493)	6.8 (233)	9.1 (198)
all causes				
40–49	2.1 (10)	3.7 (211)	3.6 (29)	9.6 (27)
50–59	6.4 (27)	9.3 (493)	16.0 (216)	19.3 (155)
60–64	5.6 (4)	17.2 (188)	23.9 (148)	26.7 (144)
age-adjusted rate	4.7 (41)	8.0 (892)	11.7 (393)	15.6 (326)

professionals and executives, 37 per cent; of the clerical grades, 53 per cent; of the 'others', 68 per cent. Smoking differences cannot provide all of the explanation for the grade differences in mortality, however. *Table 2.2* shows strong gradients for the groups of diseases found not to be associated with smoking by Doll and Peto (1976).

The two major smoking-associated diseases, CHD and lung cancer, are associated both with smoking and grade of employment. In *Table 2.3*, smoking is expressed as mg/day of tar by multiplying the number of cigarettes smoked by average tar yield of the brand. The dramatic dose-response relationship with smoking is confirmed for lung cancer, and to a lesser extent for CHD. For both diseases, however, within categories of smoking, there is a persisting inverse association between mortality and grade of employment. In non-smokers, CHD is strongly associated with grade. Only 6 of the 194 lung-cancer deaths occurred in non-smokers. Further classifying of smokers by the age at which they began to smoke still did not account for the higher lung-cancer mortality in the two lower grades.

The other risk factors, apart from smoking, on which we have information relate to CHD. *Table 2.4* shows the relative risks of CHD death as calculated from the multiple logistic equation. Controlling for age, smoking, systolic blood pressure, and plasma cholesterol reduced the risk associated with grade only to a minor extent. Similarly, leisure-time

Table 2.2 Age-adjusted mortality in ten years (and number of deaths) by Civil Service grade and cause of death

cause of death	ten-year mortality percentage (number of deaths)				relative mortality*				χ^1 test for trend (1 df)
	administrators	professional & executive	clerical	other	admin.	prof. & exec.	clerk	other	
lung cancer	0.35 (3)	0.73 (79)	1.47 (53)	2.33 (59)	0.5	1.0	2.2	3.6	54.62
other cancer	1.3 (12)	1.7 (195)	2.2 (73)	2.2 (46)	0.8	1.0	1.4	1.4	7.08
coronary heart disease	2.2 (17)	3.6 (399)	4.9 (160)	6.6 (128)	0.5	1.0	1.4	1.7	38.24
cerebro-vascular disease	0.13 (1)	0.49 (51)	0.64 (23)	0.58 (14)	0.3	1.0	1.4	1.2	1.70
chronic bronchitis	0.0 (0)	0.08 (8)	0.43 (15)	0.65 (13)	0.0	1.0	6.0	7.3	21.01
other respiratory	0.21 (2)	0.22 (24)	0.52 (18)	0.87 (15)	1.1	1.0	2.6	3.1	11.99
gastro-intestinal diseases	0.0 (0)	0.13 (15)	0.20 (7)	0.45 (15)	0.0	1.0	1.6	2.8	6.26
genito-urinary diseases	0.09 (1)	0.09 (10)	0.07 (2)	0.24 (5)	1.3	1.0	0.7	3.1	2.46
accidents and homicide	0.0 (0)	0.14 (17)	0.18 (5)	0.18 (3)	0.0	1.0	1.4	1.5	1.36
suicide	0.1 (1)	0.15 (18)	0.15 (4)	0.25 (4)	0.7	1.0	1.0	1.9	0.97
non-smoking-related causes									
cancer	0.9 (9)	1.2 (145)	1.5 (50)	1.6 (33)	0.8	1.0	1.3	1.4	4.70
non-cancer	1.0 (10)	1.9 (216)	2.8 (93)	4.2 (82)	0.6	1.0	1.5	2.0	31.83
all causes	4.7 (41)	8.0 (892)	11.7 (393)	15.6 (326)	0.6	1.0	1.6	2.1	144.05

*calculated from logistic equation adjusting for age

Class and Health

Table 2.3 *Age-adjusted mortality in ten years (and number of deaths from coronary heart disease and lung cancer) by grade and smoking expressed as tar equivalents**

cause of death and tar intake	administrators	professional and executive	clerical	other	total
CHD					
non-smokers	1.40 (2)	2.36 (44)	2.08 (8)	6.89 (16)	2.59 (70)
ex-smokers	1.29 (4)	3.06 (140)	3.32 (37)	3.98 (23)	3.09 (20)
current:					
tar ≤ 250 mg/day	2.16 (2)	3.02 (38)	5.39 (23)	4.0 (11)	3.49 (74)
251–400 mg/day	5.52 (3)	5.54 (67)	7.86 (41)	8.92 (29)	6.46 (140)
> 400 mg/day	4.97 (5)	5.62 (97)	6.03 (44)	8.49 (47)	5.92 (193)
total**	2.16 (77)	3.58 (399)	4.92 (160)	6.62 (128)	4.00 (704)
lung cancer					
non-smokers	0.0 (0)	0.24 (5)	0.0 (0)	0.25 (1)	0.21 (6)
ex-smokers	0.21 (1)	0.59 (26)	0.56 (6)	1.05 (8)	0.62 (41)
current:					
tar ≤ 250 mg/day	0.0 (0)	0.61 (8)	1.13 (5)	1.53 (6)	0.90 (19)
251–400 mg/day	0.0 (0)	1.16 (12)	1.88 (12)	3.40 (14)	1.72 (38)
> 400 mg/day	2.07 (2)	1.58 (28)	3.13 (28)	4.01 (29)	2.56 (87)
total**	0.35 (3)	0.73 (79)	1.49 (53)	2.33 (59)	2.00 (194)

*cigarettes/day × tar content of cigarette
**includes 593 men who smoked only pipes or cigars

Table 2.4 *Relative risk* of CHD death in ten years (a) controlling for age, and (b) controlling for age, smoking, systolic blood pressure, and plasma cholesterol*

control and age-group	administrators plus professional and executive	clerical	other
(a)			
40–49	1.0	1.7	3.9
50–59	1.0	1.4	1.6
60–64	1.0	1.3	1.5
(b)			
40–49	1.0	1.5	3.1
50–59	1.0	1.2	1.5
60–64	1.0	1.2	1.4

*calculated by multiple logistic regression

physical activity, although reported less often by men in the lower grades, accounted for little of the CHD difference between the grades.

Grade of employment is a guide to the social circumstances of adults. We have no direct data on the social circumstances of these men as children. *Table 2.5* shows an inverse association between height and CHD, all causes, and deaths other than CHD. Grade is strongly related to height; for example, the administrators are, on average, 4.7 cms taller than

Table 2.5 *Age-adjusted mortality in ten years from CHD and other causes by height*

height (cms)	mortality in ten years			relative risk of death*	
	CHD % (no. of deaths)	non-CHD % (no. of deaths)	all causes % (no. of deaths)	CHD	non-CHD
≤ 168	5.8 (156)	6.5 (176)	17.2 (332)	1.00	1.00
− 175	3.9 (270)	5.4 (372)	9.3 (642)	0.71	0.89
−183	3.5 (216)	5.1 (309)	8.6 (525)	0.69	0.90
> 183	3.3 (62)	4.9 (91)	8.2 (153)	0.62	0.87
total	4.0 (704)	5.4 (948)	9.4 (1652)		

*Adjusted for age and grade
Note: 168 cms = 5′ 6″, 183 cms = 6′ 0″.

Table 2.6 *Age-adjusted mortality in ten years from CHD and all causes by grade and presence of 'disease at entry' to the study**

disease at entry	ten-year mortality percentage (no. of deaths)			
	administrators	professional and executive	clerical	other
CHD				
yes	3.0 (10)	5.5 (254)	6.8 (103)	9.8 (89)
no	1.6 (7)	2.2 (145)	3.3 (57)	4.0 (39)
all-cause				
yes	7.6 (26)	11.1 (512)	15.1 (240)	21.0 (211)
no	2.8 (15)	5.8 (380)	8.7 (153)	11.2 (115)

*disease at entry = ischaemia or angina or possible myocardial infarction; phlegm or dyspnoea or wheeze; under medical treatment or diabetic

men in the 'other' grade (Marmot *et al.* 1978b). *Table 2.5* shows also the results of a multiple logistic analysis. Men under 168 cms (5 ft 6 ins) have the highest CHD mortality independent of age and grade; men over 183 cms (6ft), the lowest CHD mortality. Similarly, grade of employment is related to mortality independent of height.

Although the lowest 'other' grade contains men who were recruited because of illness, this is unlikely to be the major cause of the association between grade and mortality. *Table 2.6* shows that among men without any disease that we could detect at entry into the study, as well as among those with, there is a step-wise relation between grade and mortality.

Another way of examining the possible influence of selection of sicker men into lower grades is the year-by-year comparison of mortality. *Figure 2.1* shows that there is no tendency for the mortality difference between the grades to narrow with time. This might have been expected had the grade differences in mortality been due to different levels of pre-existing illness influencing the grade of employment.

Discussion

The differences in these civil servants reflect national differences in mortality between social classes, except that the contrasts are more marked: a greater than three-fold difference in mortality between lowest and highest grade in the civil service. This brings into clear focus social inequalities in mortality. These are all men working in one stable, sedentary occupation, in one location (London), not exposed to industrial hazards other than psychosocial ones. The fact that the gradient of mortality by grade is steeper than that by social class in the national figures may reflect more homogeneity within grades than within social classes and clearer social differences between grades. The large social differences in mortality in this study offer the opportunity to search for causes of social class differences.

We had started out to investigate the causes of the CHD mortality difference between grades, but perhaps that was too narrow a focus. The inverse association between grade and mortality is as strong for all causes and for non-CHD as it is for CHD. Is a general explanation of this general pattern likely or should we attempt to identify a set of specific causal factors for CHD, bronchitis, lung cancer, other cancer, etc.? (See Illsley 1980.) The answer is probably 'both'.

The effect of specific causes is undoubted. Smoking, in particular, is more common in the lower grades and is strongly associated with a number of specific causes of death. The particularly high relative mortality of lower grade men from lung cancer, chronic bronchitis, and other respiratory causes argues for the role of smoking in explaining social class differences in mortality (Marmot *et al.* 1978a). Nevertheless, there is still a marked gradient in mortality from CHD and other causes (excepting cancer) among non-smokers, in mortality from CHD and lung cancer when controlling for smoking, and in mortality from diseases not associated with smoking.

Most of the other established risk factors for chronic disease relate to CHD. As *Table 2.5* shows, these explain only a little of the grade differences in CHD. Similarly, differences between grades in reported leisure-time physical activity, though substantial, appear not to account for much of the mortality gradient. It is tempting to refer to the similar magnitude of the relative risk of death between lower and higher grades from the whole range of specific causes as indicating the operation of one factor common to many diseases. The confidence intervals around these relative risk estimates could, however, embrace a great deal of hetero-geneity. Nevertheless, the remarkable similarity in direction of the mortality gradients from a variety of causes does argue for a general-type explanation. 'General' and 'specific' explanations are not incompatible;

for example, diet may be 'generally' worse in lower grades, but this may reflect a relative lack of specific items such as vitamin A, fibre, vitamin C, and potassium, which may relate to specific cancers, stroke and high blood pressure.

The other kind of general explanation, proposed by Berkman and Syme (1979) and Cassel (1976), is that there is a social class difference in susceptibility to a variety of specific insults. These authors argue for the importance of psychosocial factors ('stress') in determining susceptibility. This will be considered further in the next section of this chapter.

We can only speculate as to when in life these social influences exert their effect on subsequent mortality. Forsdahl, analysing regional variations in CHD mortality in Norway, found a stronger association between CHD and poverty at the time of birth and in infancy than in adult life (Forsdahl 1977). In our study, the relation of height to death from CHD and other causes—independent of grade—suggests a correlation between factors operating early in life and factors affecting adult mortality. These factors may not all derive from the social environment—height has genetic as well as environmental determinants. One argument against a genetic determination of the CHD risk comes from the data, admittedly imprecise, on the proportion of men who reported first degree relatives with heart disease: administrators, 21 per cent; professionals and executives, 16 per cent; clerical, 10 per cent; other, 7 per cent. The relation between height and social class and possible influences of selective mobility are discussed further towards the end of this chapter.

Another type of explanation for grade differences in mortality is differences in access to or quality of medical care. Charlton *et al.* (1981) applied Rutsein's classification of diseases 'preventable' by medical intervention to the 596,662 deaths in England and Wales and calculated that only 17.2 per cent were 'preventable' medically. If this is correct, differences in medical care could explain little of the threefold differences in mortality.

PSYCHOSOCIAL EXPLANATIONS

This must remain in the area of speculation and 'more research needed'. In a later study of a different sample of civil servants, we have been trying to clarify ideas and prepare the ground for future work in this area. The strategy has been to compare psychosocial characteristics in men (and women) in different grades, and therefore presumably at different risk of disease and death. We have been interested in four types of measure: Type-A behaviour, occupational stress, social supports, and stressful life events. A fifth characteristic 'spoke to us' out of the data—leisure-time activities.

Table 2.7 *Percentage of men reporting selected psychosocial characteristics according to Civil Service grade*

characteristic	administrators	professional and executive	clerical	other
type-A behaviour	61	46	30	27
work				
underuse of skills	50	58	68	67
no variety	0	4	21	37
little or no control	7	14	18	33
not fair treatment	11	16	16	33
job of little value	2	2	6	9
activities outside work				
involved sedentary				
(solitary)	46	36	26	20
involved sedentary (social)	45	39	30	29
active (not athletic)	85	86	62	40
active sports	39	32	24	33
social supports				
see confidant daily	92	86	82	80
no contact with neighbours	37	40	55	69
no social contact with				
people at work	55	66	72	82

Table 2.7 summarizes results on some of these factors. Type-A behaviour is the so-called coronary-prone behaviour pattern. It is characterized by hostility, impatience, and time-urgency, striving and ambition. In our study, Type-A behaviour was found more frequently among men with lower CHD risk—the higher grades. This adds to a suspicion that the concept of Type-A behaviour may apply best to the population of middle-class, white Americans in which it was first studied; less well to other groups. Certainly the measures, if not the concept, of Type-A behaviour are likely to be class-biased. At the very least, these results suggest that differences in the frequency of Type-A behaviour are not the explanation of grade difference in CHD mortality.

The Karasek model of job stress (Karasek *et al.* 1982) proposes that, in the presence of psychological demands, low decision latitude is associated with an increased risk of cardiovascular disease. Decision latitude can be measured by: (a) use of skills in the job; (b) control over the work. As expected, lower grade men score adversely on both of these. They also show a lesser degree of social support *(Table 2.7)*. In Berkman and Syme's study in Alameda County (1979), a low degree of social support, assessed by measures similar to these, was associated with increased mortality from all causes. *Table 2.7* shows that not only do higher grade men apparently have more satisfying jobs, they are also involved in more active pursuits outside work. Interestingly, we found no difference between the grades in the frequency of stressful life events—assessed by a mini-version of George Brown's method (Brown and Harris 1978).

Might these psychosocial differences between grades be related to generalized differences in susceptibility to specific 'pathogens'? Presumably the next step in the research is to relate not group characteristics to group differences in mortality but individual characteristics to individual differences in mortality.

CULTURE AND SOCIAL STRUCTURE

The possible separate influence of these two is illustrated by data on mortality by social class from circulatory disease among immigrants to England and Wales, summarized in *Table 2.8* (Marmot, Adelstein, and Bulusu 1984). The pattern of mortality by social class is quite different among the three immigrant groups from the England and Wales pattern. In addition, within each social class except V, immigrants from the Indian subcontinent have higher SMRs than the England and Wales average for that class.

Table 2.8 *Mortality (SMR)* from circulatory disease by country of birth and social class, England and Wales (men), 1970–72*

country of birth	I	II	social class IIIN	IIIM	IV	V
Indian subcontinent	97	126	145	135	140	115
Caribbean	141	148	160	79	83	92
African Commonwealth	164	122	133	70	124	188
all England and Wales**	86	89	110	106	110	118

*average for England and Wales, all classes: SMR = 100
**includes all men born in England and Wales, plus immigrants

SOCIAL MOBILITY?

As shown in *Table 2.5*, adult height predicts mortality from CHD and, to a lesser extent, from non-CHD. It is therefore potentially useful to examine factors relating to adult height. If height is influenced by nutrition and environment in childhood, it might be expected to be related to fathers' social class. *Table 2.9* shows that, in civil servants, it is: mean height is 173.8 cm in men born to fathers in classes IV and V and is 176.7 cm in sons of fathers in classes I and II. It is even more strongly related to the current grade of employment of the civil servants, i.e. current social class:

Table 2.9 *Mean height (cms) of male civil servants according to current employment grade and father's social class (numbers of men)*

social class of father	own employment grade				
	administrators	professional & executive	clerical	other	total
1 & II	178.5 (95)	176.2 (58)	171.7 (36)	172.3 (12)	176.2 (201)
IIINM	178.4 (32)	175.5 (20)	175.7 (11)	176.5 (8)	176.9 (71)
IIIM	178.8 (37)	175.0 (59)	174.6 (37)	174.2 (25)	175.7 (158)
IV & V	176.7 (9)	174.8 (25)	174.3 (11)	170.0 (16)	173.8 (61)
total*	178.4 (175)	175.5 (164)	173.4 (98)	173.5 (64)	175.8 (501)

*includes ten men whose fathers' occupations were not known

173.5 cm in 'other' grades (class V) and 173.4 cm in clerical grades (class III NM), rising to 178.4 cm in the administrative grade. Within each father's social class, those who entered higher grades of the civil service were taller than those in lower grades.

What can account for this? One explanation is that among men born to fathers in a particular class there is a great deal of diversity in childhood environment: those from more 'favoured' backgrounds achieve a greater adult height and a higher grade of employment in adulthood. This implies that taller men with fathers in classes IV and V are upwardly mobile socially—the reverse being true for the few shorter men with fathers in classes I and II. An alternative explanation is that height *per se* influences life chances and hence advancement through education and subsequently the Civil Service. The selective social mobility hypothesis has been discussed more fully in chapter 1.

IMPLICATIONS

The implications of these findings on inequalities in death, and accompanying differences, are several. For epidemiological research, they imply the need for further research into social differences in mortality, at both the specific and the general level. We are now exploring further dietary and psychosocial factors. For public health, the urgent need is underlined to take action on social class differences in established risk factors, of which smoking is a prime example. No doubt for sociology, the need is to understand the general social structural causes of differences in health behaviour and mortality.

REFERENCES

Berkman, L. F. and Syme, S. L. (1979) Social Networks, Host Resistance, and Mortality: A Nine-year Follow-up Study of Alameda County Residents. *American Journal of Epidemiology* 109: 186–204.

Brown, G. W. and Harris, T. (1978) *Social Origins of Depression*. London: Tavistock.

Cassel, J. (1976) The Contribution of the Social Environment to Host Resistance. *American Journal of Epidemiology* 104: 107–23.

Charlton, J. R. H., Hartley, R. M., Silver, R., and Holland, W. W. (1981) Geographical Variation in Mortality from Conditions Amenable to Medical Intervention in England and Wales. *Lancet* i: 691–96.

Department of Health and Social Security (1980) *Inequalities in Health (Black Report)*. Report of a research working group chaired by Sir Douglas Black. London: DHSS.

Doll, R. and Peto, R. (1976) Mortality in Relation to Smoking: 20 years' Observations on Male British Doctors. *British Medical Journal* 2: 1525–536.

Forsdahl, A. (1977) Are Poor Living Conditions in Childhood and Adolescence an Important Risk Factor for Arteriosclerotic Heart Disease? *British Journal of Preventive and Social Medicine* 31: 91–5.

Fox, A. J. and Goldblatt, P. O. (1982) *Socio-demographic Mortality Differentials: Longitudinal Study 1971–75*. OPCS Series LS No. 1. London: HMSO.

Illsley, R. (1980) *Professional or Public Health: Sociology in Health and Medicine*. London: Nuffield Provincial Hospitals Trust.

Karasek, R. A., Theorell, T. G. T., Schwartz, J., Pieper, C., and Alfredsson, L. (1982) Job, Psychological Factors and Coronary Heart Disease: Swedish Prospective Findings and US Prevalence Findings Using a New Occupational Inference Method. *Advances in Cardiology* 29: 62–7.

Marmot, M. G. and Morris, J. N. (1984) The Social Environment. In W. W. Holland, R. Detels, and G. Knox (eds) *Oxford Textbook of Public Health, Volume 1.*

Marmot, M. G., Adelstein, A. M. and Bulusu, L. (1983) Immigrant Mortality in England and Wales 1970–78. *Population Trends* 33: 14–17.

—— (1984) *Immigrant Mortality in England & Wales 1970–78*. OPCS Studies of Medical and Population Subjects No. 49. London: HMSO.

Marmot, M. G., Shipley, M. J., and Rose, G. A. (1984) Inequalities in Death– Specific Explanations of a General Pattern. *Lancet* i: 1003–006.

Marmot, M. G., Adelstein, A. M., Robinson, N., and Rose, G. A. (1978a) Changing Social Class Distribution of Heart Disease. *British Medical Journal* 2: 1109–112.

Marmot, M. G., Rose, G. A., Shipley, M. J. and Hamilton, P. J. S. (1978b) Employment Grade and Coronary Heart Disease in British Civil Servants. *Journal of Epidemiology and Community Health* 32: 244–49.

Morris, J. N. (1979) Social Inequalities Undiminished. *Lancet* i: 87–90.

Registrar General (1978) *Occupational Mortality Tables 1970–72 Decennial Supplement*. OPCS Series DS No. 1. London: HMSO.

Rose, G. and Marmot, M. G. (1981) Social Class and Coronary Heart Disease. *British Heart Journal* 45: 13–19.

Syme, S. L. and Berkman, L. F. (1976) Social Class, Susceptibility, and Sickness. *American Journal of Epidemiology* 104: 1–8.

THREE

Social class mortality differentials: artefact, selection, or life circumstances?

A. J. Fox, P. O. Goldblatt, and D. R. Jones

SUMMARY

Data from 10 years' follow-up of mortality in the OPCS Longitudinal Study are used to relate deaths of men in 1976–81 to their social class as recorded by the 1971 census. Explanations of social class mortality differentials are critically reviewed in the light of these new data. The similarity between the class differentials observed for men aged 15–64 years in this study and those reported in the 1970–72 Decennial Supplement on Occupational Mortality indicate that the published gradients were not in fact grossly distorted by numerator–denominator biases. Distortions to gradients observed in the early years of the longitudinal study and ascribed to selective health-related mobility out of employment from the principal social classes to the permanently sick had largely worn off after five years of follow-up. Sharp gradients at ages over 75 years, similar to those at younger ages, suggest that, for men aged over 50 years, selective health-related mobility between social classes does not contribute to differentials in mortality.

BACKGROUND

Analyses of mortality differentials in Decennial Supplements on Occupational Mortality (see, for example, the latest report[1]) have traditionally provided the main source of data in the discussion of health inequalities by social class. For example, the recent review of inequalities conducted by a Department of Health and Social Security Research Working Group under the chairmanship of Sir Douglas Black[2] derived much of its evidence from this source. Deficiencies in the data for assessing the exact magnitude of differentials and the changing patterns over time, and for identifying causal factors, were evident from their analysis. The method of deriving occupational mortality statistics suffers from major numerator–denominator biases because the occupation reported at the registration of a death is not necessarily that reported at census. At the same time this method produces only cross-sectional data which cannot be used to shed light on the influences of social mobility. These defects in traditional data, recognized in the earliest analyses over 100 years ago,[3] have meant that even though they were unable to indicate the importance of such explanations, decennial supplements have regularly warned about the influences of artefacts,[4] namely, classification changes and numerator–denominator biases, and selection effects,[5] namely, selective movement between classes of the sick and the healthy. While the Black Report gave little credence to these explanations,[6] critics have argued, mainly on theoretical grounds,[7] that their role in perpetuating differentials is underestimated.

When, in 1973, the Office of Population Censuses and Surveys (OPCS) announced its intention to conduct a longitudinal study of a 1 per cent sample of the population of England and Wales, one of the stated purposes was to construct a data source free of numerator–denominator biases (see Cohort Studies; New Developments[8] page 6). This sample, of people born on any of four birthdays during the year, was initially selected from the 1971 census. So far, for each person in the sample, vital events between 1971 and 1981 censuses have been incorporated into the data set.

Data on mortality in the first five years of this study have been compared with those obtained by the traditional cross-sectional approach elsewhere.[9] This analysis highlighted the distortions of social class gradients to be found at the inception of prospective studies. A sizeable fraction of men aged 55–64 years were classified by the census as having an 'inadequately described occupation' or as being 'unoccupied'. The 1970 Classification of Occupations (see[12]) allocated people to social classes on the basis of their occupation and their status within an occupation. Those people who were 'inadequately described' or who were 'unoccupied' were not allocated to a social class. Since these groups included men who were permanently sick, their mortality was particularly high. Their exclusion from social classes resulted in a less marked mortality gradient from class I to class V in the Longitudinal Study than in the Decennial Supplement.

As was described in the main report of mortality in 1971–75, the prospective approach permits analysis of the change in mortality by duration of follow up.[10] When discussing the impact of health-related mobility, it was pointed out that the effect of the exclusion of the permanently sick from social classes I to V would be expected to wear off with increased duration of follow-up and that, as a consequence, the differential from classes I and V would widen in later years of the study.[10]

Failure to classify the permanently sick (and others) to one of social classes I to V is an example of health-related selection, in this case primarily representing selection out of the labour force into unemployment or health-related retirement. While this is clearly the most dramatic form of selection, it is often suggested[7] that mobility between social classes—in particular, drift down the social scale with increased disability and ill health or, perhaps, positive health enabling people to move up the social scale—could, in principle, be a major factor in explaining the wide social class gradients observed in mortality. Such arguments suggest that the gradient by social class, say, ten years before death, or even at birth, would provide a more appropriate measure of *socio-economic* differentials which would consequently be narrower than that by social class at death.

Most analyses of inequalities in health have concentrated on differentials between the Registrar General's social classes simply because these data, however crude and inadequate, constitute the most readily available national series. As earlier analyses of the longitudinal study have demonstrated, several dimensions to class differentials in mortality can now be explored. In particular, aspects of education, housing, and household possessions can now be studied, each of which is, to some degree, related to wealth and income.[10] The concentration on occupationally based social class in this chapter reflects the opportunity afforded to us by deaths occurring in the period 1976–81 to evaluate critically previous findings and hypotheses from this study concerning social class differentials. It does not indicate that we do not recognize that these other dimensions are equally worthy of further investigation;[11] indeed, it is our intention to return to these issues in later projects. While this chapter concentrates on differentials in male mortality, we are also looking at female mortality and will report this work later.

METHODS

Social class in both periods is that defined on the basis of the occupation and employment status as reported in the 1971 census and assigned using the 1970 *Classification of Occupations*.[12] Expected deaths are calculated in the standard method of prospective studies; person-years-at-risk by age for men in each social class are multiplied by age-specific death rates for all men in the Longitudinal Study. The latter were calculated by dividing all deaths (in each five-year age group) during the periods 1971–75 and 1976–81 respectively by the corresponding person-years-at-risk. A fuller account of this method is given in the report of mortality in the period 1971–5.[10] When annual figures are shown in this chapter, expected deaths are calculated using corresponding annual age-specific death rates for the entire Longitudinal Study sample.

Further editing of the original data and the addition of late death notifications mean that the data for 1971–75 presented here are slightly different from those previously published.[10]

Trends in the annual standardized mortality ratios (SMRs) for each social class with time between 1971 and 1981 have been investigated by fitting regression models[13,14] equivalent to the assumption that the observed deaths 0_{ij} in the ith social class (i = 1, 8 corresponding to classes I, II, IIIN, IIIM, IV, V, inadequately described and unoccupied) in that part of the jth calendar year in the risk period (j = 1, . . ., 11) are independent Poisson variables whose means satisfy

$$\log E(0_{ij}) = \log(E_{ij}) + \text{constant} + \alpha_i + \beta_i x$$

where E_{ij} is the number of deaths expected in the i–jth category (see above) and x is the time in years from the 1971 census to the mid-point of the jth time interval. The model was fitted using the GLIM package[15] and hence α_1 is set to zero. This model ignores autocorrelation between observations in successive time intervals, and cautious interpretation of the parameter estimates so derived is thus necessary. It should also be noted that the model does *not* assume a natural ordering of the social class categories.

Trends with age groups were investigated in a similar model using data for the six principal social class categories (i = 1, . . ., 6: social classes I, II, IIIN, IIIM, IV, V) and nine age groups: 45–49 (j = 1), 50–54 (j = 2), . . ., 80–84 (j = 8), 85 and over (j = 9). The variable x takes the value of the mid-point of each age range (j = 1, . . ., 8) and a value of 90.0 in the final age group.

CHANGE IN MORTALITY WITH DURATION OF FOLLOW-UP

Overall mortality of men aged 15–64 years at death by social class is summarized in *Table 3.1* and *Figure 3.1* for the years 1971–75 and 1976–81 separately. Several features are of interest in view of the comments made above about the contrasting findings in earlier analyses of this source and the Decennial Supplement analysis.[9] The most striking change in SMR is that observed for the unoccupied, which fell from 299 in 1971–75 to 213 in 1976–81. The effect of this fall in SMR on mortality differentials for those men who were allocated to a social class is coupled with an effect of the ageing of 'unoccupied' men beyond age 64 years to reduce substantially the fraction of deaths contributed by this group. In 1971–75 more than 10 per cent of deaths at ages 15–64 years were to men who were 'unoccupied' at the 1971 census. This fraction was reduced to little over 5 per cent by 1976–81.

This attenuation of a selection effect implies that differences in mortality between social classes in the study between 1976 and 1981 are less affected by the problem of the unoccupied than they were shortly after the 1971

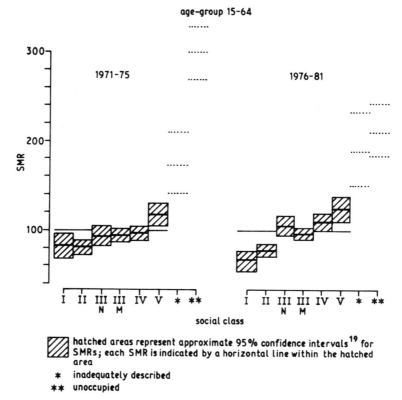

Figure 3.1   Mortality of men aged 15–64 by social class, 1971–75 and 1976–81

census. As was predicted from analysis of the time trend in 1971 to 1975 (Fox and Goldblatt[10] pages 187 and 203), the social class gradient becomes much clearer in the extended period of follow-up. The difference between class I and class V widens markedly, and progressive differentials between classes start to appear more strongly.

Figure 3.2 shows the annual changes in SMR by social class in order to provide a guide as to whether or not the gradient is continuing to widen. Although the figure gives the impression that classes I and V are continuing to diverge over the period 1976–81, the annual SMRs are based on small numbers of deaths, particularly that for 1981 which covers only the period 1 January to 5 April. *Table 3.2* gives parameter estimates and standard errors fitting the model specified above to these figures. The specified model fits the data moderately well, as a deviance of 66.0 on 72 degrees of freedom indicates. The null model ($\alpha_i = \beta_i = 0$, $i = 1, \ldots, 8$)

Table 3.1 *Mortality of men aged 15–64 by social class. 1971–75 and 1976–81*

| Social class in 1971 | Period of death | | | | | |
| | 1971–75 | | | 1976–81 | | |
	obs	exp	SMR	obs	exp	SMR
I	135	167.1	81	128	193.9	66
II	599	753.6	79	625	808.3	77
IIIN	378	414.0	91	450	429.3	105
IIIM	1,258	1,373.2	92	1,435	1,501.0	96
IV	694	720.8	96	774	710.6	109
V	369	317.3	116	358	289.1	124
armed forces	11	15.2	72	20	21.8	92
inadequately described	90	51.6	174	86	45.1	191
unoccupied	420	140.7	299	231	108.3	213
total	3,954	3,953.5	100	4,107	4,107.4	100

Table 3.2 *Parameter estimates for the model of time trends within social class*

social class	i	α_i	standard error (α_i)	β_i	standard error (β_i)
constant		−0.037	0.116	—	—
I	1	0.0	—	−0.058	0.022
II	2	−0.218	0.129	0.002	0.010
IIIN	3	−0.076	0.136	0.019	0.012
IIIM	4	−0.083	0.123	0.011	0.007
IV	5	−0.033	0.127	0.020	0.009
V	6	0.135	0.137	0.018	0.013
inadequately described	7	0.056	0.186	0.028	0.026
unoccupied	8	1.26	0.134	−0.067	0.014

yields a deviance of 745.4 on 87 degrees of freedom. The slope estimates, β_i, in *Table 3.2* confirm the impression given by *Figure 3.2* that the SMRs for social class I are declining with duration of follow-up and those for classes II, IIIN, IIIM, IV, and V show tendencies of various magnitudes to rise with duration of follow-up. The model also confirms the marked decline in SMR for the unoccupied, noted earlier.

MORTALITY IN 1976–81 BY AGE

While the longitudinal study has advantages over the decennial supplement analysis, for example, in terms of numerator–denominator biases, it suffers severely because many fewer deaths are included in the analysis. *Table 3.1* is based on analysis of just over 8,000 male deaths between 1971

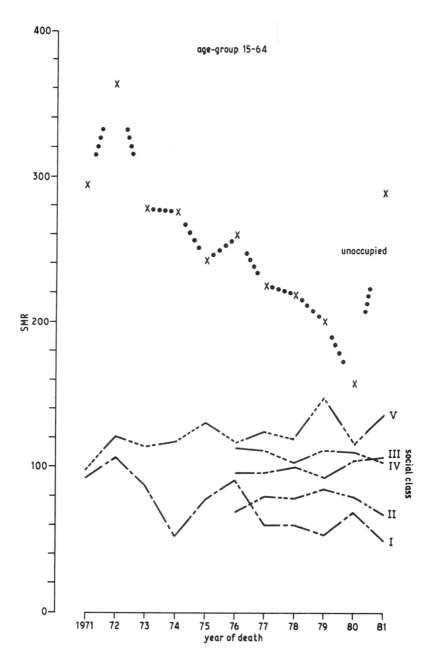

Figure 3.2 Mortality of men aged 15–64 by social class and year of death

Table 3.3 *Mortality of males in 1976–81 by social class in 1971 and age at death*

social class in 1971	age at death (yr)								
	15–64			65–74			75 and over		
	obs	exp	SMR	obs	exp	SMR	obs	exp	SMR
I	128	193.8	66	131	194.0	68	149	204.6	73
II	625	808.3	77	781	963.8	81	970	1,158.4	84
IIIN	450	429.3	105	500	580.8	86	672	731.3	92
IIIM	1,435	1,501.0	96	1,640	1,634.8	100	1,723	1,639.1	105
IV	774	710.6	109	1,107	1,045.7	106	1,202	1,110.8	108
V	358	289.1	124	597	549.1	109	697	602.1	116
armed forces	20	21.8	92	8	7.2	111	31	30.8	101
inadequately described	86	45.1	191	207	173.7	119	948	932.4	102
unoccupied	231	108.3	213	337	158.9	212	64	46.6	137
total	4,107	4,107.4	100	5,308	5,308.0	100	6,456	6,456.1	100

and 1981 at ages 15–64 years as compared with the 273,000 considered in the Decennial Supplement.[1] However, difficulty in obtaining information in the census on the previous occupation of men over retirement age has restricted traditional analysis of social class differences to those observed at working ages. At older ages the numerator denominator biases become unmanageable. Because it relies on information from only one source, the Longitudinal Study allows us to look at mortality differences beyond retirement age with some confidence, particularly as the duration of follow-up increases.

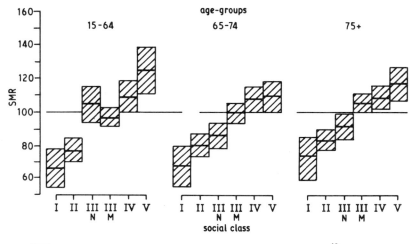

hatched areas represent approximate 95% confidence intervals[19] for SMRs; each SMR is indicated by a horizontal line within the hatched area

Figure 3.3   Mortality of men in 1976–81 by social class and broad age groups

Table 3.3 and *Figure 3.3* compare mortality by social class at ages 65–74 years and 75 years and over with that at younger ages. This is restricted to the period 1976–81 in order to allow for the selection effect of the unoccupied to wear off. At older ages this unoccupied group is less important to the analysis than at younger ages. Although more deaths of unoccupied men occurred over age 65 years than at younger ages, the deaths of unoccupied men accounted for only 4 per cent of deaths over age 65 years. The decline in importance of this category with age is expected because the cohort effect of health selection is expected to wear off with time. At the same time, people who had been permanently sick for a number of years before the census, but who were over retirement age at census, may have tended to report themselves as retired rather than permanently sick. For the retired, the census coders would seek a last occupation (which they did not do for the permanently sick). In this way men who were sick at these older ages would be included in the social class analysis.

The problem of those men with inadequately described occupation, although numerically of increasing importance at older ages, has less impact than at younger ages because the mortality of this group is nearer to that of the whole population at the same age. Again, this is as would be expected since many respondents at the older ages reported that they were retired (in response to the census question about economic position) but subsequently on the census schedule failed to give an occupation. This

Table 3.4 *Parameter estimates for the model of trends in SMR with age-group within social class*

social class	i	α_i	standard error (α_i)	β_i	standard error (β_i)
constant		−0.635	0.328	—	—
I	1	0.0	—	0.0039	0.0045
II	2	0.253	0.357	0.0024	0.0019
IIIN	3	0.859	0.374	−0.0041	0.0025
IIIM	4	0.412	0.343	0.0033	0.0014
IV	5	0.734	0.354	−0.0004	0.0018
V	6	0.896	0.382	−0.0017	0.0026

latter failure appears to have occurred as a result of a genuine mis-understanding of the census instructions and, in mortality terms at least, was unrelated to the health of the respondent.

The data presented in *Table 3.3* and *Figure 3.3* are the first reliable estimates of social class gradients in England and Wales at these older ages. The impression given is that, even if there is some narrowing of the class gradients with age, there remains a marked difference in the oldest age group. This is borne out by the age-specific mortality ratios presented in *Figure 3.4* and the model fitted to these data, which is summarized in *Table 3.4*. As with the model fitted to the time trends for each social class, the model in *Table 3.4* gives a satisfactory fit to the data. The deviance of 39.3 on 42 degrees of freedom compares with a deviance of 258.5 on 53 degrees of freedom in the null model. Much of the reduction in deviance is achieved by fitting a model with only social class terms (deviance 50.5 on 48 degrees of freedom). The parameters β_i, which represent class-specific trends in SMR with age, support the impression given by *Figure 3.4* of no clear trends with increasing age, except for men in social class IIIM, for whom the mortality ratios are higher at older ages.

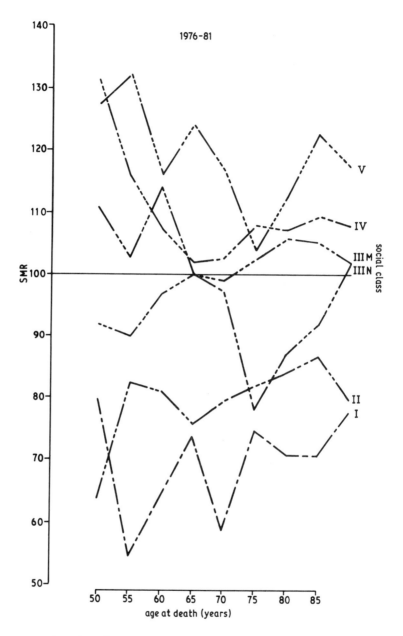

Figure 3.4 Mortality of men in 1976–81 by social class and five-year age groups

DISCUSSION

These new data on deaths of men at ages 15–64 years in the period 1976–81 from the OPCS Longitudinal Study confirm earlier estimates of mortality differentials by social class from the 1970–72 Decennial Supplement on Occupational Mortality and those from mortality in the period 1971–75 from the Longitudinal Study. In particular, the effects of selection out of the workforce, noted in the early period of follow-up, are found to have diminished substantially. While the linear models fitted in *Table 3.2* suggest that differences between social classes may continue to widen with increased duration of follow up, the data on which this model was based may fit alternative models equally well. In particular, after the widening differential during this initial period, we might now expect to see a continuing flattening of the slopes with time for each class as the follow-up period is increased. It is still too early in the study to predict when such changes will become negligible from year to year.

For men dying at ages over 65 years the present analysis extends the analysis of SMRs beyond the scope of previous data. In view of earlier comments on national data,[2] it is perhaps surprising that at ages after retirement mortality gradients in 1976–81 are almost as steep as those found in the later stages of normal working life. For example, at ages over 75 years men allocated to social class V have a more than 50 per cent higher death rate than men in social class I.

For the majority of men aged over 65 years at census, the social class recorded here represents their main occupation before retirement. Hence the existence of such steep gradients in these older age groups sheds some important light on arguments about the influence of selective mobility between social classes. The argument that a drift down the social scale may occur during periods of ill health cannot be extended with any force to people over age 75 years at death who would have retired 10 or more years before death. Differentials at these oldest ages must therefore be attributed to their socioeconomic environments, lifestyles, and cir-cumstances in the period leading up to their deaths, not to their changing social class as a result of ill health. Prospective studies of people exposed to particular occupational hazards also indicate that direct effects of occupation have greater impact on SMRs at younger than at older ages (see, for example, Case *et al.*[16]).

These comments about the mortality of men at older ages can also now be extended to men towards the end of the working age range. The data presented here, relating deaths in 1976–81 to social class in 1971, suggest that the mortality gradient by social class five to ten years before death is similar both to that by social class at death (published in the 1970–72 Decennial Supplement on Occupational Mortality[1]) and to the gradients presented here for men at older ages. This again suggests that mortality gradients at these ages, although subject to short-term effects of health-related exclusion from the social class classification, are little influenced by health-related mobility between social classes. Far more important are the effects of accumulated life experiences.

Where then does this leave arguments about the influence of inter-class mobility and its effects on mortality differentials? First, we should emphasize that most of the literature on inter-class mobility and its relation to health, both applied[17] and theoretical,[7] has concentrated on mobility at younger ages than are considered here. These studies focus on the changes between generations, comparing father's class with own class, or at the earliest stages of working life, comparing first job with job at age 30, say. These are ages when there is a much higher degree of mobility than at older ages. Some of this mobility is undoubtedly health-related, as is particularly well illustrated by the Aberdeen studies of pregnancy outcome in relation to own and father's social class.[17] Also, the effects of any health-related selection at these ages will be magnified beyond the level implied by the numerical size of those changing class because a small proportion of people at these ages are unhealthy. However, as we argued in our analysis of mortality in 1971–75 (see Fox and Goldblatt,[10] Chapter 11), such selection effects would be expected to wear off with time if they reflected only health at the time of selection.

Other mechanisms by which health selection at younger ages could have a major influence on mortality at older ages can be hypothesized. For example, it might be suggested that factors which influenced health-related behaviour after selected mobility were the same as those that influenced the direction of this mobility. As an illustration, under such a model, people who smoked or had poor diets might be more likely to be downwardly mobile; their dietary or smoking behaviour would, more-over, remain constant at least until such time as it had seriously and irrevocably affected their health.

Anyone putting forward such an argument needs to recognize that it is not health that underlies the initial social selection process at younger ages, but health-related behaviour, and that this pattern of behaviour must persist into the later stages of life, having been determined by the experiences of childhoood or early adulthood. Under the model, experiences and circumstances at older ages may, in general, only serve to reinforce the effect of these early experiences on health-related behaviour. We would favour an explanation that recognized a somewhat more variable influence of differentials in the recent experiences and circumstances of individuals on their health-related behaviour and hence on mortality. It would recognize both the influences on experience and behaviour that result from downward mobility and the major changes in behaviour that have taken place during this century.

A second mechanism might be put forward to relate mortality at older ages to mobility at younger ages. This would suggest that some types of chronic morbidity at younger ages are severe enough to have an immediate influence on social mobility but do not have a major impact on mortality until considerably older ages. A number of psychiatric conditions could be argued to operate in this way.

It needs to be recognized, however, that such conditions would have to be fairly widespread in the community to have any impact on social class differentials. Most studies of chronic diseases, moreover, indicate raised levels of mortality at every age. The effect of persistently raised levels of mortality among an unhealthy group and their subsequent influence on general mortality can best be illustrated by an example from the Longitudinal Study. The unoccupied in 1971 were sufficiently large in number in 1971–75 to have a distorting effect on social class mortality gradients. However, in 1976–81 their influence had diminished, in part because their SMRs were lower, but also because their earlier mortality experiences had reduced their numbers.

It would therefore seem improbable to us that incipient ill health could persist in a large part of the community for many years, affecting their job prospects for most of their working lives, failing to diminish the size of the group through early mortality; and yet, at the end of their working lives, resulting in excess mortality sufficient to generate observed social class differentials.

To the extent that they contribute to the interpretation of social class differentials in mortality in the 1970s, therefore, these new data add credence to the gradients published in the Decennial Supplement[1] and suggest that major explanations for such differentials should not be sought from among artefactual or selection theories. This concurs with the conclusion drawn by the Black Working Group.[2]

These observations, if supported by further data from mortality in the period 1981–85, are of major importance to the interpretation of differentials in the Decennial Supplement series. By confirming the broad findings of the 1970–72 report, this analysis adds weight to the main focus of the Decennial Supplement analysis, which looks at social class differences by cause of death. We do not suggest that such data will, in the short term, be available from the Longitudinal Study. However, the observations we have made, for example about health-related selection, should encourage those searching for explanations of class differentials for particular causes of death to look to environmental and behavioural factors rather than to social mobility.

A second major limitation of the Decennial Supplement has resulted from its inappropriateness for making comparisons of mortality differentials over time; this was seen by the Working Party under Sir Douglas

Black as one of the main shortcomings of available sources. It is clearly too early to make promises about future comparisons using new data currently being incorporated into the Longitudinal Study. However, we plan to look at mortality in the 1980s linked to social class in both the 1971 and 1981 census in the same way as we have looked at mortality in the 1970s in relation to 1971 census characteristics alone. This will, for example, allow comparison across generations, at this stage, measured ten years apart. Second, and of greater immediate significance, mobility comparisons of circumstances in 1971 and 1981 are now being made. These will, in the near future, shed important light on the extent and direction of mobility at different ages and, when linked to deaths in the 1980s, to the contribution of health-related mobility in the 1970s to mortality in the 1980s. This analysis will build on that which describes the impact of selective migration before the 1971 census on geographic differentials in 1971–75.[18]

These analyses are part of a collaborative review of the Longitudinal Study mortality data by OPCS Medical Statistics Division and the Social Statistics Research Unit at City University. The latter are supported in this work by a programme grant from the Medical Research Council.

REFERENCES

1. Registrar General (1978) *Occupational Mortality Tables 1970–2 Decennial Supplement*, OPCS Series DS No. 1. London: HMSO.
2. DHSS Research Working Group (1980) *Inequalities in Health*. London: Department of Health and Social Security.
3. Ogle, W. (1885) Letter to the Registrar General on the mortality in the registration districts of England and Wales during the ten years 1871–1880. Supplement to the 45th Annual Report of the Registrar General of Births, Deaths and Marriages in England. xxiii.
4. *Op. cit.* 1, 174–75.
5. *Op. cit.* 1, 175–78.
6. *Op. cit.* 2, 153–57.
7. Stern, J. (1983) Social mobility and the interpretation of social class mortality differentials. *Journal of Social Policy* 12: 27–49.
8. OPCS (1973) Cohort studies: New developments. *Studies on Medical and Populations Subjects* No. 25. London: HMSO.
9. Fox, A. J. (1980) Prospects for measuring changes in differential mortality. *Proceedings of the UN/WHO Meeting on Socio-Economic Determinants and Consequences of Mortality* held in Mexico City in June 1979. New York; UN Geneva: WHO.

10. Fox, A. J. and Goldblatt, P. O. (1982) *Socio-demographic Mortality Differentials: Longitudinal Study 1971–5*. Series LS No. 1. London: HMSO.
11. Jones, I. G. and Cameron, D. (1984) Social class—an embarrassment to epidemiology. *Community Medicine* 6: 37–46.
12. Registrar General (1970) *Classification of Occupations*. London: HMSO.
13. McCullagh, P. and Nelder, J. A. (1983) *Generalised Linear Models*. London: Chapman and Hall.
14. Breslow, N. E., Lubin, J. H., Marek, P., and Langholz, B. (1983) Multiplicative models and cohort studies. *Journal of the American Statistical Association* 78: 1–12.
15. Baker, R. J. and Nelder, J. A. (1978) *GLIM System Mark 3*. Oxford: Numerical Algorithm Group.
16. Case, R. A. M., Hosker, M. E.., McDonald, D. B., and Pearson, J. T. (1954) Tumours of the urinary bladder in workmen engaged in the manufacture and use of certain dyestuff intermediates in the British chemical industry. *British Journal of Industrial Medicine* 11: 75–104.
17. Illsley, R. (1955) Social class selection and class differences in relation to stillbirths and infant deaths. *British Medical Journal* ii: 1520–524.
18. Fox, A. J., Goldblatt, P. O., and Adelstein, A. M. (1982) Selection and mortality differentials. *Journal of Epidemiology and Community Health* 36: 69–79.
19. Vandenbroucke, J. P. (1982) A shortcut method for calculating the 95 per cent confidence interval of the standardised mortality ratio. *American Journal of Epidemiology* 115: 303–04.

FOUR

Serious illness in childhood and its association with later-life achievement

M. E. J. Wadsworth

The extent of social inequalities in health has been well described both in terms of morbidity and mortality (DHSS 1980; Townsend and Davidson 1982). There seems no doubt that the causes are many and may be seen, for example, as social class differentials in the uptake of preventive care and advice (Blaxter 1981), in concepts of self-care (Pill and Stott 1982), in seeking professional advice early in the course of an illness (Calnan 1982), and in exposure to experiences harmful to health (McQueen and Siegrist 1982). One of the particularly interesting questions still thoroughly to be investigated is how early in life inequalities may be detected. We already have good evidence from data on perinatal and infant mortality of considerable social class differences in these rates and reasons for these differences have been sought across a wide range of ideas.

Social class differences in childhood illness are less well documented but, in so far as they are, they seem to present a much less sharply differentiated relationship between illness and social class than the work on adults might lead us to expect (DHSS 1980). Use of preventive care services in childhood is certainly class-biased (Blaxter 1981) and there is evidence of class differences in diet and dietary habits, which shows that lower social class children have relatively ill-balanced diets that might be the beginnings of poor dietary habits for life (Black, Billiewicz, and Thomson 1976; DHSS 1975), although there are perhaps indications of some improvement (McKillop and Durnin 1982). There is also evidence that lower social class children are of shorter stature, which itself may be taken as an indicator of health status (Tanner 1962; Illsley and Kincaid 1963). We know very little about the extent to which these differences matter in the formulation of adult health, however, and very little about the extent to which the larger pool of lower social class illness in adult life is fed with streams of children from different social backgrounds, in terms of health and social circumstances. In other words, the relevance of childhood health for adult health is not well understood: nor is the effect that childhood ill-health might exert on later-life opportunities, by reducing chances of achievement in education and qualifications.

Educational achievements themselves are also beset with social in-equalities (Douglas 1964; Fogelman 1983) and in the longitudinal study reported here they, too, are associated very interestingly with social class. Educational inequalities evidently began in early life, and it was concluded from an investigation of the cohort children at age fifteen years that

'many of the major differences in performance [may be attributed] to environmental influences acting in the pre-school years. Many factors appear to have exerted their main influence on measured ability by the time the children leave the infant school . . .; children acquire, early in their years at school, attitudes to learning that are related to later success or failure.'

(Douglas, Ross, and Simpson 1968: 177–78, 180)

It is especially interesting to note that in the same study children's educational achievements, in terms of measured attainment, increased as their fathers were socially mobile in an upward direction (Douglas 1965). This is arguably the result of changing parental aspirations and of children changing school. It is, therefore, worth considering whether there might be a similar association of parental upward social mobility with improved health chances of the study child, although any similar associations between health and social mobility might take more than one generation to achieve (Illsley and Kincaid 1963). As Sorokin (1959) speculated and Illsley (1980) demonstrated, social class and health and illness are closely and dynamically associated.

'Variations in diet and the living standards which predispose to optimal growth and development are positively correlated with factors such as education and IQ (the latter being taken not as a genetic indicator but as a reflection of environmental stimulation) which predispose to occupational attainment and, in turn, through assortative mating to upward mobility on marriage. As a result, class differences, both social and biological, which occur when persons are classified by their class of upbringing, are sharpened when they are re-classified by class at marriage. The processes of social mobility thus possess an in-built differentiating quality, which continues year by year with each new cohort and produces a pressure towards disparity.'

(Illsley 1980: 21–2)

Relationships between class and health and illness pose questions that are notoriously difficult to define for research purposes (Stern 1983), and therefore to investigate and, as the Black Report on inequalities in health observed, 'in order to study the dynamics of child health—the process by which ill-health and educational under-achievement (whether a consequence of handicapping conditions, absence from school, or cultural factors) develop together and so perpetuate the link between health and social class—it is necessary to turn to longitudinal studies' (DHSS 1980: 220). This chapter describes work on inequalities in health carried out in a national longitudinal study which began at the birth of the subjects in 1946.

METHODS

The study concerned is a longitudinal study of children born in one week in March 1946 in all parts of England, Wales, and Scotland. The study began in that year and has continued ever since to follow up many aspects of the lives of a sample of those born in the study week. The follow-up sample comprises all legitimate, single births to wives of non-manual and agricultural workers and one in four of all other legitimate single births, a total of 5,362 individuals. This initial sampling procedure can be compensated for by a statistical weighting procedure.

Contacts during the infant and school years were made at intervals of two years or less and in adult life at slightly longer intervals. The data collected have always been as widely representative as possible of medical, educational, occupational, social, and psychological concerns. (A full description of the study and of the data collected is given in Atkins *et al.* 1981.) Losses have occurred as a result of death and of migration but from comparisons with published material on rates of illness, criminality, divorce, hospital admissions, and census data the sample appears still to be representative of people of this age who were born in England, Wales, or Scotland. At the last contact in 1982, 3,322 cohort members were interviewed, representing 82 per cent of those still alive and resident in England, Wales, or Scotland.

Data used in this chapter are of three kinds: social class, illness, and educational achievement. Social class is used to describe social inequalities and this information is based either on reports of fathers' occupations collected at interviews when cohort members were children or on cohort members' own social class according to occupation; those cohort members to whom a social class could not be assigned are treated separately. Ideally, cohort members' mothers' own social class should also have been taken into account but this information was not available at the time of analysis. The Office of Population Censuses and Surveys' classification (OPCS 1980) was used to ascribe social class, since this has traditionally been the classification of choice in morbidity and mortality studies, and in the tables in this chapter it is either presented in full or, if necessary, aggregated into non-manual and manual groups.

Information on illness was collected from mothers, health visitors and cohort members' own reports, from data on absence from school, and from school doctors' examinations; reports from all sources were checked with hospitals and other medical records. Illnesses were taken to be serious if they involved hospital admission of a minimum of twenty-eight consecutive days, or school or work absence of three consecutive weeks or more in total. They were coded using the International Classification of Diseases (WHO 1967) and are listed, by age, in *Table 4.1*. Information on health was assumed from the absence of serious illness and was provided by data on height, which had been collected at medical examinations carried out by health visitors and school doctors and nurses especially for the study when cohort members were four years old and fifteen years old.

Information on educational achievement at school was also collected from cohort members and from teachers' reports, and was supplied in the form of scores on three sets of attainment tests that cohort members took for the purposes of the study at the age of fifteen. The tests were of non-verbal and verbal attainment (the AH4), of reading (Watts-Vernon), and of mathematics (a test constructed for the study); details of the tests and of their reliability are given in Douglas, Ross, and Simpson (1968). Weighted norms were calculated by converting the raw scores to a combined T-score with a mean of 50 and a standard deviation of 10. Qualifications reported after the school years were checked with awarding authorities wherever possible.

It is important to note that this kind of longitudinal study design can only go part of the way towards answering questions about interactions of social class, health, and achievement in the development of inequality. Although the omission of those children who were illegitimately born is unfortunate in the study of inequalities, nevertheless the basic design is good for the study of what happens to individuals as they grow older; but because this design involves only individuals born in the same year it may in some respects be limited to interpretation of the social influences of that time. It could, for example, be argued that a cohort of individuals born in 1946 represents an unusual time in our social history. Born two years before the introduction of the National Health Service, these children spent their early years in the shadow of the Second World War, experiencing food rationing and what Marwick calls 'the frustration and austerity of the immediate post-war years' (1982: 24). The cohort's childhood years were also spent during a time when infectious disease was still far more prevalent than it is now, when death rates were higher, and when many forms of medical treatment were less effective than they are today. Nevertheless, however different life is for children today, the

Table 4.1 *Serious illness as defined in this chapter and death of cohort members at these ages—actual numbers*

serious illness (ICD codes)	age in years				
	0–5	6–10	11–15	16–20	21–25
none	4,836	4,541	4,889	4,455	4,456
tuberculosis (010–019)	23	22	9	13	12
acute specific bacterial & virus infections of childhood (032–034, 052, 055–057, 072)	49	80	0	5	3
poliomyelitis (040–046)	13	25	14	10	9
all other infective & parasitic diseases (001–009, 020–031, 035–039, 050–051, 053–054, 060–071, 073–136)	38	14	2	28	28
malignant neoplasms (140–209)	5	3	2	4	7
benign & unspecified neoplasms (210–239)	1	1	0	1	4
endocrine, nutritional and metabolic disease (240–279)	4	7	8	13	26
diseases of blood (280–289)	8	7	2	6	5
mental disorders (290–309)	0	3	3	6	7
mental retardation (310–315)	51	48	51	34	33
diseases of central nervous system (320–349)	33	37	29	38	42
diseases of peripheral nervous system (350–358)	1	0	0	2	2
diseases of eye (360–379)	1	11	8	7	7
diseases of ear (380–389)	17	20	9	14	15
rheumatic fever (390–398)	1	22	15	7	8
other circulatory disease (400–458)	1	2	1	5	14
pneumonia and bronchitis, asthma (480–493)	49	57	20	26	27
other respiratory disease (460–474, 500–519)	10	52	7	54	44
appendicitis (540–543)	3	28	2	39	18
other diseases of digestive system (520–537, 550–577)	12	6	5	29	50
genito-urinary system (580–629)	14	14	7	25	25
pregnancy and childbirth (630–678)	0	0	0	5	17
skin (680–709)	4	22	3	25	24
musculo-skeletal (710–738)	8	20	15	24	30
congenital (740–759)	90	56	40	30	27
early infancy (760–779)	52	0	0	0	0
ill-defined (780–796)	9	13	2	12	22
accident (traffic) (800)	6	16	7	82	43
accident (work) (810)	0	0	0	62	48
accident (other) (820–860)	23	39	15	83	77
more than one serious illness (880)	0	7	0	7	5
death	231	8	12	16	17

Source: World Health Organisation (1967).

cohort will still fairly represent the population who were born in this country and who are now in their late thirties. Therefore, in any attempt to extrapolate from these findings to earlier or later age cohorts it will be necessary to consider whether the subject matter concerned is specific to the time when this particular cohort was studied.

HEALTH AND ILLNESS IN CHILDHOOD

Social distribution of health and illness

From the earliest ages, morbidity is unequally distributed by social class. *Tables* 4.2 and 4.3 show that for both boys and girls there is a tendency amongst those with known social class for the ill to be of lower social class; these differences achieve statistical significance in the case of boys but not of girls. The association with social class is achieved as a result of the distribution of illness other than mental disorders, congenital problems, or injuries. The kinds of social class differences shown in these tables persist in all the five-year age-groups up to the age of twenty-five years, which is as far as our data go at present, and in each age-group the association achieves statistical significance in males but not in females.

Cohort members who could not be ascribed a social class present a problem, particularly since this is a sample of legitimate births; the lack of a social class at the age of four years therefore usually reflects a degree of disruption of family life or a loss of contact with the family. Amongst the seriously ill children, it is possible to account for the majority of those without social class. Most (105) of the 121 seriously ill boys without social class had already died by 1950, 4 had experienced family disruption through parental death or divorce, and 1 family had emigrated, thus accounting for 90.9 per cent of the seriously ill boys: we were unable to contact the remaining 11 families in this group at this time. Similarly, most of the 87 seriously ill girls who could not be classified by social class could

Table 4.2 *The percentage association of social class and illness during cohort boys' first five years*

son's serious illness 0–5 years	*father's social class when son aged four years*						
	I	*II*	*III NM*	*III M*	*IV*	*V*	*unknown & not ascribed*
none	97.8	94.1	93.1	92.5	90.3	87.7	73.7
illness, except those below	1.5	3.4	3.7	5.3	5.3	7.4	21.7
mental illness & subnormality	—	0.5	0.7	0.3	3.0	2.5	0.9
congenital problems	0.7	1.8	1.6	1.2	1.0	1.2	3.0
injury	—	0.3	0.9	0.7	0.4	1.2	0.7
total (=100%)	136	387	432	732	506	162	460*

*of these, 131 are deaths of cohort members during the first five years of life, 13 are deaths of mothers, 29 are deaths of fathers, 75 are divorces, and the remaining 212 are cases with whom no contact was made at the five-year follow-up

Note: χ^2 for those with ascribed social class = 15.66 with 5 df p < .01 (adding rows 2, 3, 4, and 5).

Table 4.3 *The percentage association of social class and illness during cohort girls' first five years*

daughter's serious illness 0–5 years	*father's social class when daughter aged four years*						
	I	*II*	*III NM*	*III M*	*IV*	*V*	*unknown & not ascribed*
none	92.9	94.5	94.1	94.2	92.4	91.4	78.3
illness, except those below	1.6	3.3	3.1	4.1	3.9	4.8	17.2
mental illness & subnormality	1.6	0.6	0.5	0.6	1.4	2.1	0.5
congenital problems	4.0	1.4	1.8	0.9	1.6	0.7	3.3
injury	—	0.3	0.5	0.3	0.7	0.7	0.7
total (=100%)	126	361	391	688	437	140	400*

*of these, 98 are deaths of cohort members during the first five years of life, 19 are deaths of mothers, 27 are deaths of fathers, 67 are divorces, and the remaining 189 are cases with whom no contact was made at the five-year follow-up

Note: χ^2 for those with ascribed social class = 2.80 with 4 df not significant (adding rows 2, 3, 4, and 5).

also be accounted for (89.7 per cent): 72 had already died, the parents of a further 4 had separated or divorced; there were no parental deaths, and 2 families had emigrated, leaving 9 families who could not be contacted.

By contrast, the most common reasons for not ascribing social class to healthy children was our loss of contact with them at this age (45.4 per cent of the 339 boys and 41.5 per cent of the 313 girls) or the emigration of their family (36 per cent of boys and 37.4 per cent of girls). Parental divorce was the next most frequent reason and this occurred at rates much higher than those experienced by seriously ill children (8.3 per cent of healthy boys compared with 1.7 per cent of seriously ill boys and 10.9 per cent of healthy girls compared with 4.6 per cent of seriously ill girls); the other cause of not ascribing social class was parental death (3.8 per cent of healthy boys and 3.2 per cent of healthy girls).

At the age of four years, boys from the non-manual social classes were significantly taller than boys from the manual classes (t = 8.92 with ∞ df p < .001) and similarly, non-manual social class girls were taller than those from the manual classes (t = 9.56 with ∞ df p < .001). By the age of fifteen years, the same kinds of differences still occurred, and were significant at the p < .001 level, but by this age the children who had had serious illness whilst they were aged 0–10 years were shorter than their healthy peers, within sex and social class groups. These differences in height do not achieve statistical significance in the non-manual social classes but manual class boys and girls were significantly shorter than their manual class, healthy counterparts if they had had serious illness

whilst they were aged both 0–5 and 6–10 years (for boys t = 1.96 with ∞ df
p = .05 and for girls t = 2.59 with ∞ df p <.01).

Childhood social mobility and serious illness

Since illness is not entirely equitably distributed by social class, it is worth
asking if changing social class is associated with chances of being ill. *Table
4.4* shows the association of fathers' social mobility, whilst their survey
member sons were aged 4–15 years, with the sons' experience of serious
illness in childhood. Boys from non-manual families were least likely to be
seriously ill if their father experienced a fall in social class, rather than a
rise or no movement, but these differences do not achieve statistical
significance. Boys from manual class families were healthier if their
fathers either rose to non-manual occupations or fell within the manual
group but these differences were not significant.

For girls, differences were somewhat greater, as *Table 4.5* shows.
Amongst girls of non-manual origin, those whose fathers did not change
their social class experienced the least serious illness, and any kind

Table 4.4 *Father's social mobility* and its percentage association with son's serious
illness in childhood*

father's social mobility whilst son aged 4–15 years	son's serious illness at these ages				total (= 100%)
	no serious illness	0–5 yrs	6–10 yrs	0–5 yrs and 6–10 yrs	
non-manual origin					
no change	84.0	2.6	9.2	4.1	533
rise	82.0	2.3	13.5	2.3	133
falling within non-manual	94.6	—	5.4	—	37
falling to manual	86.0	—	12.3	1.8	57
manual origin					
no change	81.8	3.8	10.7	3.7	708
rising within manual	77.5	6.3	13.4	2.8	142
rising out of manual	84.7	3.2	8.9	3.2	124
falling within manual	84.6	3.8	9.6	1.9	104
unknown social class in one year	88.0	3.1	7.0	1.9	482
unknown social class in both years	96.2	1.5	1.1	1.1	264

*computed on the difference between social class when child aged four years and social class when child
aged fifteen years

Class and Health

Table 4.5 *Father's social mobility* and its percentage association with daughter's serious illness in childhood*

father's social mobility whilst daughter aged 4–15 years	daughter's serious illness at these ages				total (= 100%)
	no serious illness	0–5 yrs	6–10 yrs	0–5 yrs and 6–10 yrs	
non-manual origin					
no change	87.6	1.8	7.8	2.7	510
rise	82.7	2.9	10.6	3.8	104
falling within non-manual	84.0	—	12.0	4.0	25
falling to manual	86.2	1.5	10.8	1.5	65
manual origin					
no change	85.1	2.1	10.2	2.6	678
rising within manual	80.6	5.4	10.1	3.9	129
rising out of manual	87.1	3.0	7.9	2.0	101
falling within manual	85.6	3.8	5.8	4.8	104
unknown social class in one year	86.6	3.2	7.7	2.5	403
unknown social class in both years	95.0	2.3	1.1	1.5	261

*computed as the difference between social class when child aged four years and social class when child aged fifteen years

of social mobility was associated with a greater amount of illness experienced. For those of manual origin, conspicuously less illness was suffered by those whose fathers' mobility moved them into the non-manual classes (12.9 per cent) as compared with 17 per cent of girls with serious illness whose fathers did not change their class, 19 per cent of girls whose fathers experienced downward social mobility and 21.4 per cent of girls whose fathers rose in social class but who remained within the manual social classes. If, for the sake of the statistical test, social movement is described as some or none, then significantly more serious illness is to be found amongst non-manual girls whose fathers experienced social mobility (20.1 per cent had serious illness) as compared with those whose fathers were not mobile (12.4 per cent had serious illness; $\chi^2 = 7.02$ with 1 df $p < .01$); however, the differences amongst manual class girls were not statistically significant. Thus, although there is some suggestion that children of socially mobile fathers were a little more likely to be seriously ill than others, this was not a well-defined association. For neither boys nor girls was height at fifteen years of age associated with fathers' social mobility or lack of social movement.

Any association of childhood illness in this cohort with parental social mobility is difficult to interpret. It might be that tall fathers were more socially mobile and, therefore, that what we see is a genetic effect. It might also be a cohort effect, in that in these immediate post-war years men who would under peacetime circumstances have been likely, for example, to have a social class II job might well, on first being discharged from the forces, have taken a job of a lower social class than they would otherwise have expected, thus giving in some senses a false picture of social mobility.

Educational achievement at school and health and illness

Educational achievement at the end of the compulsory school years was assessed using the combined results of three tests that children took at the age of fifteen years, as described above. Combined test scores of healthy children were compared with those of children who had had serious illness whilst they were aged 0–5 years, or whilst aged 6–10 years, or during both of these time periods, and significant differences were found for boys but not for girls. Ill boys from non-manual social class families scored significantly lower than healthy boys only if they had been ill during both time periods ($t = 2.13$ with ∞ df p <.05) and manual social-class boys had significantly lower scores if they had been ill whilst aged 0–5 years ($t = 2.06$ with ∞ df p < .05) or during both time periods ($t = 4.27$ with ∞ df p < .001). It has already been shown in this population that, during the school years, boys and girls who were high educational achievers were significantly taller than others (Douglas, Ross, and Simpson 1968).

HEALTH AND ILLNESS IN EARLY ADULT LIFE

Social distribution of health and illness

Serious illness at 21–25 years old was significantly more common in men (15.8 per cent with serious illness) than in women (11.8 per cent with serious illness) ($\chi^2 = 11.87$ with 1 df p < .001) and this was so within each social class. As expected, serious illness in early adult life was inequitably distributed by social class and, as with serious illness in this same population when they were children, there was—as *Tables 4.6* and *4.7* show—significantly more serious illness in men of lower social classes when compared with other men but there were no significant class differences in women. In both men and women, the most striking differences were in the higher rates of injury and of mental illness and subnormality in the manual social classes and these latter rates show the damaging effect

Table 4.6 *Social class and serious illness in men in early adult life, expressed as a percentage*

serious illness whilst age 21–25 years	I	II	III NM	III M	IV	V	armed forces	not working
no serious illness	89.9	87.6	86.7	80.8	77.8	79.1	75.9	66.9
serious illness, except those specified below	8.0	9.2	9.6	10.8	11.8	9.3	16.7	16.9
mental illness & subnormality	0.5	—	—	0.3	2.7	4.5	—	4.2
congenital illness	—	—	—	0.3	—	—	—	5.9
injuries	1.5	3.2	3.7	7.8	7.7	7.0	7.4	5.9
total (= 100%)	199	434	271	650	221	43	54	118

Note: Considering all types of illness together, adding classes IV & V, χ^2 = 43.98 with 5 df p < .001; considering all types of illness together, adding classes IV & V and omitting forces data, χ^2 = 22.71 with 6 df p < .001.

Table 4.7 *Social class and serious illness in women in early adult life, expressed as a percentage*

serious illness whilst age 21–25 years	I & II	III NM	III M	IV & V	armed forces	not working
no serious illness	88.4	88.3	89.2	80.5	(3)	87.2
serious illness, except those specified below	10.8	9.8	8.1	15.6	(0)	9.7
mental illness & subnormality	—	—	—	1.3	(0)	0.8
congenital illness	—	0.3	—	—	(0)	0.9
injuries	0.8	1.6	2.7	2.6	(1)	1.4
total (= 100%)	258	307	37	77	4	1,249

Note: Considering all types of illness together, comparing all non-manual with all manual and omitting those not working, χ^2 = 1.34 with Yates's correction and 1 df; considering all types of illness together, comparing all non-manual with all manual including those not working, χ^2 = 1.32 with 2 df.

on achieved class position and occupation of such illness. The extent to which these serious illnesses were of long standing is shown in the two following sections. If mental illness and subnormality, and congenital illness and injuries are excluded, however, there is still an increasing amount of other serious illness as social class falls in both men and women, although these differences are not then statistically significant.

The serious illness data presented in *Tables 4.6* and *4.7* were also checked for associations with educational achievement by the age of twenty-six and with father's social class when the cohort member was fifteen years old. The extent of serious illness was greater for both men and women with lower educational achievement and amongst those whose fathers were in the manual social classes but the statistical significances of the associations were once more found only in men (with educational achievement $\chi^2 = 11.41$ with 2 df p < .01 and with father's social class $\chi^2 = 17.20$ with 1 df p < .001) and not in women (with educational achievement $\chi^2 = 3.02$ with 2 df and with father's social class $\chi^2 = 0.30$ with 1 df).

How many seriously ill children were also seriously ill as adults?

Whilst they were 21–25 years old, 641 (12.6 per cent of the 5,079 whose health histories were known at this age) cohort members were seriously ill; of these 174 (27.1 per cent of all those with serious illness at these ages) had also been seriously ill in childhood. As *Table 4.8* shows, men had serious illness both in childhood and in early adult life more often than women ($\chi^2 = 16.08$ with 3 df p < .01).

Lifetime histories of serious illness experience are shown in *Tables 4.9* and *4.10* and they confirm that, in this population, there was an increasing difference with increasing age of serious illness in men and women. When men and women of different social classes were compared, in *Table 4.11*, it was evident that although those in the manual social classes had experienced more serious illness than others, both in childhood and in early adult life, there was nevertheless very little social class difference in the legacy of childhood serious illness present in adult life. Adult serious illness amongst men who had been healthy children was significantly

Table 4.8 *Experience of serious illness in childhood and in early adult life, by sex*

	males		females	
	no serious illness 0–10 yrs (2,258)	*serious illness 0–10 yrs* (388)	*no serious illness 0–10 yrs* (2,122)	*serious illness 0–10 yrs* (311)
no serious illness 21–25 yrs	1,984 (87.9%)	284 (73.2%)	1,929 (90.9%)	241 (77.5%)
serious illness 21–25 yrs	274 (12.1%)	104 (26.8%)	193 (9.1%)	70 (22.5%)

Table 4.9 *Subsequent serious illness of 2,122 males and 2,258 females who were not seriously ill whilst aged 0–10 years*

| | serious illness at these ages | | | | | |
| | 11–15 yrs | | 16–20 yrs | | 21–25 yrs | |
	males	females	males	females	males	females
seriously ill for the first time at this age	1.4% 32	1.3% 27	10.4% 235	8.7% 185	7.9% 178	6.5% 137
ill in one previous age band after age 11 years	—	—	0.6% 13	0.4% 8	3.8% 87	2.4% 51
ill in more than one previous age band after age 11 years	—	—	—	—	0.4% 9	0.2% 5
total seriously ill	1.4% 32	1.3% 27	11.0% 248	9.1% 193	12.1% 274	9.1% 193
total without serious illness	98.6% 2,226	98.7% 2,095	89.0% 2,010	90.9% 1,929	87.9% 1,984	90.9% 1,929

Table 4.10 *Subsequent serious illness of 388 males and 311 females who were seriously ill whilst aged 0–10 years*

| | serious illness at these ages | | | | | |
| | 11–15 yrs | | 16–20 yrs | | 21–25 yrs | |
	males	females	males	females	males	females
serious illness at this age	21.9% 85	19.9% 62	28.1% 109	28.9% 90	26.8% 104	22.5% 70
serious illness at this age and at all previous ages	21.9% 85	19.9% 62	16.2% 63	16.4% 51	13.4% 52	13.5% 42
not seriously ill at this age	78.1% 303	80.1% 249	71.9% 279	71.1% 221	73.2% 284	77.5% 241

more likely amongst those who were not employed or of manual social class rather than amongst those in non-manual employment ($\chi^2 = 19.93$ with 4 df p $<.001$) but there were no social class differences for women.

In view of the differences in height of sick children compared with well children, already described, it was necessary to ask whether shorter children were more likely to be seriously ill as adults. Although both men and women who had serious illness at any age tended to be shorter than those who had never been seriously ill, only those manual social class men who were seriously ill in both childhood and at 21–25 years old were

Table 4.11   *Sex and social class differences in serious illness in childhood and at ages 21–25 years, expressed as a percentage*

age at experience of serious illness	men*		women**	
	non-manual	manual	non-manual	manual
no serious illness in childhood or whilst age 21–25 yrs	76.3	68.1	79.0	75.6
seriously ill in childhood but not at 21–25 yrs	11.5	13.2	9.8	12.2
seriously ill at 21–25 yrs but not in childhood	8.1	13.5	8.1	9.6
seriously ill both in childhood and whilst aged 21 – 25 yrs	4.1	5.1	3.0	2.7
total (= 100%)	860	1,049	762	1,011

*χ^2 = 19.16 with 3 df p < .001
**χ^2 = 3.98 with 3 df not significant

significantly shorter than men in their own social class who had always been fit (t = 2.35 with ∞ df p < .05). Amongst the population who had not been seriously ill in childhood, there was no significantly greater likelihood of shorter men and women becoming seriously ill in early adult life. This may mean that at this age shortness of stature is to be seen as a consequence but not as a predictor of serious illness.

In linear multiple regression analyses that tested the associations of childhood illness, social class of family of origin, achieved educational position as an adult, size of family of origin when the cohort member was fifteen years old, birth rank, and height at fifteen years old, with the dependent variable serious illness in early adult life, only childhood illness remained significant for men; for women, none of the independent variables achieved significance. Thus, there were no significant differences according to social class of family of origin.

ADULT ACHIEVEMENT AND CHILD HEALTH

When they were twenty-six years old, cohort members were interviewed at home about a wide range of topics, including their educational and occupational achievements and their marital status. Contact was made with 75.6 per cent of men who had been well children and with 81.7 per cent of those who had been seriously ill in childhood, with 81.9 per cent of women who had been well in childhood and with 89.6 per cent of women who had been seriously ill in childhood.

Educational qualifications and childhood health

Men and women who had been seriously ill in childhood were significantly different in their long-term educational achievements when compared with those who had been well (Douglas 1984). As *Tables 4.12 and 4.13* show, both men and women were significantly more likely to have gained qualifications if they had been healthy children but in both sexes it looks as if serious illness experienced in the pre-school years, or for a long time in childhood, carried more potential damage for educational achievement than serious illness experienced during the early years at

Table 4.12 *Childhood health and subsequent educational achievement of men, expressed as a percentage*

childhood health	educational achievement			total (= 100%)
	no qualifications	up to 'O' level	'A' level and university qualifications	
no serious illness in childhood	39.5	20.2	40.2	1,916
serious illness 0–5 years	58.9	17.8	23.2	56
serious illness 6–10 years	43.7	20.5	35.8	229
serious illness 0–10 years	57.8	13.3	28.9	45

Note: $\chi^2 = 16.23$ with 6 df p $< .05$.

school. When children with mental disorders or mental retardation are excluded from these tables, then for men there still remains a statistically significant association between childhood serious illness and later qualifications ($\chi^2 = 13.73$ with 6 df p $< .05$) but for women the association just fails to achieve significance ($\chi^2 = 11.90$ with 6 df). Once the effects of mothers' and fathers' education and of cohort members' height at the age of fifteen had been taken into account in a linear multiple regression analysis, however, childhood serious illness was no longer significantly associated with educational qualifications, either in men or women.

Highest academic achievers were significantly taller than others. Men who gained 'A' level passes or university qualifications were taller than those who did not, whether their family of origin was non-manual (t = 5.32 with ∞ df p $<.001$) or manual (t = 3.44 with ∞ df p $<.001$). For women, there were no differences in height by educational achievement amongst those from non-manual families but those of manual origin who had gained 'A' level or university qualifications were significantly taller than those who did not (t = 4.12 with ∞ df p $< .001$).

Table 4.13 *Childhood health and subsequent educational achievement of women, expressed as a percentage*

childhood health	educational achievement			total (= 100%)
	no qualifications	up to 'O' level	'A' level and university qualifications	
no serious illness in childhood	43.3	29.2	27.5	1,817
serious illness 0–5 years	52.4	35.7	11.9	42
serious illness 6–10 years	51.4	28.6	20.0	175
serious illness 0–10 years	56.8	27.0	16.2	37

Note: $\chi^2 = 13.38$ with 6 df $p < .05$.

Adult social class, occupation, and social mobility

By the age of twenty-six, men who had had serious illness in childhood were still significantly more likely to be of a lower social class than those who had been healthy children ($\chi^2 = 6.71$ with 2 df $p < .05$). There were no social class differences amongst women who were single and employed (35.3 per cent of all women) and the proportions of women who were not employed were very similar whether they had been healthy children (64 per cent not employed) or seriously ill children (68 per cent not employed).

As *Table 4.14* shows, men who had been seriously ill as children had different experiences of social class change in early adult life when compared with those who had been healthy children and these experiences were different according to the social class of the individual's family of origin. Those from non-manual class homes who had had serious illness in childhood were more likely than the healthy to experience a fall in social class, whilst those from manual class homes were more likely to be out of work and more likely not to have risen in social class; in other words, whatever their class of origin, seriously ill boys were more likely than others to experience a fall in their fortunes, as indicated by social class. Women's social mobility is, on the other hand, more difficult to interpret, since such a high percentage were not employed by the age of twenty-six, largely because of marriage and child-bearing; educational achievement provides a better source of comparison of well and ill girls' achievements, as is shown in the previous section. The effect of marriage on women's social mobility and its association with height is discussed in the following section.

Table 4.14 *Adult social mobility of boys who were seriously ill whilst aged 0–10 years compared with well boys, controlling for social class of family of origin*

	social class of family of origin when boy aged 15 years					
social-class change from class of father	non-manual*		manual**		non-manual	manual
to cohort member's own class at age 26 years	healthy child	seriously ill child	healthy child	seriously ill child	% seriously ill in childhood	% seriously ill in childhood
no change	60.9	50.0	34.3	42.0	12.2%	19.5%
rise	12.9	11.2	52.4	42.7	12.8%	13.9%
fall	22.9	36.0	8.9	7.2	21.0%	13.9%
not working at 26 yrs	3.2	2.8	4.4	8.0	12.8%	26.2%
total (=100%)	1,051	178	699	138		

*$\chi^2 = 7.24$ with 3 df not significant
**$\chi^2 = 13.89$ with 3 df p $< .01$

Evidence was sought for the hypothesis that upward social mobility would be more common amongst taller men than others. Those men from non-manual families who had themselves fallen to manual class occupations by the age of twenty-six were significantly shorter than other non-manual class men (t =2.58 with ∞ df p<.01) and men from manual-social-class families who rose to non-manual occupations were significantly taller than other manual class men (t = 3.11 with ∞ df p <.01). Men who were unemployed were significantly shorter than others in the manual social class (t = 2.17 with ∞ df p $< .05$) but this did not hold for the non-manual group. These associations are not entirely accounted for by educational achievement, since height and social mobility remained significantly associated whatever the educational level of individuals.

Marriage

By the age of twenty-six, the majority of cohort members had married (76.4 per cent), with a higher rate of marriage amongst women (84.1 per cent) than men (69.6 per cent). There were no significant differences in rates of marriage, either of men or women, amongst those who had been seriously ill in childhood when compared with those who had been healthy.

As anticipated, marriage rates varied with educational qualifications, in such a way that the unmarried of either sex by twenty-six years old were more likely to have received the highest educational qualifications: for example, 30.2 per cent of men with 'A' level or university qualifications were unmarried at this age, compared with 18.2 per cent of men with

Table 4.15 *Difference in mean height of women marrying men in three social-class groups*

women's educational achievements	social class of husband	women's mean height at 15 years (cms)	't' test of difference in mean compared with social class I & II means
none or minimum	I & II	159.0 n = 77	
	III	157.1 n = 330	t = 2.67 ∞ df p < .01
	IV & V	156.3 n = 125	t = 3.12 ∞ df p < .01
	not married	158.0 n = 64	t = 1.02 ∞ df not significant
up to 'O' level	I & II	160.0 n = 114	
	III	158.4 n = 195	t = 2.34 ∞ df p < .02
	IV & V	159.7 n = 42	t = 0.26 ∞ df not significant
	not married	159.7 n = 54	t = 0.26 ∞ df not significant
'A' level and university	I & II	160.4 n = 182	
	III	159.2 n = 77	t = 1.47 ∞ df not significant
	IV & V	157.8 n = 18	t = 1.82 ∞ df not significant
	not married	159.9 n = 93	t = 0.66 ∞ df not significant

no qualifications, and so were 21.5 per cent of women with highest qualifications as compared with 7.6 per cent of women with no qualifications. Since the best-qualified cohort members were more likely to have been healthy rather than seriously ill children (see *Tables 4.12* and *4.13*) and more likely to have been taller (see page 59), it was anticipated that single men and women would tend to be taller than those who were married. This was not so for men but, as Illsley's (1955; Illsley and Kincaid 1963) work led us to expect, there was also in this study a tendency for taller women to marry men of higher social class than that of their families of origin; little explanation has been offered for this phenomenon but perhaps it reflects, or is reflected in, the trend in our advertisements and art for beauty and, as Gombrich (1977) notes, superiority to be represented by drawings and other representations of human form of 'fantastic slenderness and elongation' (Clark 1964: 130). Whatever the reason, as *Table 4.15* shows, women who married men in the top two social classes tended to be taller than others with comparable educational qualifications; these findings were particularly marked in women with minimum qualifications. It is also clear from *Table 4.15* that single women at each of these levels of educational achievement were very little different in height compared with those who married men in the top two social classes; this may be a cohort effect and it is discussed in more detail in the following section.

DISCUSSION

Whilst being, at least as yet, unable to answer Stern's question about whether 'the state of health of people at a given (early) age is a good proxy for the probability of early death' (1983: 38), it is nevertheless possible using data from this study to show that, in Stern's words, health is to some extent 'a systematic selection factor for social mobility' (1983: 38). There is also some predictive value for adult health from childhood health experience and in the case of respiratory illness this association seems to grow in significance as cohort members get older (Colley, Douglas, and Reid 1973; Kiernan *et al.* 1976).

This chapter shows sex differences in the experience of serious illness beginning in the first five years of life, when not only was there more serious illness amongst boys than girls but boys' chances of having serious illness increased significantly with falling social class, although there was no significant association of serious illness with social class amongst girls. These social class differences in boys' health, and the lack of them in girls' health, persisted throughout childhood and adolescence, and were found in early adult life (21–25 years). Although it has not been possible in this chapter to consider details of differences in types of illness, it was considered important to separate congenital disorders, mental illnesses, and injuries from all other types of illness, partly because of the strong class bias in the incidence of mental illness and injuries and also because of the diminishing effects of congenital abnormalities as the age of the sample increased. It is evident that these illnesses do not account for the observed class differences in serious illness in males in the study. Health was assessed by the absence of serious illness and by height, and significant social class differences in height were found in both boys and girls. Relative shortness of stature was, even within sex and social class groups, a feature of the seriously ill by the age of fifteen and seems, therefore, to have been an outcome of illness. How much later in life this outcome will continue to be detectable is yet to be seen but our most recent data collected at thirty-six years should help to answer this question.

Apparent effects of childhood ill-health were also found in reduced educational achievement at school but this too was a significant relationship amongst boys but not girls; however, serious illness in childhood did not significantly increase chances of relatively worse educational achievement in terms of qualifications achieved by twenty-six years old by both men and women, once the effects of social class of family of origin had been taken into account. It seems, therefore, that serious illness in childhood had a relatively short-term effect on ultimate educational achievements.

Highest-achieving men and women were significantly taller and height was also associated with upward social mobility in men, whereas childhood serious illness was significantly associated with subsequent downward mobility in adult life of those from manual social class families. Height was also associated with marriage, in that taller women tended to marry up the social-class scale and taller men and taller women were both more likely to be single at the age of twenty-six years.

These findings describe how children who had serious illness grew up with reduced chances of achievement in education at school, and therefore it is important to ask whether the findings are specific to this study or whether they could be extrapolated to other cohorts. In studies of mortality and its causes, this problem of cohort effect (i.e., an effect being specific to a particular time) is rarely discussed, although many of the environmental factors that are implicated as causes of death have changed very considerably. In the study of social circumstances and their interrelationships with health, the importance of social change is much more readily apparent. Although the only truly satisfactory answers can be found by comparing this birth cohort with those begun more recently (see Blaxter, chapter 8), it is worth noting the extent of relevant social change that has taken place in the lifetime of this cohort.

Some aspects of childhood that this cohort experienced have since changed quite considerably. In some senses, cohort members may represent the last of one lifestyle but, being born in the immediate post-war years, they also represent in some ways the first of a series of changes. Being born at this time, however, also makes them unusual, both in comparison with children born before the Second World War and with children born later, particuarly as regards nutrition. The cohort lived its earliest years through food rationing, which had a levelling effect on food intake and was some improvement for poor children. This kind of cohort effect is valuable, in that it provides a natural testing-ground for hypotheses about obesity and its development (Stark *et al.* 1981; Peckham *et al.* 1982).

Another source of cohort effect is to be found in serious illness in childhood, which has become increasingly less of a burden since the early years of the cohort, when it was of a very different nature—for example, poliomyelitis, diphtheria, and tuberculosis (Pless and Douglas 1971).

Illness at that period typically involved much longer admissions to hospital than nowadays, although the chances of admission to hospital in childhood are now very much greater than they were when the cohort members were children (Douglas 1975), partly because of admissions for preventive care or for care in the very early stages of illness. Thus, if the apparent effect of serious illness on educational achievement found in this study was the result of prolonged disruption of school work, then this effect may be less for children born more recently; but if serious illness has a depressing effect on self-image and self-perception of capabilities and life chances (Douglas, Ross, and Simpson 1968; Britten, Wadsworth, and Fenwick 1986), then this finding may not be simply the result of cohort effect.

Changes in education services have also been considerable. For example, only 15 per cent of the cohort went to any kind of nursery, playschool, or kindergarten before they began full-time school at the age of five years but 82 per cent of their children were able to have that experience (Wadsworth 1981). The cohort may, therefore, when compared with later-born children, be relatively lacking in the interpersonal and pre-schoolwork preparation that such experience gives and which seems to be beneficial to later educational achievement (Osborn, Butler, and Morris 1984; Wadsworth forthcoming), and in later cohorts these advantages may help to offset the apparent potential of serious illness for reducing educational achievement. Later in childhood, the cohort also experienced selective education in the form of an examination taken at about eleven years old and used as the criterion for entry to secondary school; only the highest achievers in this competitive examination were selected for entry to academically-inclined secondary schools that provided the appropriate teaching for entry to university. Now that this selective system has almost disappeared, perhaps children who have been seriously ill will have greater opportunities to catch up with their fellows in educational achievements.

There have also been changes in adolescence and early adult life that may affect the inter-relationship of social and educational factors with serious illness. Birth cohort members were amongst the first to receive the benefits of a rapidly expanding university and higher education programme, which resulted in an increase in the proportion of men who went to university when compared with earlier generations and an even bigger rise in the proportion of women (HMSO 1975). This, together with the availability of the new oral contraceptive pill and increasingly liberal views about sexual behaviour, made cohort members amongst the first to enjoy much greater opportunities to rebel against the views of their parents in some measure—and it seemed that the greatest degree of difference between cohort children's and parents' views was amongst

children who had been to university (Wadsworth and Freeman 1983)—
and to postpone marriage and child-bearing if they wished to do so, with
much greater freedom from the biological and social constraints imposed
on earlier generations. The effect of this may, perhaps, be seen in the
finding reported here that, in comparison with others, many of the best-
educated women were not yet married when they were twenty-six
years old.

Many of these changes that have taken place in medical, educational,
and social factors are assumed to be improvements and monitoring their
effects by way of inter-cohort comparison will help to demonstrate how far
this is true. There are, however, other kinds of social changes that have
undoubtedly occurred, which have not been consistently monitored but
which are of great importance in the investigation of social inequalities
(Halsey 1981) and which may well also be important in the maintenance
and change of relationships between childhood serious illness and subsequent social inequality. For example, it is necessary to guess at the dates
and extents of changes in views about sexual behaviour, illegitimacy, such
serious illness as epilepsy or diabetes, about intelligence and its
association with social class, and about the extent of perceived possible
social mobility for persons from different social origins. To some extent,
the work of Gorer (1955) and of Mass Observation (Calder and Sheridan
1984) helps to fill this gap but the intention of Jowell and Airie (1984) to
begin a regular monitoring of this kind of social change will be of great
value to longitudinal research.

Such cohort effects need to be borne in mind when interpreting these
data, not only because they are guidelines for where extrapolation is
appropriate but also because they show where further exploration of the
inter-relationships of serious illness and social factors in the development
of inequalities is necessary. In this study, for example, childhood serious
illness was associated with an increased risk of downward social mobility
in adult life, despite the particularly good and expanding opportunities in
education and occupation that were available to the cohort in 1962–72,
when they were aged 16–26 years. This indicates the need for research into
individual, familial, and school ways of coping with serious illness in
childhood and adds a new dimension to the arguments in favour of better
preventive care in childhood. Furthermore, comparisons of apparent
effects of different kinds of social change may be made by investigating
the effects of serious illness in childhood in the existing British birth-
cohort studies, which span the first twenty-four years of the National
Health Service. The first study, which has been reported on in this
chapter, is of children born in 1946; the second is of children born in 1958
(Fogelman 1983); the third is of children born in 1970 (Osborn, Butler, and
Morris 1984). These, together with the longitudinal study based on the

census (Fox and Goldblatt 1982), comprise a rich source of information for the continuing study of childhood ill-health (Wadsworth, Peckham, and Taylor 1984) and for the investigation of its role in the generation of social inequality during a time of very great social change in Britain.

©1986 M. E. J. Wadsworth

REFERENCES

Atkins, E., Cherry, N. M., Douglas, J. W. B., Kiernan, K. E., and Wadsworth, M. E. J. (1981) The 1946 British Birth Cohort Survey, An Account of the Origins, Progress and Results of the National Survey of Health and Development. In S. A. Mednick and A. E. Baert (eds) *Prospective Longitudinal Research in Europe: An Empirical Basis for Primary Prevention*. Oxford: Oxford University Press.

Black, A. E., Billiewicz, W. Z., and Thomson, A. M. (1976) The Diets of Pre-school Children in Newcastle upon Tyne, 1968–71. *British Journal of Nutrition* 35: 105–13.

Blaxter, M. (1981) *The Health of the Children*. London: Heinemann Educational.

Britten, N., Wadsworth, M. E. J., and Fenwick, P. B. C. (1986) Sources of Stigma Following Early Life Epilepsy: Evidence from a National Birth Cohort Study. In S. Whitman and B. P. Hermann (eds) *Psychopathology in Epilepsy*. Oxford: Oxford University Press.

Calder, A. and Sheridan, D. (1984) *Speak for Yourself: A Mass Observation Anthology 1937–1949*. London: Jonathan Cape.

Calnan, M. (1982) Delay in the Diagnosis and Treatment of Cancer. In M. Alderson (ed.) *The Prevention of Cancer*. London: Edward Arnold.

Clark, K. (1964) *The Nude*. London: Penguin.

Colley, J. R. T., Douglas, J. W. B., and Reid, D. D. (1973) Respiratory Disease in Young Adults: Influence of Early Childhood Lower Respiratory Tract Illness, Social Class, Air Pollution, and Smoking. *British Medical Journal* 2: 195–98.

Department of Health and Social Security (1975) *A Nutrition Survey of Pre-school Children, 1967–68*. Reports on Health and Social Subjects No. 10. London: HMSO.

—— (1980) *Inequalities in Health (Black Report)*. Report of a research working group chaired by Sir Douglas Black. London: DHSS.

Douglas, J. W. B. (1964) *The Home and the School*. London: McGibbon and Kee.

—— (1965) Education and Social Movement. In J. Mead and R. Parkes (eds) *Biological Aspects of Social Problems*. Edinburgh: Oliver and Boyd.

—— (1975) Early Hospital Admissions and Later Disturbances of Behaviour and Learning. *Developmental Medicine and Child Neurology* 17: 456–80.

—— (1984) Illness, Handicap and Ultimate Educational Achievement. In N. R. Butler and B. D. Corner (eds) *Stress and Disability in Childhood*. Bristol: John Wright.

Douglas, J. W. B., Ross, J. M., and Simpson, H. R. (1968) *All Our Future: A Longitudinal Study of Secondary Education*. London: Peter Davies.

Fogelman, K. R. (ed.) (1983) *Growing Up in Great Britain: Collected Papers from the National Child Development Study*. London: Macmillan.

Fox, A. J. and Goldblatt, P. O. (1982) *Socio-demographic Mortality Differentials: Longitudinal Study 1971–75*. OPCS Series LS No. 1. London: HMSO.

Gombrich, E. H. (1977) *Art and Illusion*. Oxford: Phaidon.

Gorer, G. (1955) *Exploring English Character*. London: Cresset Press.

Halsey, A. H. (1981) *Change in British Society*. Oxford: Oxford University Press.

HMSO (1975) *Social Trends No. 6*. London: HMSO.

Illsley, R. (1955) Social Class Selection and Class Differences in Relation to Stillbirths and Infant Deaths. *British Medical Journal* 2: 1520–524.

―――― (1980) *Professional or Public Health*: Sociology in Health and Medicine. London: Nuffield Provincial Hospitals Trust.

Illsley, R. and Kincaid, J. C. (1963) Social Correlations of Perinatal Mortality. In N. R. Butler and D. G. Bonham (eds) *Perinatal Mortality*. Edinburgh: Churchill-Livingstone.

Jowell, R. and Airie, C. (1984) *British Social Attitudes*. London: Gower.

Kiernan, K. E., Colley, J. R. T., Douglas, J. W. B., and Reid, D. D. (1976) Chronic Cough in Young Adults in Relation to Smoking Habits, Childhood Environment and Chest Illness. *Respiration* 33: 236–44.

McKillop, F. M. and Durnin, J. V. G. A. (1982) The Energy and Nutrient Intake of a Random Sample (305) of Infants. *Human Nutrition: Applied Nutrition* 36A: 405–21.

McQueen, D. V. and Siegrist, J. (1982) Social Factors in the Etiology of Chronic Disease: An Overview. *Social Science and Medicine* 16: 353–67.

Marwick, A. (1982) *British Society since 1945*. London: Penguin.

Osborn, A. F., Butler, N. R., and Morris, A. C. (1984) *The Social Life of Britain's Five-Year-Olds*. London: Routledge and Kegan Paul.

Peckham, C. S., Stark, O., Simonite, V., and Wolff, O. H. (1982) Prevalence of Obesity in British Children Born in 1946 and 1958. *British Medicial Journal* 286: 1237–242.

Pill, R. and Stott, N. C. H. (1982) Concepts of Illness Causation and Responsibility. *Social Science and Medicine* 16: 43–52.

Pless, I. B. and Douglas, J. W. B. (1971) Chronic Illness in Childhood, Part I: Epidemiological and Clinical Characteristics. *Paediatrics* 47: 405–14.

Sorokin, P. (1959) *Social and Cultural Mobility*. Glencoe, Ill.: Free Press.

Stark, O., Atkins, E., Wolff, O., and Douglas, J. W. B. (1981) A Longitudinal Study of Obesity in the National Survey of Health and Development. *British Medical Journal* 283: 13–17.

Stern, J. (1983) Social Mobility and the Interpretation of Social Class Mortality Differentials. *Journal of Social Policy* 12: 27–49.

Tanner, J. M. (1962) *Growth at Adolescence*. Oxford: Blackwell.

Townsend, P. and Davidson, N. (1982) *Inequalities in Health: The Black Report*. London: Penguin.

Wadsworth, M. E. J. (1981) Social Class and Generation Differences in Pre-school Education. *British Journal of Sociology* 32: 560–82.

―――― (1986) Effects of Parenting Style and Pre-school Experience in Children's Verbal Attainment: Results of a British Longitudinal Study. *Early Childhood Research Quarterly* 1.

Wadsworth, M. E. J. and Freeman, S. R. (1983) Generation Differences in Beliefs: A

Study of Stability and Change in Religious Beliefs. *British Journal of Sociology* 34: 416–37.

Wadsworth, M. E. J., Peckham, C. S., and Taylor, B. (1984) The Role of National Longitudinal Studies in the Prediction of Health, Development and Behaviour. In D. B. Walker and J. B. Richmond (eds) *Monitoring the Health of American Children*. Cambridge, Mass.: Harvard University Press.

World Health Organisation (1967) *International Classification of Diseases* (eighth revision). Geneva: WHO.

FIVE

Unemployment and mortality in the OPCS Longitudinal Study

K. A. Moser, A. J. Fox, and D. R. Jones

SUMMARY

The mortality of men aged 15–64 who were seeking work in the week before the 1971 census was investigated by means of the OPCS Longitudinal Study, which follows up a 1 per cent sample of the population of England and Wales. In contrast to the current position, only 4 per cent of men of working age in 1971 fell into this category. The mortality of these unemployed men in the period 1971–81 was higher (standardized mortality ratio 136) than would be expected from death rates in all men in the Longitudinal Study. The socio-economic distribution of the unemployed accounts for some of the raised mortality, but, after allowance for this, a 20–30 per cent excess remains; this excess was apparent both in 1971–75 and in 1976–81. The data offer only limited support for the suggestion that some of this excess resulted from men becoming unemployed because of their ill-health; the trend in overall mortality over time and the pattern by cause of death were not those usually associated with ill-health selection. Previous studies have suggested that stress accompanying un-employment could be associated with raised suicide rates, as were again found here. Moreover, the mortality of women whose husbands were unemployed was higher than that of all married women (standardized mortality ratio 120), and this excess also persisted after allowance for their socio-economic distribution. The results support findings by others that unemployment is associated with adverse effects on health.

INTRODUCTION

Perhaps because of the steep rises in the late 1970s in the proportion of the working populations of western countries who were unemployed, several groups have been trying to assess the impact of unemployment on health. The published work, ranging from aggregated, national data to detailed case-reports, has lately been reviewed by Brenner and Mooney,[1] Warr,[2] and Cook and Shaper.[3] Although Brenner's econometric studies,[4,5] which seek to explain variations in annual UK mortality rates in terms of the unemployment rate and various other measures of economic growth, have received wide attention, investigation of the impact of unemployment on the health of an individual (and his/her family) requires a disaggregated study design. Few results from epidemiological studies of adequate power, specifically designed to measure the mortality consequences of unemployment, have been reported. Small investigations of groups of men being made redundant have been inconclusive. In larger studies, such as the Regional Heart Study,[6] the Department of Health and Social Security cohort study,[7,8] and the Office of Population Censuses and Surveys (OPCS) Longitudinal Study reported on here,[9] the relation between unemployment and mortality has not been the primary interest. As a result, weaknesses of study size, outcome and explanatory variables, control-group selection, and response and follow-up rates have reduced the weight to be attached to the results. Although there is some evidence from these studies of raised morbidity and mortality among the unemployed, potential confounding factors remain unmeasured, and inevitably the causal mechanism remains unestablished. Some light has been shed on the morbidity consequences (in particular the psychological consequences) of unemployment in case studies and other research entailing detailed interviewing of small, but high-risk, groups (see Warr[2]). Whilst these investigations are likewise subject to methodological limitations, they suggest that, at least in some population subgroups, being, and in particular, *becoming* unemployed is associated with increased morbidity, including depression, anxiety, and stress-related behaviour such as smoking and alcohol consumption. Age, sex, occupational group, and length of unemployment are among the effect-modifying factors suggested.

In this paper we use data from the OPCS Longitudinal Study (LS) to examine further the relation between unemployment and mortality. Unemployed men in the LS sample have already been shown to have high mortality in 1971–75 and several possible explanations have been offered.[9] Firstly, men's health may suffer *as a result of* unemployment, perhaps owing to a fall in income and social status, increased stress, and consequent behaviour. Secondly, men in poor health may be more likely to *become* unemployed, and the raised mortality of unemployed men may simply reflect their health status *before* unemployment. Thirdly, the high mortality may reflect the social distribution of unemployed men *before* unemployment and the strong relation between mortality and measures of socioeconomic status.

In this paper we examine the importance that can be attached to these three explanations by (i) using mortality data for the ten years 1971–81; (ii) controlling for the socio-economic distribution of the unemployed men; and (iii) looking at the mortality of women married to unemployed men. The interpretation of our analysis is limited because our indicator of unemployment relates to one week in April, 1971, and we have no information on how long these men had been, or were subsequently, unemployed.

SUBJECTS AND METHODS

Source of Data

The LS is based on a 1 per cent sample of individuals enumerated in England and Wales in the 1971 census. Census records for sample members have been linked with information on subsequent events about which details are routinely collected, principally births, deaths, and cancer registrations. This analysis focuses on deaths in the period 1971–81. Some census information on other persons in any household containing an LS member is also linked to the information about the sample member.

In this analysis the unemployed group comprises those men who indicated, in response to the 1971 census question on economic position, that they were seeking work or waiting to take up a job in the week before the census; we shall refer to them either as 'seeking work' or as un-employed. This excludes other categories of economic position such as in employment, temporarily or permanently sick, and retired or otherwise inactive. Perception of economic position is dependent on many factors—primarily age, sex, and (especially for women) marital status and pre-vailing socio-economic climate. Women reporting themselves as 'seeking work' were a select group; 38 per cent of women aged 15–59 in our sample were placed in the inactive category to which housewives were allocated. Consequently, we have limited ourselves here to an investigation of *male* unemployment and, principally, to mortality of men in the working age range 15–64. Of the quarter of a million men in the sample in 1971, 161,699 were aged 15–64 and, of these, 5,861 (3.6 per cent) were 'seeking work'.

The 1971 census provided some sociodemographic information on res-pondents. We were able to classify men 'seeking work' into social classes from details of their most recent jobs. The LS also contains information on the household and other household members, and we have used this to investigate the mortality of women married to men 'seeking work'.

Methods

Throughout the analysis the standardized mortality ratio (SMR, the ratio of observed (O) to expected (E) deaths $\times$ 100) is used as a summary index of mortality. Expected deaths are obtained by applying the death rates by 5-year age groups in the standard group to the person-years-at-risk in the study group.[10] In most of the analyses the standard group comprises all men in the LS aged 15 and over at census. Where a different standard group is used this is indicated in the text. Approximate 95 per cent confidence limits for the ratio of observed to expected deaths are also presented.[11]

RESULTS

The SMR for 1971–81 for men aged 15–64 years at death, seeking work in 1971, was 136 with approximate 95 per cent confidence limits 122–52. It rose from 129 for 1971–75 to 144 for 1976–81. Although the mortality of these men was raised at all ages, the excess seems greater at younger ages (*Figure 5.1*). In age groups 25–34, 35–44, and 45–54 the SMR exceeded 170.

Effects of socioeconomic distribution

How much of the excess mortality among the unemployed men can be explained by their socio-economic distribution? The difference between the social class distribution of unemployed men and all men in the LS is shown in *Figure 5.2*. Unemployed men were concentrated in the lower social classes. For example, social class V contained 16 per cent of all

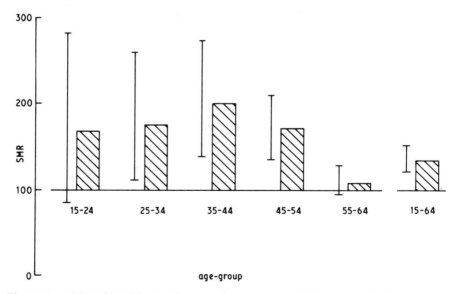

Figure 5.1 Mortality 1971–81 of men seeking work in 1971 by age at death

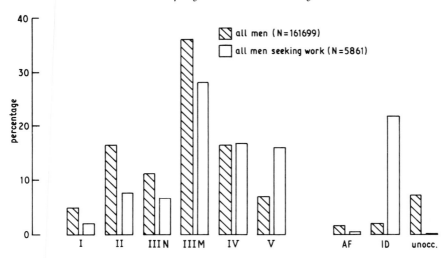

Figure 5.2 Percentage distribution of all men and men seeking work aged 15–64
I–V = social class; AF = armed forces; ID = inadequately described occupations;
unocc. = unoccupied.

unemployed men but only 7 per cent of all men. For one-fifth of the unemployed it was not possible to allocate them to a social class on the basis of their most recent job; this is the case for less than 2 per cent of all men. Those allocated to this 'inadequately described' group mainly comprised men whose failure to complete the census question on most recent occupation reflected either the fact that they were out of work or that they were enumerated in institutions such as hospitals.

There was a strong mortality gradient with social class among all men (with a social class I SMR of 73 and a social class V SMR of 120), which was also present, indeed wider, among men 'seeking work' (*Table 5.1*). Within each social class the SMR for men 'seeking work' was higher than that for all men, indicating that the raised mortality of the unemployed was maintained through all the classes. As would be expected, this is not so for the residual group, the 'inadequately described'; many of this group were in hospitals and other institutions, so those among them who were 'seeking work' would have been a comparatively healthy subset.

To take account of the social class distribution of the unemployed, new values for the expected deaths were calculated, with standardization for age and class. The SMR for all unemployed men, standardized for age and class, was 121 with approximate 95 per cent confidence limits 108–35; this suggests that some but not all of the excess mortality among unemployed men may be explained by their class distribution.

Class and Health

Table 5.1 *Mortality 1971–81 of all men and men seeking work in 1971, by social class*

social class	all men aged 15–64 at death SMR	men 'seeking work' in 1971 aged 15–64 at death	
		SMR	SMRs standardized for social class
I	73 (263)	79 (3)	103
II	78 (1,224)	109 (28)	139
IIIN	98 (828)	113 (20)	116
IIIM	94 (2,693)	123 (90)	132
IV	103 (1,468)	155 (67)	150
V	120 (727)	150 (61)	124
armed forces	84 (31)	—	—
inadequately described	183 (176)	165 (59)	87
unoccupied	264 (651)	—	—
total	100 (8,061)	136 (328)	121

Note: Figures in parentheses are numbers of observed deaths.

Table 5.2 *Mortality 1971–81 of men seeking work in 1971, aged 15–64 at death, standardized for age and social class, and age and housing tenure*

expected deaths based on:	SMR	approx 95% confidence interval
age-specific rates	136	122–152
age and social class specific rates	121	108–135
age and housing tenure specific rates	127	113–141

Standardization for the distribution of unemployed men by social class but with exclusion of men with 'inadequately described' occupations suggests that the component of the raised mortality of men 'seeking work' which could be explained by their social class composition was somewhat less than indicated above.[12] Standardization for housing tenure—an alternative measure of socio-economic status[9]—reduced the SMR of men 'seeking work' from 136 to 127 (*Table 5.2*).

The increase in SMR in unemployed men, from 129 in 1971–75 to 144 in 1976–81, seemed to be accounted for by the social class distribution; SMRs standardized for age and social class were 122 and 123 for the two time-periods. The effect of standardizing the SMRs for social class was greater in 1976–81 than in 1971–75 because there was a steeper social class gradient in mortality in 1976–81 than in 1971–75. This results largely from dis-

Table 5.3 *Mortality 1971–81 of men seeking work in 1971, aged 15–64 at death, by cause of death*

cause of death	SMR	approx. 95% CI	SMR standardized for social class	approx. 95% CI
all causes	136 (328)	122–152	121	108–135
malignant neoplasms	141 (94)	114–172	128	103–155
lung cancer	175 (48)	128–229	154	113–202
circulatory diseases	116 (132)	97–138	109	90–128
ischaemic heart disease	111 (93)	89–135	107	86–130
respiratory diseases	146 (27)	95–208	132	86–187
bronchitis, emphysema and asthma	119 (12)	60–197	117	59–193
accidents, poisonings and violence	202 (46)	147–266	149	108–196
suicide etc.*	241 (20)	145–361	169	102–254
other accidents, poisonings, and violence	179 (26)	116–257	140	90–200

*WHO (1967) *International Classification of Diseases (8th revision).* Geneva: WHO. Codes 850–77, 942, 950–959, 980–989
Note: Figures in parentheses are numbers of observed deaths.

sipation of the effects of selective health-related mobility out of employment which affected mortality differentials in the earlier period.[13]

Mortality seems to have been particularly high for malignant neoplasms and for accidents, poisonings, and violence (*Table 5.3*). Raised mortality from malignant neoplasms (O = 94, E = 66.5) appears to have been attributable in the main to deaths from lung cancer (O = 48, E = 27.4). A clear excess from this cause remained after allowance for social class.

High mortality from accidents, poisonings, and violence (O = 46, E = 22.8) was only partly explained by the very high mortality from suicide (O = 20, E = 8.3). Although SMRs for both these causes were reduced by social class standardization, substantial excesses remained.

Effects of health-related selection in the unemployed group

We now examine evidence for the suggestion that the men who were unemployed in 1971 became unemployed *because* of poor health.[14] If ill-health were a major influence on the selection of this group we would expect the health, and the relative mortality, of the group to improve over time. Such a change would be expected because of the high initial mortality of those selected on the basis of ill-health; the proportion of sick men in this category would decline over time. This and other mechanisms would lead to a reduction in mortality over time, as has been observed in

Table 5.4   *Mortality 1971–75 and 1976–81 of men seeking work in 1971, aged 15–64 at death, by cause of death*

cause of death	SMR	approx. 95% CI	SMRs standardized for social class	approx. 95% CI
all causes				
1971–75	129 (167)	110–150	122	104–142
1976–81	144 (161)	122–168	123	105–143
lung cancer				
1971–75	208 (31)	140–290	189	127–263
1976–81	137 (17)	79–212	118	68–182
ischaemic heart disease				
1971–75	108 (48)	79–142	114	84–150
1976–81	114 (45)	82–150	100	73–133
bronchitis, emphysema, and asthma				
1971–75	30 (2)	3–87	33	3–97
1976–81	278 (10)	130–481	250	117–433
suicide etc.				
1971–75	250 (9)	111–444	148	66–262
1976–81	244 (11)	119–414	186	91–316
other accidents poisonings, and violence (excluding suicide)				
1971–75	203 (16)	114–316	147	83–229
1976–81	147 (10)	69–255	156	73–271

Note: Figures in parentheses are numbers of observed deaths.

other areas of our work.[13,15] On the other hand, if this group were selected on the basis of positive health, we would expect the health of the group to worsen, and their relative mortality to rise with time. A further component of the analysis involves examination of patterns of cause-specific mortality over time, since the time scales for changes in mortality for acute causes would be shorter than those for chronic causes if the selection mechanism were valid.

Although we have 10 years' mortality data, this is a short time-span over which to observe trends in cause-specific mortality for such a small subgroup of the population. The lack of power of this analysis of short-term trends by cause of death is apparent from the wide confidence intervals around the SMRs in *Table 5.4*. As we have said, the SMRs for all causes of death standardized for social class showed no trend between the two time periods.

The fall in SMRs (standardized for social class) for lung cancer and ischaemic heart disease might be construed as evidence of ill-health selection, but they were not based on sufficient numbers of deaths for firm conclusions to be drawn about their trends with time. Interpretation of the pattern of deaths from bronchitis is even more problematical.

Although these data provide no strong evidence for a selection effect, we cannot rule out the possibility that there is one operating. The complexity of the hypothesis and the large sampling variation make conclusive interpretation of the data difficult.

Effects of unemployment on the health of other household members

Any adverse effects of unemployment—through, for example, a fall in income, or an increase in stress—may be expected to have repercussions on all members of the unemployed person's family or household. By examining mortality among people other than the unemployed man himself we partly eliminate any health-selection effect, unless the ill-health of others in the household was associated with his being less available for work. Any adverse health experience among these family members could therefore be interpreted as more directly attributable to the effects of unemployment.

Table 5.5 shows the mortality in 1971–81 of the 2,906 married women in private households whose husbands were unemployed at the 1971 census. The standard population used in calculating the expected deaths was all married women resident in private households. The overall SMR for 1971–81 was 120 (approximate 95 per cent confidence intervals 102–139), which suggests that mortality among this group of women was higher than would have been expected. The SMR rose from 108 in 1971–75 to 129 in 1976–81; the approximate 95 per cent confidence intervals were 83–138 and 105–154, respectively.

Although some cause-specific SMRs were raised, the numbers of deaths

Table 5.5 *Mortality 1971–81 of women whose husbands were seeking work in 1971, by cause of death*

cause of death	SMR	approx. 95% CI
all causes	120 (173)	102–139
malignant neoplasms	112 (59)	85–143
lung cancer	88 (7)	34–166
circulatory diseases	129 (76)	101–161
ischaemic heart disease	157 (47)	115–206
respiratory diseases	127 (14)	68–204
bronchitis, emphysema and asthma	93 (4)	23–209
accidents, poisonings, and violence	86 (5)	26–181
suicide etc.	160 (4)	40–360

Note: Figures in parentheses are numbers of observed deaths. The standard population used in calculating the expected deaths was all married women resident in private households.

from specific causes were in the main too small to make any clear interpretations of the results. However, for ischaemic heart disease the SMR was 157 with approximate 95 per cent confidence intervals 115–206. There was no apparent trend over time for this cause; the SMR for 1971–75 was 155 and that for 1976–81 was 159.

As with the excess mortality for unemployed men, part of the excess mortality among women whose husbands were unemployed may have been due to the socio-economic composition of this group. The data on tenure suggest that a high proportion of these women lived in local-authority housing; 45 per cent lived in council housing and 34 per cent owned their houses as compared with 27 per cent and 56 per cent, respectively, among married women whose husbands were *in* employment.

The tenure mortality gradient was far steeper among women with unemployed husbands (owner occupiers had an SMR of 101 while council tenants had an SMR of 144) than among women with husbands in employment (corresponding SMRs 90 and 114). Within each tenure group the women with unemployed husbands had considerably higher mortality; the overall SMR of these women was 124, compared with 100 for women whose husbands were in employment. However, standardization for tenure distribution reduced the SMR only from 124 to 121. This suggests that housing tenure explained little of the excess mortality among women with unemployed husbands.

DISCUSSION

Limitations and strengths of the analysis

This chapter has been concerned with *male* unemployment and its relation with the mortality of unemployed men and that of women married to unemployed men. Unfortunately we have not been able to consider female unemployment and its effect on health, mainly because of difficulties in interpreting responses to the question on economic position in the 1971 census.

Although we have followed about 6,000 men unemployed in 1971 for up to 10 years, the 328 deaths which occurred amongst this group were too few in number to enable us to test specific relations satisfactorily—for example, for selected causes of death and by year of death. In particular, the assessment of evidence for a health-related selection effect was severely hampered.

Our indicator of unemployment relates to one week in April, 1971, and we have no information on how long these men had been, or were subsequently, unemployed.

The principal strength of the investigation is that it is a *prospective* study of individuals who were unemployed in 1971, rather than a study of histories collected retrospectively, or an analysis of aggregate data. In this extension of the earlier analysis[9] we have examined the social class composition of unemployed men to establish the extent to which the raised mortality of these men is explained by social class differentials in mortality. As well as looking at the mortality among unemployed men, we have now started to investigate the mortality experienced by other members of households containing an unemployed man. This is useful not only because it enables us to assess the wider health effects of unemployment but also for the light it sheds on the role of health-related selection, the weakest element of our analysis of mortality among the unemployed themselves. These issues are discussed more fully in a working paper.[12]

Findings

Among men who were 'seeking work' in 1971, our data indicate high mortality (SMR 136) over the next 10 years. The analysis suggests that some of this excess mortality may be explained by the fact that unemployed men were more concentrated in social classes IV and V; nonetheless, a 20–30 per cent excess remained unexplained. However, it should be noted that, without details of the timing of unemployment in relation to social mobility, it is difficult to establish the direction of the causal relation.

The evidence in support of some health-related selection of unemployed men remains very unclear, although it seems probable that men 'seeking work' were partly selected for *good* health since the least healthy men, who were not in employment, would have been recorded either as 'out of work, sick' or 'permanently sick'. Two causes of death, lung cancer and suicide, stand out as having significantly raised levels of mortality among men 'seeking work' after allowance for social class. Both causes have been linked elsewhere to stress and stress-related activity.[16,17] However, to explain an excess of lung cancer mortality in 1971–81, one must probably invoke exposure to a risk factor *before* 1971.

Women whose husbands were 'seeking work' had raised mortality (SMR 120 compared with all married women resident in private households), most of which remained after controlling for tenure distribution. As any health-related selection effect is expected to be small among women whose husbands were unemployed—indeed the SMR rose with increased follow-up—it is reasonable to suggest that their high mortality was largely attributable to other factors, such as a direct effect of their spouses' unemployment. The excess mortality from ischaemic heart disease may support this hypothesis since this disease has been linked with stress.[18] Further work now in progress on the mortality of *other* members of households where there was an unemployed man in 1971 should therefore be of particular interest.

Between 1971 and 1981 unemployment became a more common experience among men in the working age range and durations of unemployment increased. These changes make it difficult to extrapolate from our findings to estimate the impact of unemployment on health today. Once we have access to mortality data for the 1980s and information from the 1981 census on the employment status and socio-economic circumstances of the LS sample members at this second point in time, we should be able to assess the changing health effects of unemployment.

To summarize, although effects of other factors remain to be investigated, the results of this investigation do provide evidence suggesting that *some* of the excess mortality among unemployed men may be explained by their socio-economic circumstances before unemployment. However, this alone does not account for all of the high mortality in unemployed men and in women married to unemployed men.

The analyses are part of a review by the Social Statistics Research Unit at City University of mortality data available from the OPCS Longitudinal Study. This programme is supported by a grant from the Medical Research Council. The views expressed are those of the authors.

REFERENCES

1. Brenner, M. H. and Mooney, A. (1983) Unemployment and health in the context of economic change. *Social Science and Medicine* 17: 1125–138.
2. Warr, P. (1985) Twelve questions about unemployment and health. In B. Roberts, R. Finnegan, and D. Gallie (eds) *New Approaches to Economic Life.* Manchester: Manchester University Press.
3. Cook, D. and Shaper, A. G. (1984) Unemployment and health. In M. Harrington (ed.) *Recent Advances in Occupational Health* Vol. 2. Edinburgh: Churchill Livingstone.
4. Brenner, M. H. (1979) Mortality and the national economy: a review, and the experience of England and Wales, 1936–1976. *Lancet* ii: 568–73.
5. Brenner, M. H. (1979) Unemployment and health. *Lancet* i: 874–75.
6. Cook, D. G., Cummins, R. O., Bartley, M. J., Shaper, A. G. (1982) Health of unemployed middle-aged men in Great Britain. *Lancet* ii: 1290–294.
7. Wood, D. (1982) The DHSS cohort study of unemployed men (Working Paper No. 1). London: Department of Health and Social Security.
8. Ramsden, S. and Smee, C. (1981) The health of unemployed men: DHSS cohort study. *Employment Gazette* September: 397–401.

9. Fox, A. J. and Goldblatt, P. O. (1982) Socio-demographic mortality differentials: Longitudinal Study 1971–75. Series LS No. 1. London: HMSO.

10. Berry, G. (1983) The analysis of mortality by the subject-years method. *Biometrics* 39: 173–84.

11. Vandenbroucke, J. P. (1982) A shortcut method for calculating the 95 per cent confidence interval of the standardized mortality ratio. *American Journal of Epidemiology* 115: 303–04.

12. Moser, K. A., Fox, A. J., Jones, D. R., and Goldblatt, P. O. (1984) Unemployment and mortality in the OPCS Longitudinal Study. London: SSRU, City University. Working Paper No. 18.

13. Fox, A. J., Goldblatt, P. O., and Jones, D. R. (1985) Social class mortality differentials: artefact, selection or life circumstances? Reprinted as Chapter 3 of this publication.

14. Stern, J. (1983) The relationship between unemployment, morbidity and mortality in Britain. *Population Studies* 37: 61–74.

15. Fox, A. J., Goldblatt, P. O., and Adelstein, A. M. (1982) Selection and mortality differentials. *Journal of Epidemiology and Community Health* 36: 69–79.

16. Cooper, C. L. (1982) Psychosocial stress and cancer. *Bulletin of the British Psychological Society* 35: 456–59.

17. Platt, S. (1984) Unemployment and suicidal behaviour: a review of the literature. *Social Science and Medicine* 19: 93–115.

18. Jenkins, C. D. (1976) Recent evidence supporting psychologic and social risk factors for coronary disease. *New England Journal of Medicine* 294: 987–94, 1033–038.

SIX

Income and mortality

R. G. Wilkinson

This paper describes four new pieces of statistical work on the relationship between income and health. All make use of published data from official sources and are intended to clarify the relationship between income and mortality rates in Britain. Part one of the paper analyses the relationship between relative changes in the incomes and mortality rates of various occupations over a twenty-year period. Part two looks at the relationship between the changing real value of state old-age pensions and death rates of people of pensionable age. Part three is concerned to see whether the narrowing of class differences in postneonatal mortality that took place during the 1970s can be explained in terms of a narrowing of class differences in income. Finally, Part four looks at the likely effects of changes in income distribution on mortality rates.

It is widely accepted that, in some contexts, income and the standard of living are important determinants of health. The contrast in life-expectancy between rich and poor countries and the historical association between the increasing standard of living and declining mortality rates within industrial societies carry an inescapable message. Yet, when it comes to explanations of the socio-economic differences in health in industrial societies, there is no consensus on the role of income and almost no good evidence.

The issue of the relationship between income distribution and inequalities in health was raised in the Black Report. The Report's recommendations were divided into two parts, the first on policies for health and personal social services, and the second on 'measures to reduce the difference in material standards of living' (Townsend and Davidson 1982: 173). The main thrust of the second part was directed towards incomes: both reducing inequalities and raising the incomes of the worst-off. The Report pointed out that the number of people below the supplementary benefit level was increasing and said that 'at these levels there is evidence of multiple deprivation in diet, housing and environmental amenities, leisure activities and at work' (Townsend and Davidson 1982: 174).

Recommending 'a new approach to the fairer distribution of resources', they said:

'If the share of disposable income of the top 30 percent . . . were only moderately reduced, the sum available for redistribution in social security benefits . . . could be doubled. . . . we shall need to develop greater restrictions on the amount of wealth which may be inherited and accumulated, together with more effective measures to inhibit the growth of top incomes and reduce present differentials in incomes. . . . we believe that it may be desirable to establish national minimum and maximum earnings . . . as indispensable elements of a nationally approved framework of incomes.'

(Townsend and Davidson 1982: 175–76)

These proposals were made not so much on the basis of any direct research evidence on the association between income and health as in the belief that low incomes are central to the various measures of deprivation with which ill-health is associated. As the Report says,

'Unfortunately the opportunities for examining directly the association between income and health are restricted. Relatively few data about personal health can be related even to occupation and fewer still to income and wealth. More frequent adoption in studies of a more reliable measure of income is desirable.'

(DHSS 1980: 161)

Comparisons of class mortality and median incomes (see chapter 1, *Tables 1.1* and *1.3*) are too crude to throw much light on the influence of income on life expectancy. Even the fact that people in social class III non-manual appear to have lower incomes as well as lower death rates than those in social class III manual should not necessarily be taken at face value. As Peter Townsend has pointed out, the income differential between these two groups is reversed when differences in employees' fringe benefits and assets are taken into account (Townsend 1979: 386–88).

Part of the difficulty of working in this field is that it is not clear what we should be aiming at. Are annual or lifetime incomes the most appropriate? Should one measure total household income, per capita household income, or perhaps income of the so-called 'head of household'? As almost all of the few studies in this field have relied on routinely collected statistics, they have had little choice as to how income is measured, and on this point the present research is no exception. Unlike most of the published work, however, it does not rely simply on correlations of cross-sectional statistics for geographical areas (Grossman 1972, Kitagawa and Hauser 1973). In the hope that the results may be a little more relevant to

policy, the analysis described here uses data that are more closely related
to source of income.

PART ONE: OCCUPATIONAL INCOMES AND MORTALITY

Data on occupational incomes were linked with occupational mortality
rates for a group of twenty-two occupations in England and Wales in 1951
and 1971. Age-specific mortality rates were used to follow the mortality
experience of occupational cohorts over the twenty-year period. Significant inverse correlations were found between the percentage change in
incomes and mortality rates among these occupations during the period.
The results suggest that income differentials are likely to make an
important causal contribution to social-class differences in health.

Data sources

It was initially intended to match occupational earnings with the
decennial occupational mortality figures for 1951, 1961, and 1971;
however, the only reliable series of income figures classified by
occupation (rather than by industry) for this period are tabulations of
basic weekly wage rates. Unfortunately, as overtime and bonus payments
became increasingly important, basic weekly wage rates were a declining
proportion of total weekly earnings. In 1950, basic weekly wage rates
amounted to 95 per cent of total weekly earnings; they declined to 84 per
cent in 1960 and to 70 per cent in 1970 (Department of Employment 1972:
Table 129; DOE 1970b: Table 44). As the gap between earnings and basic
wages widened faster in some occupations than in others, a comparison of
changes in basic weekly wage rates over this period would not have given
a reliable indication of movements in the relative earnings.

Figures of total weekly earnings by occupation became available with
the start of the New Earnings Survey at the end of the period. This allowed
figures of basic weekly wage rates at the beginning of the period, when
they amounted to 95 per cent of total earnings, to be compared with total
weekly earnings figures at the end. The lack of sound earnings data in the
middle of the period meant that the occupational mortality rates for 1961
had to be excluded from the analysis.

The published sources of wage and mortality data use different
occupational classifications and these classifications are periodically
revised. As a result, only those occupations which could be matched on
four different classifications (incomes and mortality classifications at the
beginning and end of the period) could be used. This limited the analysis
to the twenty-two occupations listed in *Table 6.1*. Most of them are

Table 6.1 *Occupations for which income and mortality data could be matched*

occupation	1961 popn (thousands)
agricultural workers (excl. farmers)	286
miners (underground)	290
miners (surface)	54
bakers and pastrycooks	50
maintenance fitters and engineers	522
bleachers & textile finishers	17
tailors & dressmakers	20
sawyers & woodworking machinists	49
compositors	38
bricklayers, masons, plasterers	212
steel erectors	38
plumbers & gas fitters	147
railway engine drivers, motormen, etc.	70
porters & ticket collectors	37
bus & coach drivers	86
bus conductors	50
stevedores & dockers	58
postmen & mailsorters	103
roundsmen (milk, etc.)	60
motor mechanics	142
shoemakers & repairers	22
shop salesmen & assistants	189

classified as skilled or semi-skilled manual, belonging to social class IIIM or IV. In 1961, they accounted for some 2.5 million men. The lack of sufficiently detailed information on women's mortality classified by their own or their husband's occupations confined the analysis to men.

Occupational mortality rates were taken from the 1951 and 1971 decennial supplements on occupational mortality tables (Registrar General 1958 and 1978). Figures on wages for the first period were taken from the Department of Employment's British Labour Statistics and for the later period from the New Earnings Survey (DOE 1970a and 1970b). Wage figures used for the beginning of the period were basic weekly wage rates in 1948. This year was chosen for the wage data as it is the year immediately preceding the five-year period (1949–53) for which deaths were aggregated to calculate the 1951 occupational mortality rates. Earnings figures for 1970 were used at the end of the period, partly because a full list of occupations was not published in the New Earnings Survey until its second edition in 1970, and partly because the 1971 occupational mortality rates were based on deaths for the three years 1970–72.

Standardized mortality ratios and four age-specific mortality rates (25–

34 years, 35–44 years, 45–54 years, 55–64 years) for all causes of death combined were used for each occupation. Unpublished tabulations of the age-specific occupational death rates for 1971 were provided by OPCS.

Methods

Two methods were used to analyse the relationship between changes in occupational incomes and death rates. Both avoid the danger of producing spurious associations reflecting nothing more than the secular tendency for death rates to fall while wage rates rise. First, the four age-specific death rates were used to calculate the percentage change in death rates between 1951 and 1971 in each age-group in each occupation. This was correlated with the percentage change in wages. Second, it was decided to look at the mortality changes within occupational cohorts of men over this twenty-year period. This would not only avoid any problems of changes in recruitment that might result from occupations moving up or down the 'earnings league' but, by relating changes in income to changes in mortality within cohorts, it would remove extraneous cohort differences in mortality. The data allowed changing occupational mortality and earnings to be compared within two cohorts. The first was the cohort who were 25–34 years old in 1951 and 45–54 years old in 1971. The second cohort was ten years older than the first and consisted of those men in each occupation aged 35–44 in 1951 and 55–64 in 1971.

As the use of cohorts involves the comparison of variations in death rates at one age with variations in their much higher death rates when they were twenty years older, the age-specific death rates were expressed as percentage variations around the means at each age. The position of an occupational cohort in relation to the mean age-specific death rate at the beginning of the period could then be compared with its relative position at the end. For each cohort, the different occupational changes in relative mortality were then correlated with the changes in occupational incomes expressed in the same way. As standardized mortality ratios already take the form of variations around the age-standardized mean mortality in each period, changes in the occupational SMRs between 1951 and 1971 could be directly correlated with changes in occupational incomes in relation to their means at the beginning and end of the period. Pearson product–moment correlations were used throughout.

Results

The results of the correlations between the percentage change in each of the four age-specific death rates and the percentage change in occupational incomes are shown in the first row of *Table 6.2*. Changes in two of

Table 6.2 *Age-specific death rates and occupational incomes (correlation coefficients of percentage changes)*

	25–34 yrs	35–44 yrs	45–54 yrs	55–64 yrs
unweighted	0.089 n.s.	−0.385*	−0.370*	0.056 n.s.
weighted	−0.363	−0.439	−0.541	−0.361

* p < 0.05

Table 6.3 *Cohort death rates and SMRs with occupational incomes (correlation coefficients of changes in distributions around means)*

	cohort A 25–34 yrs in 1951 to 45–54 yrs in 1971	cohort B 35–44 yrs in 1951 to 55–64 yrs in 1971	SMRs
unweighted	−0.417*	−0.249 n.s.	−0.224 n.s.
weighted	−0.664	−0.658	−0.643

* p < 0.05

the four age-specific death rates show statistically significant negative associations with changes in incomes. In small occupations, age-specific death rates may be based on a number of deaths too small to be stable, so the correlation coefficients are also shown when the data are weighted by the population in each occupation (taken at the mid-point of the period from the 1961 census). The weighted correlation coefficients are higher and range between − 0.36 and − 0.54. (Levels of statistical significance are not meaningful for these weighted coefficients and are therefore not shown.) Despite the poor quality of the data and the small number of occupations, both the unweighted and weighted data provide some evidence of an inverse association between changes in occupational incomes and death rates.

Table 6.3 shows the results of the cohort analyses and of the correlations between changes in SMRs and occupational incomes. Mortality rates and incomes are expressed as changes in position around their respective means in 1951 and 1971. Once again, the correlations are shown using unweighted and weighted data. All coefficients are negative but only one of the three unweighted coefficients is high enough to reach statistical significance on just twenty-two occupations. With weighting, however, all three correlation coefficients are close to − 0.65.

Discussion

That this study analyses the relationship between changes in incomes and death rates within specific occupational groups means that it has tight internal controls that make it unlikely that the correlations could be attributed to other factors. Although there are statistically significant correlations on the unweighted data, it is clear that weighting substantially increases the strength of the correlations, implying that the outlying occupations are the smaller ones. It is difficult to know what confidence can be placed in the weighted coefficients. Normally, if the results were used to indicate the relationship between changes in incomes and death rates over the population as a whole, the use of population weights would provide a better guide. The increased strength of the weighted correlations here, however, seems largely due to the very heavily weighted category of maintenance fitters and engineers. The other puzzling element is the lack of even week correlations in the top and bottom age-specific death rates shown in *Table 6.2*. These relationships should become clearer after the completion of a similar analysis of the 1981 mortality figures, using better earnings data.

PART TWO: STATE PENSIONS AND MORTALITY RATES OF THE ELDERLY

Following the occupational analysis, there were two reasons for examining the relationship between national figures of the changing value of state old-age pensions and the death rates of old people in England and Wales. The first was simply that this was an additional area where published data provided an opportunity to look for a relationship between changes in incomes and mortality. The second was that the Family Expenditure Survey (Department of Employment) and the National Food Survey (Ministry of Agriculture, Fisheries and Food) show expenditure and consumption figures for pensioner households, so making it possible to see what might underlie the broad associations between income and mortality for at least one sub-group of the population.

Most old people have other sources of income besides their state pensions. This means that any correlations between pensioners' death rates and the real value of pensions cannot be associated with an absolute level of real income. Fluctuations in the real value of pensions will, however, produce fluctuations in total incomes, despite the fact that contributions are also derived from other sources.

Methods and results

The analysis was confined to the sixteen years 1965 and 1968–82 inclusive. Although some variables were available for a longer period, these were the only years for which it was possible to obtain Family Expenditure Survey

Table 6.4   *Variables used in Part 2*

age-specific death rates*	categories of expenditure	foods & nutrients per capital	others
all causes	housing	energy	pensions
cancers	fuel & power	protein	personal disposable
circulatory	food	fat	income p.c.
respiratory	alcohol	carbohydrate	GDP p.c.
influenza	tobacco	calcium	av. winter temps**
accidents	durables	iron	
	clothing	vitamin A	
	transport	thiamine	
	services	riboflavin	
		nicotinic acid	
		vitamin C	
		vitamin D	
		potatoes	
		green vegetables	
		fruit	
		bread	

*death rates were taken for each sex separately for the three age groups 45–54, 65–74, 75–84, giving 36 death rates in all
**daily temperatures were averaged over four months: January, February, March, December

Note: All monetary variables were expressed in real terms after deflating by price indices from *Economic Trends*, annual supplements.

Sources: Column 1: death rates from Registrar General's *Statistical Review* and *Mortality Statistics*, Series DH No. 1. Column 2: expenditure variables are for households in which the head of household is over 65 years old and are taken from the *Family Expenditure Survey* — including some unpublished tables. Column 3: foodstuffs and nutrients are those for 'pensioner households' from *Household Food Consumption and Expenditure*, annual reports of the National Food Survey Committee. Column 4: pensions from DHSS *Social Security Statistics*; personal disposable income p.c. and GDP p.c. from *Economic Trends*, annual supplements; temperatures from Registrar General's *Statistical Review* and CSO *Annual Abstract of Statistics*.

data by age of head of household. Data were collected for the variables listed in *Table 6.4*. (The sources are given below the table.)

The analysis of aggregate time series data such as these is dependent on the use of control variables. Several approaches to the problem of avoiding or detecting spurious correlations were used. First, the death rates for people in the age range 45–54 were used as controls, to see whether correlations with pensioners' expenditure and consumption variables were really specific to their death rates. Second, indices of real gross domestic product (GDP) per capita and real personal disposable income per capita were included for use as control variables in partial correlation analysis. Third, although the main interest was in the 'all causes' death rates, cause-specific death rates were used as a way of checking on the credibility of correlations between the 'all causes' death rates and the independent variables. The choice of statistical methods was restricted by the small number of degrees of freedom and the close intercorrelations between the independent variables. As a result, partial correlations were used for all but the initial analysis.

As shown in *Table 6.5*, simple (zero-order) correlations suggest that the changing real value of pensions is indeed more closely related to deaths of people of pensionable age than to deaths in the 45–54-year-old control age-group. The correlations with the all-causes death rates for men and women in the 65–74 age-group were both − 0.92. For the 75–84 age-group, they came out at − 0.86 and − 0.91 respectively. On the other hand, for people in the 45–54 age-group the correlations were both − 0.79. This lower, but still very high, correlation shows the size of the problem of misleading time-series correlations. The differences in the proportion of the variance explained in the death rates of age-groups receiving and not receiving pensions, however, are statistically significant for both sexes in the 65–74 age-group, and for women but not men in the 75–84 age-group.

Table 6.5 *Correlations between changing real value of state pensions and age-specific death rates*

age-groups controls		pensionable ages			
45–54 yrs male	female	65–74 yrs male	female	75–84 yrs male	female
−0.79	−0.79	−0.92*	−0.92*	−0.86	−0.91*

*these correlations are significantly higher than those with death rates for the control age group

Although real expenditure on tobacco was the only other independent variable (among those listed in *Table 6.4*) to rival the strength of the pensions correlations with the all-causes death rates, there seems little doubt that a sizeable part of the statistical importance of pensions should be attributed to other factors.

Much of the secular decline in death rates among the elderly is presumably related to the general tendency for the standard of living to rise throughout society. Real GDP per capita provides the most general measure of changes in consumption summed over public and private sectors. For this reason, it was decided to test the specificity of the correlations between the changing real value of state old-age pensions and death rates of people of pensionable age by controlling for real GDP per capita. Partialling out GDP revealed significant first-order partial correlations of between − 0.57 and − 0.68 between pensions and the all-causes death rates for men and women in the older two age-groups (see *Table 6.6*). The validity of these correlations seemed confirmed by the fact that, on the same basis, there were no significant correlations between death rates for the elderly and personal disposable income per capita, which primarily reflects the earnings of people of working age.

Having established that at least an important part of the correlation between the real value of pensions and the death rates of people of pensionable age was likely to be valid, the next task was to identify the items of consumption and expenditure that accounted for the relationship. Before doing so, however, several attempts were made to identify and remove parts of the variation in death rates that were unlikely to be income-related. First, the possibility that there were significant variations in death rates related to average winter temperatures was excluded, after looking at simple correlations. Although correlations with age-, sex-, and cause-specific death rates were—as expected—almost universally negative, none reached significance. Partial correlations between death

Table 6.6 *Partial correlations between age-specific death rates and changing value of state pensions controlling for GDP p.c.*

	age-groups 65–74 yrs male	female	75–84 yrs male	female
correlation coefficient	−0.68**	−0.57*	−0.62**	−0.66**

* $p < 0.05$
** $p < 0.01$

rates and winter temperatures, controlling for expenditure on fuel and power, were also consistently negative; although they approached significance with death rates from 'flu in both sexes, in no case did they reach significance.

It seemed possible that the influence of the standard of living on health could be divided between those factors emanating from the public sector that affect everyone, regardless of personal income, and those aspects related to personal circumstances, which are primarily a function of personal income. In the first category would come factors such as improvements in health services, in road safety, and in air pollution, while in the second would come factors such as nutrition and housing. An attempt was made to separate these by correlating personal disposable income per capita with the all-causes death rates for men and women in the 45–54 age-group. If that correlation represented the personal income component, then the residual variation in the death rates represented the contribution from the public sector. This residual variation was then used as an independent variable. If it did indeed represent the effect of the public as opposed to the private environment, it should be possible to improve correlations between pensions and death rates for the older age-groups by using it as a control variable. In the event, the correlations between pensions and the all-causes death rates for the two older age-groups were marginally improved but the initial simple correlations were so high that there was little room for improvement. Because the improvement was necessarily small and there was no way of assessing the validity of the concepts which lay behind it, it was decided not to try to remove a public environmental component from the death rates to be used in the subsequent analysis.

Among the cause-specific death rates, it seemed implausible that cancer deaths could be significantly affected by environmental influences in the year of death. Most cancers have long histories. While it could be argued that the rate of spread of the disease and the precise timing of the death of a cancer patient may be influenced by the patient's current environment, it was decided on balance to exclude cancer deaths from the all-causes death rates used in subsequent analysis. While diseases such as stroke and heart attack also have long histories, the disease process is more likely to be additive, depending on a continuous series of environmental increments. In contrast to cancers—where the disease process, once firmly established, appears self-sustaining—the additive model suggests that a more favourable environment could halt (though not necessarily reverse) the disease process at any point. After these attempts to refine a component of death rates that could be expected to be influenced maximally by annual fluctuations in personal income, the analysis was continued using death rates that were unaltered except for the exclusion of cancer from the all-causes rates.

Two criteria were used in the attempt to identify the items of consumption and expenditure that accounted for the association between pensions and death rates. It was hoped to identify a *group* of variables that satisfied the following three conditions: first, that, used together as control variables, they should remove the significance of the partial correlation between pensions and the all-causes (excluding cancer) death rates; second, that each variable in the group should show significant partial correlations with the all-causes (excluding cancer) death rates while controlling for all the other variables in the group; third, that, while controlling for all the variables in the group, there should be no consumption or expenditure variables left outside the group that retained significant partial correlations with the all-causes (excluding cancer) death rates.

After rotating the consumption and expenditure variables, the following list was found to satisfy these conditions: expenditure on tobacco, and consumption of vitamin C, vitamin A, green vegetables, and carbo-hydrates. Expenditure on tobacco and consumption of carbohydrates had significant positive partial correlations with the all-causes (excluding cancer) death rates, while the others had negative ones. Together, these five variables removed all traces of significance between pensions and the four age- and sex-specific all-causes (excluding cancer) death rates. They also left no significant correlations between death rates and any other expenditure and consumption variables. Using any four of these five variables as conrols, however, left significant partial correlations between death rates and the excluded variable. Interestingly, despite the ability of this group of five controls to remove any significant associations from the correlations between death rates and the other consumption and expenditure variables, correlations with the residuals (derived as described above to serve as a proxy for the effect of the public environment on health) were significant and positive for the all-causes (excluding cancer) death rates for each sex in the 65–74 age-group.

Discussion

What do these correlations mean? As we noted earlier, the danger with any time-series analysis is that there will be a myriad significant but meaningless positive or negative correlations resulting from the tendency for all the relevant variables to go consistently up or down over time. This problem is largely eliminated when using control variables in partial correlations. Correlating residual variations in death rates with residual variations in the independent variables means that one is no longer dealing merely with the gross trends. This is particularly important where it is unlikely that the variables in the analysis could be considered res-ponsible for the gross trends in the dependent variables but, in the present context, it is perfectly reasonable to think that measures of trends in the standard of living are the *prime* candidates in any attempt to account for the overall downward trend in death rates.

This analysis was hampered by the small number of cases available (sixteen years of data). Even important, income-related influences on old people's death rates will have escaped attention. The five consumption and expenditure variables that were picked out in the partial correlations analysis probably should not be taken at face value. They may well be proxies, either for factors that were not covered by data in the analysis or for complicated interactions between larger numbers of factors. At the very least, it seems likely that a variable such as 'carbohydrates' is acting as a proxy for sugar and nutritional problems associated with other refined carbohydrates. In emphasizing tobacco and nutrition, however, the analysis does seem to point in a plausible direction. The statistical methods could equally well have pointed the finger at quite implausible factors such as expenditure on 'other goods', services, or even on transport and vehicles.

The correlations between the all-causes (excluding cancer) death rates and the five selected variables (consumption of carbohydrates, vitamins A and C, green vegetables, and expenditure on tobacco) were supported by a large number of disease-specific correlations. There were eighty possible correlations between these five independent variables and one of the four groupings of specific causes of death (circulatory diseases, respiratory diseases, 'flu, and accidents) in the two older age groups in either sex. Of these eighty simple (zero-order) correlations, some fifty-three (66 per cent) were statistically significant. Of the eighty partial correlations controlling for GDP p.c., some thirty-three (41 per cent) were statistically significant. All signs (+ ve or − ve) were in agreement with the correlations with the all-causes (excluding cancer) death rates. Together, these considerations lend credibility to the view that an important part of the correlation between pensions and old people's death rates reflects a causal relationship.

The small number of years for which data are available and the close relationships between most of the independent variables prevented any attempt at partitioning the variance in death rates between the five selected independent variables.

PART THREE: NARROWING CLASS DIFFERENCES IN INCOMES AND POSTNEONATAL MORTALITY

After looking at the relationship between incomes and mortality in the previous two sections, it was decided to see if the unexplained narrowing of class differences in postneonatal mortality could be explained in terms of changing class differentials in income. In 1970–72, the postneonatal mortality rate (deaths between 28 days and 1 year old) for social class I was 2.9 per 1,000 live births. For social class V, the rate was 13.1—that is, 4.5 times as high. By 1978, the social class I rate had hardly changed and stood at 3.0. In contrast, the social class V rate had dropped to 7.1—less than 2.4 times as high. As *Table 6.7* shows, the lower the social class, the more rapid the fall in postneonatal mortality rates. Although it is clear that most of the fall took place before 1975, the lack of annual figures before that date means that its exact timing is unknown.

Records since early this century suggest that this narrowing of class differentials is unprecedented (Registrar General 1978: 174; DHSS 1980: 74–81). Although the gap has narrowed in absolute terms as infant mortality rates have fallen during this century, the raw figures suggest that relative class differences have remained extraordinarily constant. The extent to which this may be influenced by factors such as revisions in the social class classification of occupations is uncertain but the figures of postneonatal mortality 1970–79, shown in *Table 6.7*, are all based on the 1970 classification of occupations. The narrowing of differentials over this period must, therefore, be regarded as real. What, then, is the explanation for the change?

Figures on the causes of postneonatal mortality are not published separately for each class. Nonetheless, the stability of social class I rates means that it is likely that the causes of death that have declined nationally are responsible for the decline in the class differential. The changing

Table 6.7 *Postneonatal death rates by social class 1970–79 (per 1,000 live births)*

year	social class I	II	IIIN	IIIM	IV	V
1970–72	2.9	3.7	3.9	5.6	6.7	13.1
1975	3.0	3.3	3.5	4.4	5.7	8.7
1976	2.6	2.8	3.1	4.0	5.1	8.4
1977	2.9	3.0	3.2	3.7	5.0	8.0
1978	3.0	3.1	3.2	4.2	4.3	7.1
1979	3.2	2.8	2.6	3.9	5.0	9.1
1978 as % of 1970–72	103	84	82	75	64	54

Note: The 1970 social class classification is used throughout.
Sources: MacFarlane and Mugford (1984), p. 135; OPCS *Monitor* DH3 82/85.

causes of postneonatal death for England and Wales are shown in *Figure 6.1*. It appears that the narrowing class differential is unlikely to have resulted from a decline in any single cause of death. Each causal category declines, with the exception of cot deaths, which increases. Diagnosis of causes of death among babies is known to be extremely difficult and it is likely that the overall picture reflects changes in diagnosis as much as real changes. The impression gained from *Figure 6.1*, however, is of a broadly based decline in mortality from a number of quite different causes.

One of the more surprising features of the class trends in postneonatal mortality is that there appears to be no corresponding narrowing of the differences in perinatal deaths (stillbirths and deaths in the first week of life). As *Table 6.8* shows, there was a fairly even decline in perinatal mortality in all classes during the 1970s. Although one might expect that many of the factors associated with pregnancy and birth that determine perinatal mortality rates would carry through to influence postneonatal mortality rates, the fact that the trends differ tells us that the processes which lie behind them differ. This means that we should not look for the

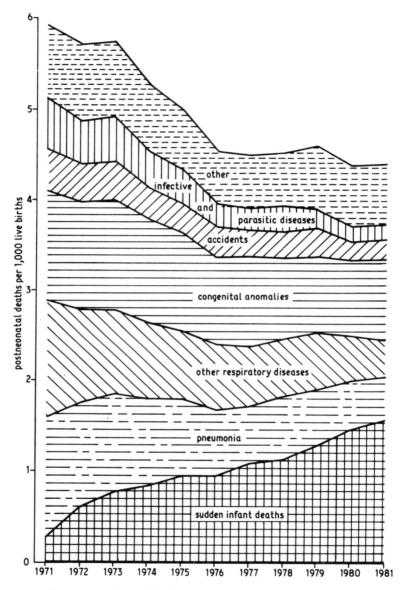

Figure 6.1 Postneonatal mortality by cause (England and Wales 1971–81)

Source: MacFarlane and Mugford (1984) *Birth Counts: Statistics of Pregnancy and Childbirth Volume I. Figure 3.7, p. 39. London: HMSO.*

Table 6.8   *Perinatal death rates by social class 1970–79 (per 1,000 total births)*

year	social class I	II	IIIN	IIIM	IV	V
1970–72	16.3	18.6	20.6	22.1	23.9	32.1
1975	13.8	15.6	16.0	18.9	21.4	27.0
1976	12.7	14.3	15.6	17.1	19.2	24.9
1977	11.6	13.0	14.1	17.1	18.8	22.0
1978	11.9	12.3	13.9	15.1	16.7	20.3
1979	10.7	11.8	12.6	14.3	16.4	19.0
1978 as % of 1970–72	73	66	67	68	70	63

Note: The 1970 social-class classification is used throughout.
Sources: MacFarlane and Mugford (1984), p. 135; OPCS *Monitor* DH3 82/85.

Table 6.9   *Income by class and sex (1970 prices)*

	annual earnings (£) 1970	1978	real increase (%) 1970–78
men			
higher professional	2,928	3,072	5
lower professional	1,885	2,015	7
managers, etc.	3,400	2,984	−12
clerks	1,337	1,372	3
foremen	1,669	1,737	4
skilled manual	1,440	1,614	12
semi-skilled manual	1,289	1,419	9
unskilled manual	1,154	1,257	9
women			
higher professional	2,460	2,488	1
lower professional	1,224	1,443	18
managers, etc.	1,870	1,880	1
clerks	839	1,012	21
forewomen	1,014	1,192	18
skilled manual	677	833	23
semi-skilled manual	645	873	35
unskilled manual	610	844	38

Sources: Routh (1980), p. 120; HMSO (1984).

explanation of the narrowing class differences in postneonatal mortality among factors that would also have affected perinatal mortality, such as maternal age, parity, birthweight, obstetric practice, etc. The impression is that the explanation we are looking for becomes influential only after pregnancy and birth are over. This suggests that we should probably be looking at the changing home environment to which mother and child return after leaving the maternity hospital.

Class differences in mortality are an indication of the continuing sensitivity of health to socio-economic factors. Few can doubt that, in one form or another, class differences in the standard of living are likely to be of primary importance. This is confirmed by the negative association found between relative changes in occupational incomes and occupational mortality rates and between annual changes in pensions and the mortality rates of old people discussed in parts one and two above. Is there, then, evidence that the narrowing class differences in postneonatal mortality were accompanied by narrowing class differences in the standard of living?

Table 6.9 shows changes in income in different occupational classes between 1970 and 1978. It shows a slight narrowing of differences among men and a dramatic narrowing among women. Social class I in *Table 6.7* approximates to the 'higher professionals' and a proportion of the 'managers, etc.' (which include senior administrators) in *Table 6.9*. Social class V is almost identical to the 'unskilled manual' category in *Table 6.9*. On this basis, the percentage increase in the earnings of social class V men was probably at least two or three times as great as that for social class I men. Among women in social class I, earnings scarcely increased at all, while for those in social class V, they increased by almost 40 per cent.

The movement in women's earnings reflects the impact of the 1970 Equal Pay Act, which required employers to establish equal pay for equal work by the end of 1975. The Act did nothing to help those women throughout the economy who were paid less than men by virtue of holding lower-status jobs. The women it did help were those who were paid less although doing identical work to men: it was because this situation was very much more common in the lower classes that women's pay differentials narrowed so dramatically. Insofar as this narrowing was a result of the Equal Pay Act, the changes shown in *Table 6.9* would have taken place before the end of 1975 (Zabalza and Tzannatos 1985).

From the point of view of the differentials in postneonatal mortality, what matters is the changing class distribution of *total household* income. Unfortunately, the narrowing of income differences between *social classes* has received very little attention and there are no continuous or even comparable figures of total household income by class covering the 1970s. Nor is there any easy way of matching the occupations of husbands and wives, during this period when women's employment rates were increasing so rapidly. As the 1971 census showed, working wives of men in any class tend to be spread over occupations allocated to neighbouring classes. This means that the combined effects of the changes in men's and women's incomes will produce a smoother gradient of increases in total household income than that shown for either sex alone. At the extremes, increases in household incomes will range from something like a 2 per cent increase for couples both of whom are in social class I occupations, to almost a 20 per cent increase for couples both of whom are in social class V occupations.

In 1974, working wives provided between 25 and 50 per cent of family income (Hamill 1978). By the end of 1975, when the Equal Pay Act should have been fully implemented, this proportion would have risen still higher. Although we know that the part-time employment of married women increased particularly rapidly during the early 1970s, there is once again no clear indication of how this increase was related to the social class of their husbands. That it was part-time work rather than full-time (the dividing line is 30 hours per week) made little difference to the narrowing in family earnings: presumably reflecting a comparatively small difference in hours, women's part-time manual earnings averaged only 6.5 per cent less than full-time earnings in 1975 (Robertson and Briggs 1979).

Another factor affecting class differences in expenditure during this period was the change in the proportion of income saved. Nationally, the proportion of income saved increased from an average of 8.7 per cent for the years 1970–72 to 12.5 per cent in 1975; after which it remained at roughly that level for the rest of the decade (CSO 1984). This figure of a 4 per cent switch of income from expenditure to savings is an average of what are likely to have been quite different figures in different classes. The increase in savings is widely believed to have been a response to inflation (Thomas 1984). The assumption is that as the rapid inflation of the 1970s decreased the real value of people's capital, they responded by saving more. If this is correct, then the increased savings ratio was probably largest amongst those with the largest capital savings at risk from inflation. Those with no savings at risk would have been unaffected.

The trends in class earnings and saving imply that the early 1970s were characterized by a substantial class difference in the rate of increase in expenditure and so presumably by a narrowing of class differences in the standard of living.

Direct evidence that class differences in the standard of living narrowed is available from several sources. Expenditure on food, which accounts for about a quarter of personal disposable income, is one of the few major items of expenditure that is flexible enough to respond quickly to changes in income: its short-term income elasticity is high. *Table 6.10* shows differences in food expenditure and nutrient consumption classified by the income of the so-called 'head of household'. During the three years 1975–77, the lower-income groups not only spent the same absolute amount on food per head as the upper-income groups did, they also succeeded in getting more nutrients for their money. This contrasts very sharply with the picture over the previous quarter of a century. Each year since the National Food Survey began until 1975, the records show that

Table 6.10 *Nutrient consumption and food expenditure per capita: differences by income of head of household (per capita consumption and expenditure of bottom 10 per cent of households as a percentage of top 10 per cent)*

	1970–72	1975	1976	1977	1978	1979
energy	99	106	107	107	104	101
protein	94	104	104	98	95	95
calcium	88	98	99	108	96	91
iron	97	107	107	198	100	102
thiamine	97	104	104	95	98	95
riboflavin	84	94	95	89	88	90
nicotinic acid	89	100	98	92	90	93
vitamin C	68	73	98	75	68	67
vitamin A	82	90	99	102	97	107
vitamin D	108	125	105	120	109	116
average of nutrients:	91	100	102	99	95	96
expenditure:	85	98	98	95	91	93

Note: Gross weekly incomes of heads of households with earners: in 1975 the top 10 per cent had incomes of £82 and over, compared to the bottom 10 per cent with incomes of £28 or less.
Source: Household Food Consumption and Expenditure (Ministry of Agriculture, Fisheries and Food, annual publication).

poorer people spent less money on food and ended up with less of almost every nutrient than the better-off.

While it is important to note that the changes recorded in food consumption during the 1970s are as unprecedented as the change in the postneonatal mortality differential, this does not mean that nutritional factors were primarily responsible for the postneonatal mortality trends. The narrowing of class differences in food expenditure is probably more important as an indicator of the overall narrowing of class differences in living standards.

The National Food Survey's data, shown in *Table 6.10*, should not be interpreted as meaning that poorer families suddenly increased the proportion of income they spent on food. What is happening follows from the sex differences in income growth shown in *Table 6.7*. As lower-class women's wages rose faster than men's, total household income would also have risen faster than male wages. Thus, if families were to spend (for example) a constant proportion of *household income* on food, we would expect to see the observed narrowing of differences in food expenditure and consumption between groups classified by the incomes of the predominantly *male* heads of households.

It should be noted, however, that although the trends in food consumption show the impact of the more rapid rise in lower-class women's earnings, they are blind to the benefits resulting from the narrowing of class differences in men's wages. As the National Food Survey's income-group classification is based on the income of the, usually male, 'head of household', changes in wage differentials between men will shift them between income groups rather than narrow the gaps between the groups. While the narrowing of wage differences was much smaller among men than women, for couples where both man and woman were employed in manual jobs some 40 per cent of the 1970–78 increase in real household incomes still came from the increase in male earnings (see *Table 6.9*).

Figures that indicate changes in other aspects of the home environment by class are less plentiful than might be expected. Unlike the National Food Survey, the difficulty with the Family Expenditure Survey is, para-doxically, its classification by total household income. The only indication that families may have moved into higher income categories from one year to the next is in the changing proportions of families in each income category. Any accurate assessment of such changes is confounded by the annual revision of the size and number of income categories used and by the inevitable sampling variation.

Table 6.11 (which comes from the General Household Survey) shows the changing social-class distribution of households with various amenities and consumer durables between 1971 and 1978. The available figures suffer from the fact that the upper classes are near saturation point on most items covered, but they do suggest that the physical environment was improving more rapidly at the bottom than at the top of the social scale. On five of the six items shown, the gains made by semi- and unskilled manual workers were greater than the gains made by professionals, employers, and managers. Only the changes in ownership of washing machines showed no real narrowing of the gap between classes. All the items on which lower classes made absolute gains—baths and showers, central heating, telephones, fridges, and vacuum cleaners—may be expected to ease the problems of baby-care and so contribute to raising standards. As well as the direct contribution they make, the changes in class access to these household amenities and consumer durables are, like the nutritional changes before them, also important for the confirmation they provide of a general narrowing of class differences in living standards. The question that remains is whether the rise in lower-class living standards would have reached homes with babies between one month and one year old.

The OPCS Women and Employment Survey (Martin and Roberts 1984) found that about 16 per cent of all mothers having their first babies in the period 1970–74 were back at work within six months of the birth. Almost all the women would have worked before the first pregnancy and some 77 per cent of women continued to work while pregnant with their first child (Daniel 1980). The narrowing class differences in men's wages would have

Table 6.11 *Household facilities and ownership of consumer durables by social class*

	percentage of households with: bath or shower	CH	telephone	washing machine	refrigerator	vacuum cleaner
professional & employers/mgrs						
1971–72*	96	59	82	80	93	97
1978–79**	97	74	92	88	98	98
increase	1	15	10	8	5	1
intermediate & jnr non-manual						
1971–72*	89	41	53	69	84	92
1978–79**	94	57	81	78	96	95
increase	5	16	28	9	12	3
skilled manual						
1971–72*	89	29	37	76	81	90
1978–79**	95	48	70	85	95	95
increase	6	19	33	9	14	5
semi & unskilled manual						
1971–72*	82	19	22	66	66	82
1978–79**	91	37	54	75	91	89
increase	9	18	32	9	25	7

*bath-or-shower and central heating figures are for 1971; all consumer durables are for 1972
**figures for telephone are 1979; all others are 1978
Source: General Household Survey (HMSO, annual publication).

affected all families, regardless of whether or not they had children. (Illegitimate births are excluded from the social class classification.)

The levelling-up of class differences in earnings would have paved the way for higher standards of home-making among couples in the lower social classes. Whether setting themselves up in a new home, buying some of the necessary household equipment and clothing in preparation for a baby, or meeting the daily expenses of life, a higher joint income would have eased the problems of many parents and improved the survival chances of their offspring.

Conclusion

In essence, what we were looking for was a socially graded improvement in living standards petering out in class I but capable of tipping the balance between life and death for some four or five babies in every thousand in class V. It appears that a narrowing of class differences in living standards did occur at about the right time in the early and mid-1970s. That such a dramatic narrowing of class differences in mortality and in living standards are equally unusual lends credibility to the suggestion that they were related. What is lacking is any detailed knowledge of changes in the home environment and in the causes of death that they might have affected.

PART FOUR: INCOME REDISTRIBUTION

In the context of socio-economic inequalities in health, evidence of a relationship between income and mortality leads naturally into a discussion of income distribution. The first issue facing any proposal for redistribution concerns the relative health gains and losses that might result from redistributing income from the rich to the poor. Would the health of the poor improve by more than the health of the rich deteriorated? This is essentially a matter of the shape of the relationship between income and health.

To establish the shape of the relationship between income and mortality, 1971 occupational mortality rates (Registrar General 1978) were matched with occupational earnings taken from the 1970 New Earnings Survey (DOE 1970b). It proved possible to match some eighty occupations on both classifications. Using these data, the correlation between income and mortality rates was compared on the assumption of a linear and loglinear relationship. The linear relationship gave a correlation coefficient of -0.447, compared to -0.565 for the loglinear relationship. The *improvement* in the correlation is significant at the 0.001 level of significance. The best fit relationship is illustrated in *Figure 6.2*.

It is clear from *Figure 6.2* that successive increases in income bring diminishing health returns. The shape of the curve suggests that income transfers from the rich to the poor might be expected to bring substantial health benefits to the poor while having little effect on the health of the rich. Every pound transferred from people earning (in 1970) £60–70 per week to people earning £10–20 would reduce the death rates of recipients by five times as much as it increased those of the donors. Given the distribution of personal disposable income, there would seem to be a great deal of scope for redistribution. In 1980, the bottom 20 per cent of incomes could have been doubled by reducing the top 20 per cent of incomes by only 17 per cent (Townsend 1982).

To infer that major advances in health would result from such a policy of income redistribution may seem to involve too much extrapolation but fortunately there are other sources of evidence on this issue. If income redistribution does benefit the poor by substantially more than it harms the rich, then a more egalitarian income distribution should lead to an

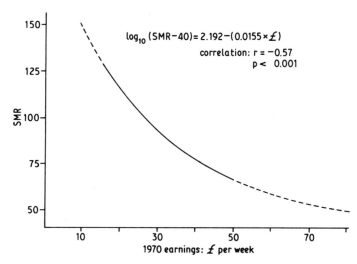

Figure 6.2 Cross-sectional relationship between occupational earnings and standardized mortality ratios

affected all families, regardless of whether or not they had children. (Illegitimate births are excluded from the social class classification.)

Let us look first at the cross-sectional evidence from international comparisons. As Mildred Blaxter pointed out to me, there is a very close association between the degree of income inequality and the overall life-expectancy or mortality rates of developed countries. Across the 11 OECD countries for which there are reliable gini coefficients of income inequality, there is a correlation coefficient of better than -0.8 between gini coefficients of post-tax income inequality (standardized for differences in household size) and both life-expectancy and infant mortality. The correlation is significant at better than 1 in 1,000 and suggests that the overall population mortality increases with income inequality. The association is shown in *Figure 6.3*.

We have already seen some longitudinal evidence of the possible effect on postneonatal mortality rates of the reductions in class differences in income that took place during the early 1970s. More important, however, is Winter's analysis of increases in life expectancy in England and Wales during this century (Winter forthcoming). Using data from Preston, Keyfitz, and Schoen, he shows that the decades 1911–21 and 1940–51, covering the two world wars, saw much the most rapid improvements this century in the life-expectancy of civilian men and women. Men's and women's life expectancy at birth increased by 6.5–7 years in each of those decades compared with an average of 2.6 years for other decades. These

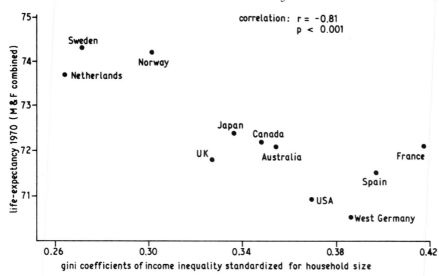

Figure 6.3 Life-expectancy (male and female) and gini coefficients of post-tax income inequality (standardized for household size)
Sources: Sawyer (1976) *Table 11*; World Bank (1983)

improvements resulted from a decline in deaths from a wide range of diseases. He argues that the improvements in life-expectancy during these decades were actually concentrated in the war years and says that 'the worse-off a section of society was in 1914, the greater were the gains registered in life-chances in the war years'; he goes on to identify 'an unanticipated but real improvement in the standard of living of the home population' as the most important reason for these advances (Winter forthcoming). He emphasizes particularly the development, as part of the mobilization of the population during the two wars, of the concept of citizenship as carrying an entitlement to certain minimum standards. Food-rationing during the Second World War is perhaps the most obvious example but there is also clear evidence of narrowing income differences during the two wars. In the First World War, wage differentials narrowed because increases took the form of lump sum, rather than percentage, bonus payments (Von Tunzelmann 1985). In the Second World War, wage increases were supposed to be linked to a cost-of-living index but, as Dudley Seers has shown, this did not stop a considerable narrowing of post-tax income differentials (Seers 1949). Between 1938 and 1947, real incomes (after tax) of those Seers identified as working-class rose by over 9 per cent. This compares with a fall of more than 7 per cent for those identified as middle-class (Milward 1984: 41).

In the light of this cross-sectional and longitudinal evidence taken from national and international sources, there can be little doubt that substantial health benefits could be expected to accrue from a policy of income redistribution in Britain. There are, however, a few remaining points on which it may be useful briefly to speculate. From the evidence we have seen, it would seem reasonable to suppose that within most countries one could find a pattern of diminishing health returns with successive increases in income. The easiest way of understanding the international relationship between measures of income inequality and life-expectancy (*Figure 6.3*) is to assume that the relationship between income and mortality in other countries is something like the curve shown for England and Wales in *Figure 6.2*.

No doubt the position and precise shape of such curves will vary from one society to another. In less developed countries, it seems likely that diminishing returns may set in earlier, preventing the rich from achieving such low mortality rates as they do in more developed societies. Similarly, the minimum levels of income that are just adequate to keep people off the section of the curve where death rates rise particularly steeply will also vary. With economic development, it seems likely that the curves move down and to the right. If this is so, then it suggests that in each society there is something amounting to a historically determined minimum real cost of living. The developing material and social culture establish a minimum income level necessary to support a normal life in each society. It seems likely that one of the effects of economic development is to transform the material and social environment in ways that raise the real cost of living for most of the population in each society. This gives rise to the notion that there is a rising, historically-determined, minimum wage.

The levels of income below which it becomes exponentially difficult to manage have presumably always been an important factor in wage determination. From the point of view of social policy, it is clearly extremely important to identify that level of income and ensure that tax and benefit arrangements are adequate to keep people off the steeply rising part of the mortality curve.

There is a tendency to believe that income redistribution is just an alternative to economic growth in producing rising living standards for the poor. It may be, however, that the problem is not simply one of ensuring that people are minimally equipped to deal with a particular socio-economic environment. More rapid increases in real income throughout society might not compensate for great inequalities in income.

In his analysis of the international relationship between income and mortality, Preston found a relatively poor cross-sectional fit between per capita income levels and life-expectancy in each country (Preston 1976).

While he recognized that income distribution was likely to be part of the explanation for this, he did not include the data in his analysis and so had no indication of how important it might be (Preston 1976: 78–80). This weakness has since been made good by Rodgers (1979). Looking at industrial and third-world countries he shows that around three-quarters of the international cross-sectional variation in life expectancy can be explained in terms of average incomes and income distribution alone.

What it would be nice to know now is whether income distribution is important simply because a given change in income benefits the poor more than the rich, or whether at higher levels of average income greater equality is beneficial *per se*. In other words, are increases in top incomes actually detrimental to the poor?

This work was made possible by a research grant from ESRC which is gratefully acknowledged.

REFERENCES

CSO (1984) *Economic Trends, Annual Supplement.* Central Statistical Office. London: HMSO.
—————— (annual publication) *General Household Survey.* London: HMSO.
Daniel, W. W. (1980) *Maternity Rights: The Experience of Women.* Policy Studies Institute No. 588. London: Policy Studies Institute.
Department of Employment (annual publication) *Family Expenditure Survey.* London: HMSO.
—————— (1970a) *British Labour Statistics: Historical Abstract 1886–1968.* London: HMSO.
—————— (1970b) *New Earnings Survey.* London: HMSO.
—————— (1972) *Department of Employment Gazette.* London: HMSO.
Department of Health and Social Security (1980) *Inequalities in Health (Black Report).* Report of a research working group chaired by Sir Douglas Black. London: DHSS.
Grossman, M. (1972) *The Demand for Health.* NBER Occasional Paper 19. Cambridge, Mass.: National Bureau of Economic Research.
Hamill, L. (1978) *Wives as Sole and Joint Breadwinners.* Government Economic Service Working Paper No. 13. London: DHSS.
Kitagawa, E. M. and Hauser, P. M. (1973) *Differential Mortality in the United States.* Cambridge, Mass.: Harvard University Press.
MacFarlane, A. and Mugford, M. (1984) *Birth Counts: Tables.* London: HMSO.
Martin, J. and Roberts, C. (1984) *Women and Employment: A Lifetime Perspective.* Department of Employment and OPCS. London: HMSO.
Milward, A. S. (1984) *The Economic Effects of the Two World Wars in Britain* (second edition). London: Macmillan.
Ministry of Agriculture, Fisheries and Food (annual publication) *Household Food*

Consumption and Expenditure (annual reports of the National Food Survey Committee). London: HMSO.

Preston, S. H. (1976) *Mortality Patterns in National Populations*. New York: Academic Press.

Registrar General (1958) *Occupational Mortality Tables, 1951 Decennial Supplement*. London: HMSO.

—— (1978) *Occupational Mortality Tables, 1970–72 Decennial Supplement*. OPCS Series DS No. 1. London: HMSO.

—— (annual publication to 1973) *Statistical Review of England and Wales*. OPCS. London: HMSO.

—— (annual publication from 1974) *Mortality Statistics for England and Wales*. OPCS Series DH No. 1. London: HMSO.

Robertson, J. A. S. and Briggs, J. M. (1979) Part-time Working in Great Britain. *Department of Employment Gazette* July: 671–77.

Rodgers, G. B. (1979) Income and Inequality as Determinants of Mortality: an International Cross-section Analysis. *Population Studies* 33: 343–451.

Routh, G. (1980) *Occupation and Pay in Great Britain 1906–79*. London: Macmillan.

Sawyer, M. (1976) *Income Distribution in OECD Countries*. OECD Economic Outlook, Occasional Studies. Paris: OECD.

Seers, D. (1949) *Changes in the Cost of Living and the Distribution of Income Since 1938*. Oxford: Blackwell.

Thomas, R. L. (1984) The Consumption Function. In D. Demery (ed.) *Macroeconomics*. London: Longman.

Townsend, P. (1979) *Poverty in the United Kingdom*. Harmondsworth: Penguin.

—— (1982) An Alternative Anti-poverty Programme. *New Society* 62 (1038): 22–3.

Townsend, P. and Davidson, N. (1982) *Inequalities in Health: The Black Report*. London: Penguin.

Von Tunzelmann, G. N. (1985) Personal communication.

Winter, J. M. (forthcoming) Public Health and the Extension of Life Expectancy in England and Wales, 1901–60. In M. Keynes (ed.) *The Political Economy of Health and Welfare*. Eugenics Society Symposium.

World Bank (1983) *World Tables, Volume II*. Baltimore: Johns Hopkins University Press.

Zabalza, A. and Tzannatos, Z. (1985) The Effect of Britain's Anti-discriminatory Legislation on Relative Pay and Employment. *Economic Journal* 95 (379): 679–99.

SEVEN

Inequalities
in health and health care:
a research agenda

J. Le Grand

SUMMARY

There are five basic questions that can be asked about inequalities in health and health-care:

1 How much ought there to be (objectives)?
2 How great are they (extent)?
3 What causes them (causes)?
4 What consequences do they have (effects)?
5 What can be done about them (policy implications)?

In what follows, I group together a number of possible research topics under these headings. The chapter is, therefore, basically a taxonomy of topics, although under each heading I have given some indication as to which topics seem to me to offer the most potential.

OBJECTIVES

How much inequality in health (or health-care) ought there to be? At first sight, the answer might seem obvious: none. But the issue is actually much more complex. For the objectives of social policy with respect to health or health-care are—or should be—derivative of more fundamental objectives of social and economic organization, such as the promotion of social justice, the attainment of economic efficiency, and the preservation of individual liberty. Achieving any or all of these might require certain inequalities in areas of social policy such as health, rather than full equality. For instance, the promotion of economic efficiency might require that health (and health-care) be concentrated on the more productive members of society and less on, say, the elderly or the disabled; whereas social justice might require the reverse.

A limited amount of work has been done on specifying the possible objectives of health policy in terms of various interpretations of equality (Le Grand 1982, chapters 2 and 3; Muurinen and Le Grand 1985; Mooney 1982). This has discussed objectives such as, for health-care, equality of public expenditure on health-care, equal treatment for equal need, and equality of access to health-care; and, for health, equality of access to health, and equality in health itself. These 'secondary' objectives have not been firmly located in philosophical discussions of the aims of the wider society, however. They have not been derived from basic considerations of the requirements of social justice, efficiency, liberty, etc.; nor has much effort been made to relate them to the grander philosophical systems, such as those of the utilitarians and John Rawls (exceptions include Weale 1978 and Plant, Lesser, and Taylor-Gooby 1980).

As a result, confusion abounds. Consider, for instance, the term 'equality of access'. Often used in discussions of health-care policy (as, for instance, by the Royal Commission on the National Health Service 1979: 9), this has never been defined in a rigorous fashion; its vagueness is exemplified by the fact that it often appears under other guises, such as 'equality of opportunity', as in the 1944 White Paper, *A National Health Service* (HMSO 1944); or even, in the RAWP report, 'equality of opportunity of access' (DHSS 1976: 7). The fact that the concept appears so often in government documents and elsewhere indicates its importance as an objective for social policy in the health field; but its imprecision means that it offers little by way of clear implications for that policy.

It is possible, however, to refine the conception in such a way that its policy conclusions become more apparent. For instance, it has been suggested (Le Grand 1982: 15) that an appropriate interpretation—one consistent with wider notions of social justice—is that of equal private costs per user. That is, every individual should face the same personal cost for each 'unit' of use made of health services. This yields the, unsurprising, conclusion that greater equality of access, in the sense of greater equality of private costs, will be achieved if medical facilities are relocated so as to reduce inequalities in travelling distances. A perhaps less obvious policy implication is that the income losses associated with receiving medical care should be equalized so far as possible, a requirement that might, for instance, imply awarding less sickness benefit to salary-earners in hospital (who generally will continue to be paid) than to wage-earners in the same position (who generally will not).

There are other possible interpretations of the objective. Some might argue, for instance, that it is not equality of access to health-*care* that is important but equality of access to health itself (see Muurinen and Le Grand 1985: 23). However, the purpose of the example is not to argue for one specific objective or one specific interpretation of an objective. Rather, it is to show what could be gained by the exploration of policy objectives in a more rigorous fashion than has been customary up to now. Little has been achieved in this area so far; much remains to be done.

EXTENT

The Black Report (DHSS 1980) devoted much of its efforts to documenting the extent of inequalities in health and health-care. On the whole, it did this well. Indeed, there is little doubt that it is the best collection so far of the evidence relating to inequalities in death, sickness, and the use of health services.

Nonetheless, the Report was not—and could not hope to be—the last word on the topic. The problems associated with its discussion of inequalities in health can be categorized under the headings of health indicators, groups and inequality measures. So far as *health indicators* are concerned, the Report concentrated heavily on mortality rates, with some side-glances at self-reported morbidity. There are well-known problems with these as indicators of health (and ill-health) and there is plenty of work to be done that uses other indicators to supplement the Report's analyses. On *groups*, the Report primarily considered the differences between social classes. This emphasis on class suggests that it is occupational differences that are the prime focus of social concern. More subtly, it also supports a causal hypothesis: that occupation is the major determinant of ill-health and that inequalities between other groupings are simply reflections of the more basic occupational inequalities. But neither of these propositions is likely to command universal agreement. The respondents to Hart's survey (1981) argued that inequalities between income groups, the sexes, races, or regions may be just as important for policy purposes as those between occupational groups. There is, of course, indeed considerable evidence to suggest that occupational differences, although very important, are by no means the sole factor creating health inequalities.

Finally, *inequality measures*: in making its more controversial assertions—for instance, that inequalities in health have been widening over time—the Report used some crude inequality measures, such as the absolute difference between the standardized mortality ratios for the top and bottom social classes. Those can be criticized on two main grounds. First, as explained by Illsley (forthcoming), they do not adequately take account of changes in the relative sizes of the groups over time. Second, the measure used is only one of a wide class of inequality measures, others of which might yield quite different impressions. For instance, again as shown by Illsley, a comparison between the absolute difference in numbers of deaths in the two social classes over time suggests that there has been a dramatic reduction in inequality. Analyses based on differences in mortality between *individuals* rather than between groups also give rather different conclusions. Elsewhere (Le Grand 1985), I have calculated Gini coefficients measuring the dispersion of age-at-death in the population as a whole; again these show a fall, rather than an increase, in inequality. Although such estimates are measuring something rather different from the social-class measures, they nonetheless pertain to important aspects of inequality and are ripe for further investigation.

So far, we have concentrated on the problems of ascertaining inequalities in health. Inequalities in *health-care*, however, are also a matter of concern. There is currently much dispute over whether such inequalities actually exist—particularly, whether the lower social groups use the health services as much, relative to need, as the higher ones. The conventional view of the 1970s was that they do not (Alderson 1970; Forster 1976; Le Grand 1978) but this has recently been challenged (Collins and Klein 1980; see also Le Grand 1982: 29–30). There is an urgent need to resolve this dispute for it underlies much current debate concerning the role of the Health Service.

CAUSES

The Black Report (DHSS 1980) considered four possible explanations of health inequalities: artefact, natural or social selection, materialist, and cultural/behavioural. The first concerns the statistical issues discussed in the previous section. The second concerns the direction of causation in the relationship between health and inequality. Are unhealthy individuals in a lower social class ill because they are in that class or are they, as the selection hypothesis would imply, in that class because they are ill? Are individuals in a particular region healthy because of factors connected with that region or are they in that region because they are healthy? Illsley (forthcoming) has argued strongly that the Report did not pay enough attention to quantifying the importance of social mobility and hence to social selection; a concern apparently also expressed by many of the respondents to Hart's survey. Richard Wilkinson, in Chapter 6, addresses the issues involved, together with some suggestions as to how they might be resolved; this is clearly an important area for future work.

The two remaining explanations are the materialist—that inequalities in health are determined by the fundamental inequalities in resources and power in the society—and the cultural/behavioural—that they are determined by differences between the classes in individuals' behaviour concerning health-damaging or health-promoting activities. Of the two, the Report favoured the former; indeed, it argued that, over all, 'it is our belief that it is in some form or forms of the "materialist" approach that the best answer lies' (DHSS 1980: 170).

However the Report's attempts to distinguish between the behavioural and the materialist explanations seem misguided. In practice, people's behaviour is greatly influenced by the material constraints they face on their activities. The outcomes of the choices they make will, of course, be partly a function of their tastes or preferences but it will also depend heavily on their constraints (such as their income). Moreover, even their tastes may, in part, be determined by their, or their parents', constraints. Individuals brought up in poor households, whose parents found it cheaper to buy white bread rather than brown, or to smoke a packet of cigarettes rather than take a walk in the country, are likely to develop tastes that accord with their situation. Hence explanations for health inequalities in terms of behaviour differences are not necessarily alternatives for explanations that rely on differences in the socio-economic environment; rather, behaviour may be one of the routes through which the environmental influences work.

What are the research implications of this? First, it seems necessary to use large samples to establish on a statistical basis what are the principal factors in the socio-economic environment that affect health. At the moment, there is considerable dispute about this; for instance, an individual's economic resources are revealed as being of major importance in some studies (such as Wilkinson 1976) and as insignificant in others (Burchell 1981). Much of the data necessary to resolve this and other issues is likely to be available only from longitudinal studies, such as those discussed in Blaxter's contribution to this volume (chapter 8). Second, once the basic statistical relationships have been established, it will be desirable to explore in depth—necessarily, using a much smaller sample—the exact way in which the factors indicated operate. For instance, does a low income affect health (if it does) directly through impeding the purchase of nutritious food, or indirectly through 'creating' tastes for non-nutritious food? From a policy point of view, it is important to be able to answer these kinds of questions; for instance, in this case, if the former were true, it would imply that raising incomes would be more effective than, say, dietary education, whereas, if the latter were true, it might imply the opposite.

Third, it seems important to establish the relative significance of medical care as an influence on health states. Again, this is a matter of considerable controversy. There is a growing volume of evidence that much medical care is ineffective and some actually harmful. This has apparently convinced some observers that it is *all* ineffective. Victor Fuchs (1974: 6) has argued that 'differences in health levels between the United States and other developed countries, or among populations in the United States are not related to differences in the quantity and quality of medical care'. The Black Report did not even consider inequalities in medical care as a possible explanation for inequalities in health.

At first sight, this might seem solely a medical problem but such an interpretation would be incorrect. The relative importance of medical care as an influence on health can be properly assessed only in conjunction with an investigation of the other influences, particularly socio-economic ones. The appropriate research strategy would be to include the utilization of medical care as one of the factors to be investigated in both the large-scale statistical analysis and the small-scale in-depth studies already proposed.

Inequalities in health-care

There has been no overall study of the reasons for differences between social classes in their utilization of health-care services. This may be because, as was discussed earlier, it has yet to be established to everyone's satisfaction that such inequalities exist. If, for the sake of argument, it is assumed that they do exist, then there are a number of possible explanations. These include: the absence of medical facilities in poorer areas; the poor having worse access to such facilities as do exist, owing to their possessing fewer cars and telephones: manual workers, unlike the salaried middle class, losing money when they take time off to go to the doctor; failures of communication between essentially middle-class medical staff and working-class patients. Of these, some are under the control of the Health Service (relocation of medical facilities); some are more likely to be affected by changes in the overall income distribution, through taxation and social-security policies; some, such as communication difficulties between the classes, may not be amenable to any short-term remedy.

For policy purposes, it is obviously important to establish which of these factors, if any, are the most important. It seems unlikely, however, that anything can be done using published data. New data are required, possibly from surveys of the kind discussed in the previous section. Over all, this seems to be an important field for research but one that is currently relatively uncultivated.

EFFECTS

Obvious issues that arise here concerning inequalities in *health* include the effect of inequalities in health on employment, incomes, quality of life, and other aspects of living. The impact of inequalities in health on attitudinal differences between groups also seems a potentially fruitful area. The principal issue so far as *health-care* is concerned is, presumably, the extent to which inequalities in health give rise to different needs for health-care and inequalities in health-care contribute to inequalities in health.

POLICY IMPLICATIONS

In some ways, there is little need for extra research under this heading: if the other areas discussed have been properly researched, then the policy implications should automatically follow. Thus, if we have a clear idea of what we are trying to achieve (objectives), what the present situation is (extent), and what are the major factors determining it (causes), then it ought to be relatively simple to fashion the policies appropriate for changing what is into what ought to be.

In practice, of course, things are not that simple. Even though ends are the same, policies differ. What is needed is extensive research on the effects of different institutional structures on inequalities in health and health-care. In this connection, international comparisons are likely to be very useful. Different countries have different institutions and different experiences of inequalities in health and health-care; hence each offers the possibility of acting as a 'laboratory' for the others. There seems to be room, therefore, for a number of studies comparing the institutional structure and effectiveness of social policy towards inequalities in health and health-care in various countries.

Another, more specific, proposal is an investigation of the effects of the recommendations of RAWP (DHSS 1976). They have now been, or are currently being, implemented, at least after a fashion; it would be of interest to explore the effects, both on the re-allocation of health-care resources and on the variables that the re-allocation was intended to affect (such as mortality rates).

Three other types of questions arise under this heading. First, what is the impact on inequalities in health of social policy directed at other ends (for instance, pensions policy)? Second, what is the impact of social policy directed at other ends on inequalities in health (e.g., anti-smoking campaigns that have a greater impact on the better-off and hence actually widen health inequalities)? Third, what are the political and other impediments to policy-making in this general area?

This last was particularly emphasized by some of the respondents to Hart's survey:

'Several respondents raised the issue of why it is senior managers, health authorities and politicians show so little interest in the problem of health inequality. What are the political processes whereby health inequalities are identified and acted upon? How is information handled and processed? What are the priorities of those with power to decide? Who has the power to decide? In what way does local "discretion" facilitate the thwarting of central government's attempts to reduce inequality through a diversion of funds from hospitals to community services?' (1981: 10–11)

Again, the experience of RAWP seems to be an obvious area to explore in this context.

CONCLUSION

Under each heading, there are enormous opportunities for research. As Alan Williams put it in his reply to Hart's survey (Hart 1981: 1), 'there is enough work to keep a thousand researchers going for a thousand years.' However, the following seem to stand out as the key issues that should figure on any research agenda:

1 What are (and what should be) the objectives of policy towards inequalities in health and health-care? Can these be formulated in a fashion that is both generally acceptable and sufficiently specific to be useful?
2 What is the most useful way of defining and measuring health from the point of view of health inequalities? Once that is decided, which inequality measure should be used, and what do the different measures tell us?
3 To what extent are observed health inequalities the outcome of social selection?
4 Is there substantial inequality in the utilization of health services? If so, what are the main factors that create that inequality?
5 What are the principal socio-economic factors that affect health? In what way do they affect health; how does their influence operate?
6 How much of an influence on health is medical care? What is its importance relative to that of socio-economic factors?
7 How effective have different countries been in reducing inequalities in health and health-care? How far can differences in effectiveness be explained by differences in institutions?
8 What has been the effect of RAWP on regional differences in resources and in health?
9 What are the principal political impediments to the implementation of effective inequality-reducing policies?

Precisely how these questions are to be answered is a matter of research strategy and hence beyond the scope of this paper. It is worth noting, however, that they are not all equally resource-consuming. (1) is a matter of philosophical investigation and need take up only the time of the principal investigator. The first part of (2) also does not require extra research resources; the second part does, but perhaps not an enormous amount since it could be implemented using published data. (7) will be expensive but the cost could be shared by researchers in several countries.

The really expensive items are likely to be (4), (5), (6), and (9), since they are all likely to require the generation of new data. The issues they deal with, however, are of immense significance for the future allocation of resources in the health field generally; hence, the money would be well spent.

In writing this paper, I have had help from a variety of sources. These include the members of the Subcommittee on Inequality in Health and of the Social Affairs Committee of the ESRC (then SSRC), particularly Jack Barnes, John Fox, Raymond Illsley, and Richard Wilkinson. Also useful was a review of responses to a survey of researchers in the field undertaken by Hart (1981).

© 1986 J. Le Grand

REFERENCES

Alderson, M. R. (1970) Social Class and the Health Service. *Medical Officer* 124: 51–9.

Burchell, A. (1981) Inequalities in Health: Analysis of the 1976 General Household Survey. Government Economic Service Working Paper No. 48.

Collins, E. and Klein, R. (1980) Equity and the NHS: Self-reported Morbidity, Access and Primary Care. *British Medical Journal* 281: 1111–115.

Department of Health and Social Security (1976) *Sharing Resources for Health in England*. Report of the Resources Allocation Working Party. London: HMSO.

——— (1980) *Inequalities in Health (Black Report)*. Report of a research working group chaired by Sir Douglas Black. London: DHSS.

Forster, D. P. (1976) Social Class Differences in Sickness and General Practitioner Consultations. *Health Trends* 8: 29–32.

Fuchs, V. (1974) *Who Shall Live?* New York: Basic Books.

Hart, N. (1981) Research on Inequalities in Health. Report to the Sociology and Social Administration Committee of the SSRC.

HMSO (1944) *A National Health Service*. Cmnd 6502. London: HMSO.

Illsley, R. (forthcoming) Occupational Class, Selection and the Production of Inequalities. *Quarterly Journal of Social Affairs*.

Le Grand, J. (1978) The Distribution of Public Expenditure: The Case of Health Care. *Economica* 45: 125–42.

——— (1982) *The Strategy of Equality*. London: Allen and Unwin.

——— (1985) *Inequalities in Health: the Human Capital Approach*. LSE Welfare State Programme Discussion Paper No. 1.

Mooney, G. (1982) Equity in Health Care: Confronting the Confusion. *Effective Health Care* 1: 179–87.

Muurinen, J. M. and Le Grand, J. (1985) The Economic Analysis of Inequalities in Health. *Social Science and Medicine* 20: 1029–035.

Plant, R., Lesser, H., and Taylor-Gooby, P. (1980) *Political Philosophy and Social Welfare*. London: Routledge and Kegan Paul.

Royal Commission on the National Health Service (1979) *Report*. Cmnd 7615. London: HMSO.

Weale, A. (1978) *Equality and Social Policy*. London: Routledge and Kegan Paul.

Wilkinson, R. G. (1976) *Socio-economic Factors in Mortality Differentials*. M. Med. Sci. thesis, University of Nottingham. (Unpublished.)

EIGHT

Longitudinal studies in Britain relevant to inequalities in health

M. Blaxter

This review of longitudinal studies is presented in two main sections. The first presents tabulated, summarized information about each study examined, which attempts to set out exactly what data have been or are being collected, on what samples, by what method, at what time intervals, and with what success in retracing or retaining the cohorts or samples involved. The second gives a discussion dealing with (a) theoretical issues relating to the different potentialities and achievements of longitudinal or cross-sectional studies, and population cohorts or selected samples, in analysing or explaining inequalities in health; (b) issues relating to the nature of the data collected and the social/medical categories by which inequality is distinguished; (c) practical problems of attrition, representativeness, and the long-term organization and funding of studies.

It has, of course, been necessary to decide, firstly, what counts as a longitudinal study and, secondly, what studies have most relevance to the question of inequalities in health. Studies have been included only if:

1 they have investigated subjects at more than one point in time or have the potential for doing so;
2 they have data on an individual (i.e. longitudinal) rather than a group (i.e. cross-sectional) level, so that individuals at time (1) can be identified at time (2) (a few studies are, of course, of mixed cross-sectional and longitudinal design);
3 they have some data both on health variables and on the possible social causes, correlates or consequences of states of health—the ideal, of course, is to have both health and social data at each time-period covered. Studies are, however, included if at least one of the cross-pathways of association shown in *Figure 8.1* is available.

It is, perhaps, useful to spell this out in a simple way, to emphasize that the pathways that are covered vary in different studies. Even if both health

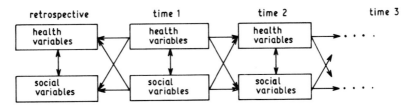

Figure 8.1 Potential pathways in longitudinal studies

and social data are collected at each follow-up, the extent to which each box is full may differ at different periods (e.g. there are commonly more health data in infancy than in adolescence). In the more focused studies, the health data may be viewed as possible consequences or as possible antecedents of social variables; this will determine the pathway followed.

There are three types of relevant study and the tabulated information which follows deals with them in this order:

Studies based on total population data banks

Study 1:   OPCS Longitudinal Study
Study 2:   Aberdeen Maternity and Neonatal Data Bank

These two studies, one national and one local, obviously do not represent all existing data banks. There are many others with a medical orientation and in some there is longitudinal linking of events occurring to the individual; the Oxford Record Linkage Project (Acheson 1967) is one of the best examples. However, these data banks, even if records are linked and even if some social data are included, have been used almost exclusively for epidemiological or health-service administration studies: they have not been intended to explore socio-medical inequalities, nor do any of them appear to offer easy potential for doing so. The two data banks included differ from the others in that they are not simply linked records but are essentially longitudinal *studies*.

Cohort studies of representative normal populations

Study   3: National Survey of Health and Development
Study   4: Second Generation Study
Study   5: National Child Development Survey
Study   6: Child Health and Education Study
Study   7: National Study of Health and Growth
Study   8: National Surveillance of Growth in Pre-school Children

Study 9: Newcastle Thousand Families Survey
Study 10: Aberdeen Child Development Study
Study 11: MRC Derbyshire Schoolchildren Smoking Study
Study 12: Aberdeen Styles of Ageing Study
Study 13: MRC Glasgow Cohort Studies

An attempt has been made to offer a complete list, whether national (3–8) or local (9–13). Most are births cohorts (3–6, 9, 10) or cohorts identified in early years (7, 8). Longitudinal studies that begin in adult life are rare (12, 13). Most of the population studies are concerned with the whole of development or life circumstances but some have focused on only one or two specific measures of health or development (7, 8, 11).

Longitudinal studies of samples of 'deviant' populations

Study 14: Mothers at Risk
Study 15: Children in Day Care Study
Study 16: Children of Young Mothers
Study 17: Pre-school Language and Behaviour Study
Study 18: Childhood Experiences and Parenting Behaviour: children in
     care
Study 19: Aberdeen Mental Subnormality Study
Study 20: Sheffield Problem Families

These are studies that, rather than following total populations, select their samples for a particular characteristic (e.g. children of single parents, mentally subnormal children, etc.). There may or may not be matched control groups without the characteristic. These studies are more focused and are akin to the type of study usually described as prospective; they are likely to be testing a hypothesis or looking for an expected association over time. They are, of course, also likely to be smaller in scale than the cohort studies and there is a large number of them. The list, which is certainly not complete, has been selected to represent studies of different kinds that are particularly relevant to inequalities in health. It may be noted that the large national cohorts have also provided studies of sub-samples of special groups: at least twelve deviant sub-groups have been studied in the National Child Development Survey, for instance, and for some of these (one-parent families, children in care, the physically and mentally handicapped) extra data have been collected. Similarly, the Child Health and Education Study examines groups of children with disabilities more extensively.

 The selection of these more focused studies is intended to illustrate current trends. At previous periods, studies of the sequelae of birth conditions would perhaps have been prominent. At present, there are no cohort studies of infants at risk that have any substantial social content, though there are clinically-oriented longitudinal studies, such as the series of studies on high-risk newborns of the Department of Paediatrics of University College, London. Similarly, studies of groups of problem families, particularly those going through social agencies, were once much more common. The most fashionable characteristics now or recently studied as the possible precursors of later childhood or adult maladjustment or lack of achievement would seem to be single parenthood, youthful child-bearing, and family stress. Single parents are a group that many of the national studies (e.g. 3, 5, 7) have also chosen for special analysis.

The bibliography with which the review ends includes, under the heading of each study, only a selection of the publications based on it, focusing particularly on those that are relevant to inequalities and to health. (There is no bibliography for Studies 13, 15, or 16.)

Table 8.1 *Study 1: OPCS Longitudinal Study*

investigators	*index sample*		
A. Brown, P. O. Goldblatt, B. Werner, Office of Population Censuses and Surveys; A. J. Fox, K. A. Moser, E. M. D. Grundy, M. Rosato, J. Webster, R. Barker, Social Statistics Research Unit, City University	1% of population of England and Wales, updated by including births and immigrations; base population that of 1971 census		
	number 513,073 at commencement		*year of birth* all ages *year of identification* 1971, continuing

data available (all generations in population, 1971, and continuing with subsequent births)
continuous, social data at ten-year (census) intervals

age of index sample	*health data*	*social data*	*method*
—	age and cause of death	occupation and marital status at death	death records
		and at each census	census
	fertility	births of children	birth records
	birthweight	all census information e.g. household, housing, marriage, internal migration, immigration, education, etc.	census

age of index sample	health data	social data	method
	deaths of infant children and of spouses (after 1971)		death records
	entry into long-stay psychiatric hospital (after 1971)		DHSS
	entrance into cancer register (after 1970)		cancer register

Notes on bias, potential for future study, etc.: As there is continuous updating with births and immigrations, the sample will always be representative of the population. The subjects at commencement represented 96.8% of the potential sample; the small shortfall consists disproportionately of those in institutions and defence establishments. *Ad hoc* tabulations are being made available, and visiting researchers are invited to participate in the analysis of the 1981 Census data.

Table 8.2   *Study 2: Aberdeen Maternity and Neonatal Data Bank*

investigators	index sample
Professor R. Illsley, Dr B. Thompson, M. L. Samphier; MRC Institute of Medical Sociology, Aberdeen	all women with obstetric and fertility-related events resident in Aberdeen District

number	year of birth
over 120,000	—

	year of identification
	continuous since 1951

data available (data are now available on two generations of child-bearing women)

age of index sample	health data	social data	method
—	individually linked clinical, demographic, and social data on all fertility-related events, e.g. pregnancy, child-bearing, spontaneous and therapeutic abortion, sterilization; a basic 55-item data file, for instance, contains items on:		medical records
	mother's height, outcome of pregnancy; abortion, termination of pregnancy and sterilization; delivery details and condition of infant; eclampsia and PET; mother's smoking	residence, marital status, father's occupation; mother's occupation, education, place of upbringing; ages of parents; date of marriage(s); fertility history	
	other data are available, including particular data on special groups, at certain time-periods, or on special topics		

Table 8.3   *Study 3.: National Survey of Health and Development*

investigators	*index sample*
Professor J. R. T. Colley,	sample of all children born in one week in England,
Dr M. E. J. Wadsworth,	Wales and Scotland, composed of all non-manual,
Dr R. Midwinter, B. Rodgers,	all agricultural, and one in four sample of remaining
N. Britten	families, illegitimate and multiple births excluded

number	*year of birth*
5,362	1946
	year of identification
	birth

data available (parental generation at child's birth and throughout childhood; index generation to 36 years; children of index generation)

age of index sample	health data	social data	method
4–6 weeks (1946)	antenatal and postnatal care, birth conditions	mother's education and work, father's occupation; care of child	interview by health visitor
2 (1948)	development, illnesses, accidents, hospitalizations; mother's health	family circumstances, mother's employment and care of child, use of welfare services and nurseries	interview by health visitor
4 (1950)	as at 2	as at 2	interview by health visitor
6 (1952)	as at 2	as at 2 and sleep and play, training, etc.	interview by health visitor
	general examination and history		medical examination by school doctor
	school absences		school records
7 (1953)	general examination and history		medical examination by school doctor
	school absences	school information, teacher's accounts of parental interest	school records, teacher's reports
8 (1954)	mother's account of health, hospital and clinic use, accidents, etc.	family and household; attitudes to school	interview by health visitor
	school absences	school information	school records
		teacher's accounts of parental interest	teacher's reports

age of index sample	health data	social data	method
9 (1955)	as at 8	as at 8	interview by health visitor
10 (1956)		achievement and behaviour, parental interest, home environment	teacher's reports
11 (1957)	as at 8	as at 8	interview by health visitor
	general examination and history, sexual development		medical examination by school doctor
		ability and attainment	tests completed by children
		school environment, transfer to secondary school	school information
13 (1959)		ability and attainment	tests completed by children
		achievement, ratings of attitude to work, behaviour, personality	teacher's reports
		job ideas, hobbies, interests; personality inventory	questionnaire completed by child
15 (1961)	as at 8	family and household; attitudes of parents to work and further education of child	interview by health visitor
	general examination and history, sexual development		medical examination by doctor
		ratings as at 13 years, school-leaving and careers guidance	reports by teachers
		ability and attainment	tests completed by child
		occupational interest inventory, attitudes to jobs and further education	questionnaire completed by child

age of index sample	health data	social data	method
16 (1962)		examinations and school leaving	school records
	(if at school) self-reported health	(if at school) course, future career, activities, personality inventory	questionnaire completed by child
17 and 18 (1963–64)		(if at school) examinations and school leaving	school records
		(if left school) job choice, job history, training, apprenticeship, further education, ambitions, pay, hobbies, personality inventory	questionnaires and interviews with subjects
		training and technical college, facilities, courses, achievements	information from colleges
19 (1965)	self-reported health, use of medical services	further education and jobs, marriage, babies	interview by health visitor
		examinations and school leaving, college courses and achievements	school and college records
		(if still in education) examination records, degree course details, personality inventory	questionnaires completed by subjects
		undergraduate group discussions	
20 (1966)	self-reported health, including height, weight, chest trouble	jobs, household, etc.	postal questionnaire completed by subject
20–24		courses and achievements	university and colleges
21 (1967)	parents and siblings' eyesight		questionnaire
22, 23 and 25 (1968–71)	similar to 19 years	similar to 19 years, including income, housing	postal questionnaire completed by subjects

age of index sample	health data	social data	method
26 (1972)	height and weight, home and work stress, nervous troubles	marriage, children, housing, religion, training, employment of spouse, father, father-in-law, spouse's education, perceptions of society, voting, union membership, activities	interview
36 (1982)	height, weight, blood pressure, respiratory function, diet, mental health (Present State Examination), stress	as at 26 years, but with the exception of voting and union membership	interview and examination by nurses

Notes on sample: In 1977, 88% of the survivors in the sample were living in Great Britain, and losses have been low (even after the children left the educational system) because of the frequent contact. At 26 years, losses totalled 12%. There has been a slight excess loss of S.C. IV/V, but the resultant bias is very small. The proportions of the original sample were, of course, biased towards non-manual and agricultural families. At 36 years, contact was maintained with 85% of those still living in Great Britain, i.e. approximately 3,500 individuals.

The possible distortion of events which might be introduced by such frequent and close study of individuals has been partially checked by using as a control group one-third of the original birth cohort of manual social class families who were not included in the sample. Some very minor differences in service-use appear to have been introduced.

Since 1969, interviews have been carried out with each survey member whose first child reaches four years (see Study 4).

Table 8.4 *Study 4: Second Generation Study*

investigators	*index sample*		
Dr M. E. J. Wadsworth, MRC National Survey of Health and Development, University of Bristol	first-born children of the members (both male and female) of the National Survey of Health and Development		
	number at present over 2,000	*year of birth* 1965 onwards *year of identification* at four years old 1969–85	

data available (see Study 3)			
age of index sample	*health data*	*social data*	*method*
4	admissions to hospital, accidents; respiratory illness, asthma, eczema	child's behaviour, training, activities, education, relationship with parent, separation, etc.; mother's self-assessment and assessment of child, recollections of own childhood	interview
8	as at 4	as at 4, plus tests of child's verbal ability	interview
		school progress	questionnaire to teachers

Notes on sample: Rate of refusal has generally been low, ranging from none when the parent was aged 27 years to 11.6% when the parent was aged 22 years: the mean is 6.3%. The parental generation reached their peak of first-child bearing at 25 years.

Table 8.5   *Study 5: National Child Development Survey*

investigators	index sample		
National Children's Bureau; R. Davie, K. Fogelman, P. Shepherd	all births occurring in one week in 1958 in England, Scotland and Wales, augmented by those born in the same week who came into the country by 1974		
	number 17,733	*year of birth* 1958 *year of identification* at birth	

data available (parental generation, at child's birth and throughout childhood; index generation to 23 years of age; children of index generation)

age of index sample	health data	social data	method
birth	obstetric and antenatal history, complications of pregnancy, labour; birth condition, weight, progress of infant	social and family background; management of child; mother's smoking	interview and medical records
7 (1965)	height, weight, clinical examination and tests, sight, hearing, speech, motor co-ordination		medical examination
	medical history, hospitalizations, accidents, clinic attendance, dental care, primary care consultations	family size, housing, parental situation, occupations, etc.; pre-school experience, periods 'in care', behaviour, separation from mother	interview with mother (health visitor)
		attendance records, ratings of parental interest, assessment of abilities, attainment and behaviour; variables of schools	teachers' questionnaire
		achievement tests	tests completed by child
11 (1969)	medical examination as at 7		medical examination
	medical history and service-use as at 7	family circumstances as at 7, and financial situation, satisfaction with housing, neighbourhood	interview with mother (health visitor)

age of index sample	health data	social data	method
11 (1969) cont.		teachers' assessments as at 7 achievement tests	teachers' questionnaire tests completed by child
		interests and aspirations, essay describing predicted life at 25	questionnaire completed by child
16 (1974)	medical examination as at 7		medical examination
	medical history and service-use as at 7	family circumstances as at 7 and parental expectations for further education and employment	interview with mother (health visitor)
		teachers' assessments as at 7 and expectations for future education and employment	teachers' questionnaire
		achievement tests	tests completed by child
		activities and attitudes, smoking, drinking, sex education, and preparation for parenthood; family relationships, marriage intentions, educational and occupational intentions	questionnaire completed by child
21 (1979)		Public Examination results	school records
23 (1981)	self-rating of health, long-standing illness or disability, limitation on functioning; height; weight, sight, migraine, fits, asthma, wheezy bronchitis, cough and phlegm, any other condition with regular medical supervision; disability in the	extensive data on employment, unemployment, training, further education, qualifications, job searching, pay (since school leaving); literacy/numeracy, attitudes school/work; birth of children; breastfeeding of children; household composition, marriage, cohabitation; employment	interview

age of index sample	health data	social data	method
	employment field; accidents since 16, hospitalizations; specialist consultations for depression; malaise index; miscarriages and abortions; birthweight of children; infant deaths; whether parents alive and working	and education of partner; housing, income and other financial; family plans and contraception; leisure activities, voluntary work; alcohol, smoking, voting, TV, activity, religion	

Notes on sample: The total of known deaths and emigrations within the cohort, by age 23, represents approximately 5% in each case of the original birth cohort.

It has proved possible to trace between 98% of the target population (at birth) and 85% (at 23). Refusals, few in the early years, have totalled approximately 5% of the target population at 11 years, 6% at 16 years, and 7% at 23 years. (Refusal, inability to trace, and even emigration, at one stage has not, of course, necessarily meant that the individual could not be included at a later age.)

These inevitable losses have reduced the cohort, by age 23, to approximately 12,500, or approximately 70% of the original birth cohort. The nature of any bias in the 1981 follow-up is not yet available, but in 1974 there was no bias at 16 years of age in relation to, e.g. parent's occupation, education, indices of child's physical development. There was a small bias against some minority groups of disadvantaged children, e.g. those in special education or those born illegitimate, but this was very slight (for instance, 3.4% of cohort were known to be illegitimate at birth, 3.2% of the 16-year-old respondents were illegitimate).

It is the hope and intention that the index cohort can be retained for further follow-up in adult life. There are data about whether their parents are still living and the parental generation could be traced through them. Limited health data have been collected about the young children of the index generation.

Table 8.6 *Study 6: Child Health and Education Study*

investigators	*index sample*	
Professor N. R. Butler, A. F. Osborn, M. N. Haslum, B. C. Howlett, J. Golding; Department of Child Health Research Unit, University of Bristol	all children born in one week in 1970 and resident in England, Wales, and Scotland; originally studied at birth in the British Births Survey (1970), which also included children born in Northern Ireland	

	number		*year of birth*
	Birth (1970) – England, Wales and Scotland	16,567	1970
	N. Ireland	629	*year of identification* 1970
	5 years (1975)	13,135	
	10 years (1980)	14,906	
	Subsamples: (a) study of low-birth weight children and 10% randomly selected controls (England, Wales, and Scotland). Carried out by Dr R. Chamberlain; 22 months (1972) and 3½ years (1973)	3,375	
	(b) regional study in south-west region of England and South Wales; 3½ years (1973)	978	

data available (index generation from birth; parental generation from child's birth)

age of index sample	health data	social data	method
birth (1970)	pregnancy, childbirth and care during the first week of life	social class, parents' age, education and country of origin; marital status; mother's employment, smoking	interview by midwife
22 months (1972) and 3½ years (1973) (sample surveys)	assessment of child's physical, cognitive and social developmental progress; child's illnesses and disabilities	social class, housing, family size	interviews with mother and tests with child by medical officer
3½ years (1973) (regional study)	personal/social development; use of health services; medical history	family structure, socio-economic/ housing conditions; TV, reading, outings,	health visitor interview with mother

age of index sample	health data	social data	method
		parent-child interaction; maternal employment; pre-school education and day care	
		child-rearing attitudes; social attitudes	maternal self-completion
5 years (1975)	use of health services, medical history, chronic illness and handicap, hospital admissions	family structure, socio-economic/housing conditions; mother-child separations; TV and reading; pre-school education and day care; maternal employment	health visitor interview with mother
	health visiting, child health clinic attendances, risk registers		questionnaire completed from health visitor and CHC records
	scale of maternal depression	assessment of child's behaviour; maternal child-rearing attitudes; cognitive and vocabulary tests; child's height and head circumference	maternal self-completion questionnaire; test booklet
10 years (1980)	medical history, illness and handicap; accidents; family health; scale of maternal depression	family composition; education and occupation of parents; housing and amenities; assessment of child's behaviour; child's activities at home; parent's view of school; parent's assessment of child's life skills	parental interview by health visitor; maternal self-completion form
	school medical service; examination for deficiency in vision, speech, hearing, pulse, and blood pressure; measures of height, head circumference and weight; systematic examination; test for laterality; motor co-ordination	need for special education	medical examination by medical officer

age of index sample	health data	social data	method
10 years (1980) cont.		organisation of school day; special education; social relations in the classroom; child's educational aptitude; parental interest; child's behaviour at school; incentives and discipline in the classroom; social composition of school; neighbourhood in which school is located	educational questionnaire completed by head and class teachers
		self-esteem and locus of control; smoking; diet	pupil self-completion questionnaire; tests administered by class teacher
		tests and assessments: 1 language 2 diagnostic reading 3 writing and spelling 4 left/right test 5 sequential recall 6 social judgement 7 reading comprehension 8 mathematics 9 British Ability Scales	

Notes on sample: The cohort at age five and ten includes a small number of children born during the week 5–11 April, 1970, who were not born in the UK.

The cohort at age five includes 64 children of service families posted overseas in 1975. The children and mothers were interviewed by nurses of the Soldiers', Sailors', and Airmen's Families' Association (SSAFA) in West Germany, Malta, Gibraltar, and Singapore.

Longitudinal analysis between birth and five years is possible for 12,732 children, this being 77% of the British cohort at birth.

Table 8.7   *Study 7: National Study of Health and Growth*

investigators	*index sample*
Dr R. Rona, S. Chinn, Professor C. du V. Florey, Professor W. W. Holland; Social Medicine and Health Services Research Unit, United Medical and Dental Schools of Guy's and St Thomas's Hospital	birth cohorts of children in primary school in 28 areas in England and Scotland (chosen by stratified random sampling, with proportionately more areas from poorer social groups); sample increased 1982–86 to include ten inner-city areas, chosen to represent high unemployment, overcrowding and lack of household amenities, and five areas with high Afro-Caribbean communities, five areas with high Asian populations and eight Scottish areas

number	*year of birth*
500–680 (England) and 120–200 (Scotland) in each age–sex cohort; by 1981 over 29,000 children had taken part at least once	1961 onwards *year of identification* 1972 onwards

data available (limited data on parental generation; annual data on index generation 5–11 years)

age of index sample	*health data*	*social data*	*method*
5–11 annually	height, weight, triceps skinfold, handgrip		examination
(from 1982 biennially)	height and weight of parents, birthweight of child, respiratory illness of child	parents' occupational status and occupation, education, household, etc.; number of older siblings; uptake of school meals and school milk	questionnaire to parent
	Other information which may have varied from year to year: e.g. parental smoking, parental obesity, respiratory symptoms of child or other members of household; parents' attitudes to school meals		

Notes on sample: This is a large-scale, mixed cross-sectional and longitudinal study. Cross-sectionally the analyses of development in relation to unemployment, area, one-parent families, etc., are, of course, relevant to inequalities in health. Longitudinally, the linking of the records of individual children enables e.g. rates of growth to be examined in relation to social trends or specific social policies, such as the provision of school meals.

In each year, measurements have been obtained from at least 95% of the target population. The number of years for which individual records can be linked depends, of course, upon the cohort: at least two measurements are available for 76% of the total sample, and seven measurements (1980) for 1,461 children.

The social data obtained by questionnaire varies between 60% and 80% according to birth cohort and item of information. There has been some decline in response to questions about employment in later cohorts. The children whose social class is unknown tend to be smaller than the mean heights of their contemporaries.

Table 8.8 *Study 8: National Surveillance of Growth in Pre-school Children*

investigators	index sample
P. T. Fox, E. M. Hoinville, London School of Hygiene and Tropical Medicine	1 cross-sectional study (1973) of children who were 2, 3, and 4 years old in 4 areas (Northampton, Southampton, Stoke, Co. Durham), sampling frame birth notification register;
	2 longitudinal study (1973–79) of children in same areas;
	3 cross-sectional study (ongoing) of 1- and 2-year-old children, primary sampling unit LA areas on Webber and Craig classification, modified for use with families with young children, sampling frame child benefit register

number	year of birth
1 6,000	1 1968–71
2 4,000	2 1973
3 10,000	3 1980–81
	year of identification
	1 1973
	2 1973
	3 1980

data available

age of index sample	health data	social data	method
longitudinal study (2) data collected on 12 occasions between 3 and 60 months	anthropometric measurements, chronic illnesses of child, respiratory infections, diarrhoea, infectious diseases, hospitalizations		measurement by field worker and interview
6 months	feeding information		
24 and 42 months	developmental questionnaire and assessment (as used in British Births Survey)		
60 months	anthropometric measurements of members of natural family		
3, 30, 42, and 60 months		household, family, housing, income, parents' education, employment, welfare benefits	

data available age of index sample	health data	social data	method
cross-sectional study (3) 1–2 years	similar anthropometric measurements and limited morbidity data	similar socio-economic data	

Notes: Response rates in the longitudinal study were 87–89% at each follow-up. The study (3) was designed as a model for monitoring trends over time in the measurements and social data of 1–2-year-old children. It is hoped that new cohorts will be studied by the DHSS using this system.

Table 8.9 *Study 9: Newcastle Thousand Families Survey*

investigators	index sample
Dr F. J. W. Miller, Professor S. O. M. Court, Professor W. S. Walton, Professor E. G. Knox, Professor S. Brandon; (currently) Professor I. Kolvin, Nuffield Psychology and Psychiatry Unit, Fleming Memorial Hospital, Newcastle-upon-Tyne	all births occurring in two months in Newcastle-upon-Tyne
	number 1,142
	year of birth 1947 *year of identification* at birth

data available (parental generation at child's birth and throughout childhood; index generation to 15 years of age, limited data to 22 years, retraced at 33 years; children of index generation to 1979–81)

age of index sample	health data	social data	method
0–7 (1947–1954)	birth condition, etc.		medical records
	medical examination at end of year 1, 3, 5		examination by paediatrician
	illnesses and other health events		clinics and hospital records; visits from health visitor or doctor when illness was notified
	consultations and use of services; health of parents	housing, occupation, household, income, etc.; assessment of care and 'family performance'	health visitor interviews every 10–12 weeks

age of index sample	health data	social data	method
7–15 (1954–1962)	height/weight at 9, 13, 14, 15 years		school health records and examinations
	illnesses requiring medical care, with special enquiries on e.g. stuttering, enuresis, age of menarche	family structure and 'performance'	health visitor interviews annually
		school performance and teachers' assessments	information from teachers
		attainment and personality tests	tests completed by child
		children's attitudes to school, activities, etc.	questionnaires and group interviews with children
		teachers' assessment of attitudes to school-leaving, etc.	teachers' questionnaire
		examination results	educational records
18½ (1966) (boys only, 277 subjects)		employment, use of f.e. facilities	interview: part of larger study
22 (1969) (500 subjects)	growth 15–22		

retraced sample at 33 years

847 children who remained in the sample at five years; subsample of 292 followed up and of those alive 266 interviewed

four subsamples selected for intensive study:
(a) random sample of families in which there was no evidence of 'deprivation' (on the six areas then identified) at five years
(b) random sample of all the families known at five years
(c) random sample of families deprived in at least one respect at five years
(d) random sample of families in at least three respects at five years

Notes on sample: Refusals in this study have always been very low. Because of deaths (approximately 4% in the first five years) and, more especially, because of moves out of the city, the cohort was by fifteen years reduced to 763 children, or 67% of the original subjects. Drop-out rate was very much higher in S.C. I/II than in S.C. IV/V, representing moves out of the city by the more advantaged families. At five years, only 56% of the children were in the same house as at birth.

The tracing and interviewing of 92% of the selected samples (whether remaining in the city or not) at thirty-three years, eighteen years after the last systematic contact, is a considerable achievement. The bias represented by the loss is not currently available but its relevance is less because the cohort is now being treated as a source of selected subsamples, for the examination of possible continuities in deprivation.

There is every intention of retaining the retraced sample for longitudinal study.

Table 8.10 *Study 10: Aberdeen Child Development Study*

investigators	*index sample*
Professor R. Illsley, G. Horobin, MRC Medical Sociology Unit, Aberdeen	children in City of Aberdeen schools aged 7–11 in 1962; one in five random sample selected for further study

	number	*year of birth*
	approx. 14,000 in main cross-sectional study; approx. 2,500 (in 1964) in subsample	1950–1955 *year of identification* 1962

data available (some data on parental generation at birth of children; parental generation when children aged 7–11; children in 1962–64)

age of index sample	*health data*	*social data*	*method*
at birth (for those, the majority, born in Aberdeen)	pregnancy history of mother, birth parameters, complications, etc.	parents' ages, occupations, etc.	maternity records
1962–1964 (in main cross-sectional study)	health records		school medical records
		reading, intelligence, and achievement tests	completed by children
		behavioural assessments	completed by teachers
1964 (in interviewed sub-sample)	health, hospitalizations, clinic attendances, asthma, allergies, etc.	household, housing, parental employment, education, family activities, contact with extended family, etc.; attitudes to child-rearing and schools, children's future, etc.; children's activities, social networks, behavioural assessment	interview

Notes on sample: There are plans to follow up the 'interviewed' sample. It is considered that it will be possible to trace and contact at least two-thirds.

Table 8.11   *Study 11: MRC Derbyshire Schoolchildren Smoking Study*

investigators	*index sample*		
Professor W. W. Holland, Dr M. Murray, A. V. Swan, Social Medicine and Health Services Research Unit, St Thomas's Hospital Medical School	cohort of children entering secondary schools in Derbyshire (also comparison groups: a 'secular trend' group of 14–15-year-olds in 1974, and 11–12-year-olds in 1977; also a 'Hawthorne group' of 15–16-year-olds investigated in 1978 only)		
	number 6,330 (and 2,500 in each comparison group)	*year of birth* 1963 *year of identification* 1974	

data available (parental generation; index generation 11–12 years to school-leaving (15–16 years), subsequently to 18–19 years, and planned extension to 20–21 years)

age of index sample	*health data*	*social data*	*method*
annually, age 11–12 to school-leaving (1974–78, 1981)	reported respiratory symptoms	smoking behaviour; attitudes and activities	questionnaire completed by children
(1974, 1978)		parental smoking behaviour, occupation, etc.	questionnaire completed by parents
(1974, 1978)		assessments of children	questionnaire completed by teachers

Notes on sample: Initial response rate to produce cohort of 6,330, 86% of target group. Response rates of children, 1974–78, 75%–86%; of parents, 1974 and 1978, 88% and 75%; of teachers, 1974 and 1976, 69% and 56%.

Number of children remaining in sample from 1974 to 1978, 4,270.

The sample has been retraced for a follow-up study of smoking among young adults. 6,617 young people remained from the original target group and the follow-up response among these was 86.3%, giving a cohort of 5,712. The follow-up study will also include an intensive qualitative study on a random subsample of 50.

Table 8.12   *Study 12: Aberdeen Styles of Ageing Study: longitudinal study of coping behaviour and adjustment in later life*

investigators	index sample
Dr R. C. Taylor, G. Ford, MRC Medical Sociology Unit, Glasgow	population over 60 years living in own homes in Aberdeen City; sampling based on GP records, random sample of GPs preceding sample of patients

number	year of birth
619 in 12 equally-sized age/sex strata, 5-year cohorts	1920 and earlier
	year of identification
	1980

data available age of index sample	health data	social data	method
variable (1980)	health and functioning (self-rated); psychological functioning	socio-economic background variables; activities and interests; social support	interview
— (1982)	repeat measures of health; psychological and physical functioning; impairments and handicap	experience of threatening life events and associated coping behaviour	interview
— (1984)	repeat measures as above	as above	interview

Notes on sample: Attrition to date: 18% dead; 6% movers/out-migrants; 5% refusals; 3% institutionalized.

Additional studies:
(a) on those who die, information from 'principal supporter' on circumstances and cause of death, pattern of last illness, formal and informal care, recent important life events;
(b) on all movers within the Aberdeen area;
(c) on all arthritis sufferers;
(d) on all disabled.

Table 8.13 *Study 13: MRC Glasgow Cohort Studies*

investigators	index sample		
Dr S. MacIntyre and colleagues, MRC Medical Sociology Unit, Glasgow	15-, 35- and 55-year-olds in an area around Glasgow, with oversampling in a 'good health' neighbourhood and a 'poor health' neighbourhood		
	number c. 400 in each age-group in each neighbourhood, plus c. 800 in each age-group from the surrounding area	*year of birth* 1971, 1951, and 1931 *year of identification* 1986	

data planned *age of index sample*	*health data*	*social data*	*method*
15, 35 and 55 (1986)	physical and mental health and functioning (self assessment, some physical measures and some NHS data)	personal and local life circumstances, beliefs/values, behaviours	interviews and physical measures
17 (1988)	as above	as above	as above plus telephone interviews, diaries and reports of health service contacts
19, 39 and 59 (1990)	as above	as above	as above

Notes: At the time of writing (1985), these prospective cohort surveys are in an initial planning stage. It is intended to follow up the youngest cohort more frequently than the older ones, and to follow out-migrants from the study neighbourhood. The two neighbourhoods will be systematically compared to assess area (i.e., social and physical environmental) effects on health. Other studies undertaken in the Unit will cross-refer to these area-based cohort studies.

Table 8.14 *Study 14: Mothers at Risk: studies of predictive factors of psychopathology in childhood*

investigators	index sample
Dr S. Wolkind, Family Research Unit, The London Hospital Medical College	all British-born women with a first pregnancy attending antenatal booking clinics serving Tower Hamlets; from these, a random sample of all women and various groups of vulnerable women – single, those with psycho-social difficulties, those who had received institutional care as children, those from broken homes – and a sample for observational study

	number	year of birth
	population of 534 women random sample (131), risk group samples (of various sizes 30–90), comparison sample (83 women conceiving after marriage, to compare with those conceiving before marriage or stable cohabitation), and observational sample (80)	(of children) 1974 *year of identification* 1974

data available (some retrospective data on mothers' family of origin; index generation from late pregnancy; children of index generation to seven years)

age of index sample	health data	social data	method
late pregnancy and at 4, 14, 27, 42 months after birth, and when children 7 years (1974–82)	pregnancy and delivery data, birth conditions of children; child's health—clinic visits, consultations, OP and specialist consultations, in-patient spells, accidents, dental health; mother's health, psychiatric screening tests	family of origin, attitude to pregnancy; occupation, income, housing, relationship with husband, social networks, husband's health, stress, etc.; child's behaviour, sleep, training, management, etc.; separation from mother; development	interview
	child's health and development	child's development and behaviour	health visitor reports, nursery teacher reports, teacher reports
	school medical examination		school doctors' reports

Notes on sample: 95% of women initially agreed to interview, and 82–95% of interviews were completed at each stage. At the last contact in 1982 it was possible to trace approximately 90% of the families. Contact has been retained even where families have left the area.

Table 8.15   *Study 15: Children in Day Care Study*

investigators	*index sample*
P. Moss, E. Melhuish; Thomas Coram Research Unit, London	children of mothers taking maternity leave – 4 samples: 1 not returning to employment, 2 returning, children cared for by relatives, 3 returning, children in day nursery, 4 returning, children cared for by child-minder; each sample divided between families in which mother's pre-birth occupational status was S.C. I/II, or S.C. III/IV/V

number	*year of birth*
250 in total sample	1982–83 *year of identification* at birth

data available

age of index sample	*health data*	*social data*	*method*
4/5, 10, 18, and 36 months	developmental assessment at 4/5, 18, 36 months		examination
	mother's account of birth details, child's health; mother's account of own health, short GHQ, tiredness, psychological state	biographical, social, housing, employment, education, etc., history of mother and father; attitudes to work and job, ideologies; attachment to motherhood, child care history, ideology of gender roles and child care, perception of child; resources, support networks, coping strategies; diary of child's activities; temperament questionnaire for child	interviews by interviewers and psychologists

Notes on sample: The samples were originally being collected through health visitors and employers but it has been found more satisfactory to contact the women directly in post-natal maternity wards. Seven hospitals are covered. The sample cannot be regarded as totally random but represents a compromise given the problems of finding women who represent a very small proportion of all mothers with babies. It is hoped that the sample may be further followed up, if funding is available.

Table 8.16 *Study 16: Children of Young Mothers*

investigators	*index sample*		
P. Moss, E. Melhuish; Thomas Coram Research Unit, London	women aged 16–19 having a first child, attending antenatal services at one of two large London general hospitals		

	number	*year of birth*	
	two tiers:	(of children)	
	80–90 intensively,	1983–84	
	100–110 less so	*year of identification*	
		late pregnancy	

data available (mothers from childbearing; index children to 21 months)

age of index sample	*health data*	*social data*	*method*
late pregnancy, 6 and 21 months after birth	course of pregnancy; child and maternal health; maternal tiredness and psychological state	background to pregnancy; biographical, housing, employment, education history of mothers and fathers; satisfaction with motherhood; social support and resources	interview
	developmental assessment of child		examination

Notes on sample: There have been problems with response rates and attrition. At later contacts, losses from the intensive group are made up by replacements from the second group.

Table 8.17 *Study 17: Pre-school Language and Behaviour Study*

investigators	*index sample*		
N. Richman, J. Stevenson, P. J. Graham, Department of Child Psychiatry, The Hospital for Sick Children, London	1 One-in-four sample of all children born in Waltham Forest (immigrant families the subject of a separate analysis); 2 sample of the 101 most disturbed children (by BSQ score) in the main sample, and controls		

	number	*year of birth*	
	(a) 705 cross-sectional	1966–67	
	sample, (b) 198 intensive	*year of identification*	
	follow-up sample	1969–70 at 3 years	

data available (parental generation; index generation) ·

age of index sample	*health data*	*social data*	*method*
(a) 3 (1969–70)	mother's account of child's health problems, clinic and GP consultations, accidents; birthweight	parental occupation, education, housing, stresses, etc.; behaviour screening, questionnaire on child, behaviour check list; tests of language and development	interview

age of index sample	health data	social data	method
(a) 3 (1969–70) cont.	weight and skinfold thickness		examination by interviewer
		clinical rating of disturbance	psychologist
(b) 3 (1969–70)	as (a) but more intensive interview including parental background, mother's health, Cornell Medical Index, stresses, marital relationships, social contacts, etc.		interview
		psychological tests of child; observation of behaviour	psychologist
4 (1970–71)	as at 3	as at 3	
8 (1974–5)	as at 3, with additional data about child's school experience, parental attitudes and involvement in education	behaviour screening questionnaire; parent behaviour questionnaire	interview
	in subsample of 47 boys, fathers separately using a modified version of the same parental interview		
		repertory grid on child's perception of school activities	completed by child
		intelligence and achievement tests; behaviour rating	psychologist
		behaviour questionnaire	completed by teachers

Notes on sample: At the original contact at three years, 9.4% of the children on the birth register could not be traced and 3.3% of families refused. There are at present no plans to follow up the cohort.

Table 8.18 *Study 18:Childhood Experiences and Parenting Behaviour: children in care*

investigators	index sample
Professor M. Rutter, Dr D. Quinton; Institute of Psychiatry, London	1 retrospective study: families with children admitted to care in one Inner London Borough during an eight-month period; comparison group (sampled from two general practices) with no child ever in care

index sample
2 follow-up sample: individuals who were in care
in 1964 (originally studied by Tizard); contrast group
of individuals of same age in same area never in
care (originally studied as control group for another
study)

number	*age*
1 48 families	—
(comparison	*year of identification*
group of 47)	1 1975
2 93 women, 124	2 1977
men (sample still	
being completed);	
comparison group of	
51 women, 55 men	

---

data available (parents and children, with systematic data on general health and psychiatric problems)

age of index sample	*health data*	*social data*	*method*
1 parenting of children age 5–8 studied	malaise inventory; history of hospitalizations, psychiatric contacts, standardized psychiatric evaluation	recall of childhood, family, peer and work experience, current circumstances, housing history, etc.; assessment of parenting skills, parent–child interaction	interview
2 parenting of children age 2–3½ studied	as 1	as 1	interview
		home observation of mother–child interaction	observation
		contemporary background family and personal data from childhood; behavioural questionnaire by teachers; parental questionnaire by house parents	social service records, data from original study of Tizard

---

Notes: This study is included as only one example of the extensive and important programme of family studies which has continued for many years at the Institute of Psychiatry. Their focus is, of course, upon mental health and psycho-social functioning rather than physical health. Other groups studied include the children of mentally ill parents, institution-reared and fostered children, children with educational or psychiatric problems, children with handicapping disorders, various groups of children in infant schools, etc.

This programme has always been characterized by designs which (as in this study) link cross-sectional and longitudinal studies, retrospective and prospective data, or total-population studies from which sub-groups are identified. The use of control groups, the development and validation of testing instruments, and procedures that achieve high response rates are also particular features of the programme.

Further follow-up is proposed in this study.

Class and Health

Table 8.19 *Study 19:Growing Up as a Mentally Subnormal Young Person*

investigators	*index sample*
Professor S. Richardson, Albert Einstein College of Medicine, Bronx, NY, USA; J. McLaren, MRC Medical Sociology Unit, Aberdeen	three samples of children born in 1951–55 and resident in Aberdeen in 1962: 1 all children administratively classified as mentally subnormal and placed in special education or residential care during school years 2 all borderline subnormal children remaining in ordinary schools 3 comparison group of matched controls selected from 20% random sample of all non-subnormal children

	number	*year of birth*
	1 258	1951–55
	2 61	*year of identification*
	3 258	8–10 years

data available (parental generation; index generation)

age of index sample	*health data*	*social data*	*method*
8–10	psychometric, psychiatric, neurological and reading measures		evaluation by team of psychologists, psychiatrists, neurologists
	detailed information from parents on social environment, health, education, and social history		interview
22 (1972–79)	health history, accidents, hospitalizations, handicaps, psychiatric disturbance; health problems in primary family	life history 10–22; educational and vocational activities, social relationships; subjective valuations of self, experience of stigma, discrimination, goals and aspirations; parents' child-rearing experiences and problems, evaluation of services, etc.	interview with parents and young people

Notes on sample: Because of the stability of the relevant population, over 80% of the children studied were still, at 22, living in the community. At this follow-up, at least 90% of interviews were achieved with parents and/or young people. Follow-up at later ages would be possible.

Table 8.20 *Study 20: Sheffield Problem Families*

investigators	*index sample*	
Dr J. E. Lunn, Department of Community Medicine, University of Sheffield	second generation (married sons or daughters) of an earlier sample; the earlier sample consisted of families from two housing estates in Sheffield, in contact with a large number of social agencies (and a comparison group from the same estates not in contact with agencies)	
	number	*year of identification*
	34 adult children from 'problem' families; 25 adult children from 'comparison' families	first generation identified 1968–69, second generation identified 1976, aged early/mid 20s

data available (parental generation from earlier study; index generation; limited data on children of third generation)

age	*health data*	*social data*	*method*
1st generation (1968–69) (1976)	extensive data (Tonge, James and Hillam 1975): employment, housing, marriage, etc.		interview
2nd generation (1976)	mental state inventory, medical history of children	family, housing, work history, occupation, income expenditure, debt, ownership of consumer durables, etc.; extended family, neighbourhood interaction, family relationships, attitudes to children, schools; personality and intelligence tests	interview
	sickness absence records	unemployment records, criminal records	official records

Notes on sample: The sample has not been retained and there is no expectation of another follow-up. It is thought that further response might be more reluctant.

THE ACHIEVEMENTS AND POTENTIAL OF THE LONGITUDINAL STUDIES

The potential of longitudinal studies obviously lies not so much in the demonstration of inequalities as in the possibility of finding causal mechanisms and examining the *process* by which inequality is created (or, perhaps, redressed). It is true that, for reasons discussed later, many analyses produced from longitudinal studies have been at a cross-sectional level, producing a description of the health and social circumstances of particular groups of the population at successive moments of time. This is not necessarily to be deplored, since the examination of an identified cohort, or the taking of a 'snapshot' from a data bank, may in fact be a relatively economical way of producing repeated descriptions, if this is what is wanted. However, it is in the examination of process, the testing of hypotheses, and the prediction of outcomes, that these studies make their distinct contribution. The distinction between longitudinal and cross-sectional study is not necessarily simply one of interest in the individual, as opposed to the group—though, of course, the search for individual predictors of 'career' outcomes has been a major preoccupation of longitudinal research. Rather, the distinction is between explanatory power (however difficult, primitive, and partial this may so far be) and a descriptive purpose.

This first section of this discussion attempts to show some of the ways in which the different types of study reviewed have been, or are being, used in order to explore the social causes or effects of health inequality. Some examples of the sort of questions that are relevant are:

What is the association of later-life health status or health events with earlier ones; how do these associations vary by social factors; what intervening 'protective' factors may there be; what periods of life show greater vulnerability to the effects of social factors on health?

What are the effects of health factors on life patterns—education, marriage, occupation, mobility; does a known association of health and social factors remain (increase, decrease) if the individual moves to another environment; which is the more important, family of origin or later environment?

What is the stability or randomness of intergenerational patterns of association; what are the health effects in the second generation of social factors in the first, or the social consequences in the second generation of health factors in the first?

What are the social consequences of the way in which health events are dealt with by services; what are the effects of social policy changes or changes over time in the general social environment?

Data bank studies

The distinction between the three types of longitudinal study distinguished in the introduction to this chapter is largely, though not entirely, one simply of scale. Where, as in a data bank, a very large number is involved, obviously the data about individuals will be less comprehensive and the group, rather than the individual, will be the focus. There is, however, a clear distinction between data-bank studies and the rest, whether large or small, in that record-keeping (data collection) is continuous, as opposed to repeated surveys at however long or short intervals. The 'events' recorded will necessarily be selected and relatively few for each individual but this is an event-oriented rather than a time-oriented approach. The questions likely to be appropriate are those that concern the relationship of health and mobility and changing patterns of fertility, health experience, and mortality over time, with their associated 'advantages' or 'disadvantages' for the groups concerned. The achievements and potential of large data bank studies, exemplified by Studies 1 and 2, cannot be over-emphasized, though they necessarily represent many years of work before that potential can fully be realized.

OPCS Longitudidnal Study

The OPCS Study (1), being relatively young, is only beginning to demonstrate its value. The data are, of course, limited. It must be noted, however, that the simple outcome measure of mortality by occupation or social class/age/geographical area is the one that is most consistently used in order to demonstrate inequality in health. Indeed, most of the concern about inequalities is based principally on mortality ratios by social class (e.g. in the Black Report, Townsend and Davidson 1982). It is only with the advent of the OPCS 1 per cent study that these data become longitudinal, in that they relate to the deaths and social characteristics of the same individuals over time. Already, the first analyses have demonstrated how national occupational statistics can be improved or better understood and have begun to produce important findings relating to occupational change and health-related mobility.

Some of the topics, relevant to inequality in health, where the longitudinal study has already provided important results are summarized below. These are derived from the analysis of only a brief and preliminary period during which the study has been in operation—mortality in 1971–75 in relation to the socio-demographic characteristics in 1971 of those who died.

A limitation of conventional mortality statistics is that characteristics (especially occupation) recorded on death certificates may be misleading, partly because of misreporting at death and partly because the chronic conditions more likely, nowadays, to be the cause of death may have their roots in previous occupations, behaviour, or environments. The longitudinal survey, using census-declared occupations, is more likely to be accurate and will in time be able to relate mortality to occupations at ten-year intervals throughout life. Again, the mortality of women classified by social class according to their own occupations is problematic using conventional methods and the longitudinal study can examine alternative methods. In fact, in the 1971–75 analysis, differentials among married women were found to be clearer when they were based on their husband's occupation.

A particularly important contribution of the prospective study is in the clarification of health-related selection. The first analysis demonstrated selection effects for occupation, migration, and household structure (but little for mortality differentials in marital status). Preliminary evidence was also presented about the importance of evaluating the contribution of social mobility to social-class gradients. There will always be difficulties in separating the effects of selection and survival from the more direct effects of socio-economic circumstances. As the Report notes, however, it is hoped that by separating out the effects of health-related mobility, subsequent analyses will provide a better measure of structural inequalities.

The longitudinal data emphasize the importance of separating mortality by economic position, as well as occupation. In the 1971–75 analysis, those who were in work at the census were found to have low mortality and those who were out of work (especially if they were sick), those who were off work sick, and those who were permanently sick were found to have higher mortality.

The analysis also emphasized the importance, in studies of the relationships between health and social circumstances (especially among the elderly), of the potential influence of support, and of health, in determining social circumstances. The elderly living alone, for instance, were shown to be relatively healthy, the expected relationship of poor circumstances leading to poor health having been obscured by the movement of those with poor health to live with children or in institutions.

Since the 1971 census included detailed questions on the marital and fertility histories of married, widowed, and divorced women under sixty, it was possible to examine (though with, as yet, relatively few deaths) mortality differences by age at first marriage, parity, age at first child, etc. A number of specific hypotheses, some of which were very relevant to inequality in health, were confirmed.

Based on the migration histories from 1966–71 ascertained by the questions in the 1971 census, the relationship between mortality and migration could be explored. Migrant status, it was found, identified people with the most serious short-term health problems (those moving for support or those, not at work at census because of sickness, moving for employment) as well as those with particularly good long-term health prospects (the 'healthy migrant' effect).

New topics on which study is planned or in progress include: family and household formation, transition and dissolution; changes in the circumstances of the elderly; changes in the characteristics of certain types of locality; social and occupational mobility and the unemployed; life-cycle changes and migration; the circumstances of the descendants of immigrants and ethnic minority groups.

This is only a limited selection of the important but very early results of the longitudinal study. It may be suggested that the continuance and support of this study is of the utmost importance: though it may be limited (largely) to mortality differentials, it is already answering some of the questions that have bedevilled research on differential mortality by socio-economic variables.

Aberdeen maternity and neonatal data bank

The Aberdeen data bank is, of course, different in scope, restricting both its population (to a defined area) and its focus of interest (to fertility-related events). It is, however, unique in that it relates to the total population of this area, and in its completeness over a period of more than thirty years. All the medical and social data used have been recorded contemporaneously. The large core of families permanently resident in the district allows familial studies, since it is possible to identify sisters and sisters-in-law, and mothers of a second generation.

This material has been used extensively for a wide range of medical and sociological research. Originally, the focus was on the contribution of social factors to obstetric performance. Groups at high risk of pregnancy or delivery complications, or abnormality or death of the foetus, were identified by the social and physical characteristics of the mother (e.g. age, parity, social class, marital status, height, physical condition) and the relationships between these factors were explored. Sub-groups of infants (e.g. low-birthweight babies, twins) or mothers (e.g. the very young) have been selected for intensive study. Since medical and social data are both available, it has been possible to study many aspects of fertility behaviour and of service use.

At the widest sociological level, Illsley's early work on the interpretation of class differences was particularly relevant to inequalities in health. The apparent persistence in the gaps in perinatal death rates was examined in the light of selective exchange between social classes at marriage, whereby those with favourable characteristics marry 'upwards' and vice versa. Current work is taking this further by examining rates of perinatal death and low birthweight over two generations (primiparae in 1969–75) by social class of upbringing and social class of marriage, and also the effects of changes in fertility patterns, to illustrate 'the process which underlies and sustains the class structure' (Illsley 1980). This work by Illsley and colleagues will include examination of the effects of class size and internal heterogeneity on the characteristics of mobility profiles, analysis of sibling and mother–daughter comparisons, the intensification or weakening of selection processes by assortative mating, characteristics of intragenerational mobility, and the adequacy of class allocation as a reflector of living conditions.

Other studies in progress or proposed also relate very specifically to the causes or consequences of social inequalities in child-bearing efficiency and social differences in fertility behaviour. A major study is investigating the consequences, for the health of the mother and the growth and development of the child, of different patterns of child-bearing at various ages, with particular reference to early and later reproducers and the changes that have occurred over time among sub-groups of the population.

This work demonstrates, as does the OPCS study, that the basic 'health' events—birth and death—provide a very fertile ground for the study of the widest and most fundamental sociological issues relating to the structure of society and unequal life-chances. The work is of methodological and theoretical, as well as substantive, importance.

Cohort studies and explanation at the individual level

The distinction, among cohort studies, is between those that follow total, 'normal' populations and those (probably, though not necessarily, smaller) that select high-risk or disadvantaged samples in advance. If the objective is the testing of one hypothesis, or the examination of one, fairly restricted process or set of relationships, studies of risk-groups may well be the most effective method and such studies can examine in greater detail the precise nature of a given relationship. This type of study is exemplified by the surveys of children thought to be at risk (14–18).

The representative population cohorts are sometimes criticized as 'catch-all', unable (since they begin with no particular hypothesis) to know from the start what data they are interested in. A great deal may be collected, much of which may prove to be of little importance and much of which may remain unanalysed. This view may be strong in medical circles (see, for instance, *Lancet* 1983), perhaps because the hypothesis-testing model is a more familiar one and is seen as more 'scientific'. Studies 3,5, and 6 began, of course, with a specific interest in births and birth conditions, which fixed their initial focus.

On the other hand, it is claimed (and the record of the major cohort studies substantiates the claim) that, in the long run, population cohorts are equally useful for retrospective hypothesis-testing and are essential for hypothesis development. They have the advantage that explanatory models can grow out of the data and are not confined to models that may become out of date. They can be tested retrospectively, by reference to data that were collected contemporaneously and are not subject to the perils of recall or the use of data collected for other purposes. Rutter (1981) points out that wrong conclusions have been drawn in studies of 'deviant' groups because retrospective data are misleading or because a valid association between two variables is, in fact, due to some prior variable, which could not be assessed retrospectively.

The main thrust of the cohort studies has been the attempt to distinguish the predictors of disadvantage of various sorts—ill-health, deviance, poorer development, disturbance. The combination over time of measures and assessments has been shown to be one way in which measures can be strengthened; e.g., the combination of behavioural measures at thirteen years and fifteen years (Douglas 1976); the scoring of 'disadvantage' at eleven years and at sixteen years (Wedge and Essen 1982); the increase of the strength of a measure of deviance by concentrating on children selected by a teachers' questionnaire on at least three occasions over a four-year period, which demonstrated that behavioural deviance was more *persistent* in the children of mentally ill parents (Rutter 1977).

The existence of a wide range of data has also meant that predictor variables (or, indeed, outcome variables) can be found without their possible significance having to be known or planned for. An example of this is the retrospective association, in the NSHD (Study 3), of abnormally slow pulse rates in children with emotional deprivation and with later delinquent behaviour, which has enabled Wadsworth (1976) to offer a psycho-physiological explanatory model linking violent behaviour and autonomic response to stress.

It can be noted that studies of groups with a 'deviant' outcome (with controls) often show stronger associations, retrospectively, than representative population cohorts. The longitudinal studies have shown that, if you start from a 'deviant' population, common factors are frequently found in the past but if you start from a 'normal' population, it becomes clear that these factors often do *not* lead to deviance. Especially in childhood, the predictive power of single factors is low: this is one of the major lessons of the longitudinal studies. Relatively small high-risk groups, studied prospectively, may not provide strong evidence of adverse consequences. It is, of course, possible—as Rutter advocated—to combine a prospective study of a high-risk group with some 'follow-back' enquiry to check whether the cases do not differ from others with the same factor in their background.

Representative population studies have the advantage of allowing for a whole *range* of possible outcomes and involve less danger of relying on chance associations or associations that depend on intervening variables. For instance, both the NSHD (3) and the NCDS (5) have shown that though birth factors have some importance as causes or predictors of health and development, their effect is relatively weak when compared with social variables.

Longitudinal studies also have potential for the description of the natural history of deviant or disadvantaged states. Rutter (1981) notes that they have been crucial, for instance, in validating the broad difference between emotional disturbances and disorders of conduct, showing that the two have different prognoses, responses to treatment, and linkages with adult psychiatric disease. Similar achievements in the describing of the natural history of disadvantaging physical illnesses or states of chronic ill-health are so far lacking, except perhaps for a body of work on respiratory complaints.

The greatest gains specifically attributable to longitudinal studies are perhaps related to the examination of long-term effects and the *timing* of associations. For instance, the effect of childhood emotional disruption is well documented in the short term. Longitudinal studies following children to adulthood, however, have produced particularly important findings about the longer term. In the NSHD (3) cohort at twenty-six years—taking into account social class, birth order, and family size—psychiatric affective disorders and, in males, peptic and duodenal ulcer were more frequent in a group predicted as vulnerable because of childhood family disruption.

Some interesting and important 'sleeper' effects have been demonstrated, where effects of adverse circumstances may seem to diminish, only to reappear later. Again in the NSHD, for instance, chest illnesses in childhood had been clearly linked with air pollution and with overcrowding in the home. At twenty-five years, the association of cough with early chest illnesses was stronger than it had been at twenty and moreover these early associations with poor home conditions reappeared, whereas at twenty they had not been associated (Douglas 1976). As the members of the early cohorts go on to reach middle age, it seems likely that findings such as these about life-long vulnerabilities, especially to chronic conditions, will become more and more important. 'Sleeper' effects have also been demonstrated in the delayed or long-term effects of educational methods.

An example of the importance of the timing of events refers again to the study of long-term vulnerability in the NSHD cohort (Wadsworth, Peckham, and Taylor 1984). In the association with later disturbances, it was the age at which family disruption occurred that appeared to be important: delinquency by the age of twenty-one was associated with disruption in early infancy; psychiatric illness and illegitimate births to women were associated with disruption in infancy or in adolescence and young adulthood; stomach ulcers and colitis were associated with disruption in early infancy for males but not for females.

The differences between the sexes in the timing and magnitude of adverse consequences of disadvantaging factors is another important topic on which the longitudinal studies have shed some light. Boys have been shown to be more likely to suffer psychosocial disturbance as a result of family stress. The studies of Sheffield problem families (20) have suggested that married sons' households were more likely than those of married daughters to show repeated patterns of problems across the generations.

At the opposite end of life, the Styles of Ageing Study (12) is producing important findings related to stressful life events, coping strategies, and trajectories of decline towards dependency and death.

It is perhaps true that *protective* factors have been somewhat neglected in the analysis of longitudinal studies. Protective factors for psychosocial health have received some study: it was found in the study of single mothers (14), for instance, that the existence of a close, confiding relationship protected against vulnerability. The factors favouring 'unexpectedly' good achievement in school were, of course, examined in both the NSHD (3) and NCDS (5) and both studies were influential in the educational field. In considering health and its social causes or consequences, however, the 'deviant' individuals in the childhood cohorts who do not succumb to adverse factors have not so far been studied and this is an area to which— now that child-to-adult analysis is possible in the oldest cohorts— attention might be turned. Who are the individuals for whom an unhealthy adulthood would have been predicted, who appear to have escaped? Or the individuals whose disadvantage in health might have been expected to be a hindrance to their social achievement in adulthood but who have overcome it and prospered? What are the relative importances of the environment of childhood and the environment of later life? What effects can be shown of an environment having changed notably, at different periods of life, through the geographical or social mobility of parents or of the individual himself?

Cohort studies and secular change

The cohort studies cover a period of considerable change, in service structures, in marriage and child-bearing patterns, in economic conditions, in education, and in occupational opportunities. These changes complicate the analysis greatly and it is probably true that the methodological problems they present remain largely unsolved. A cohort is defined by its date: all its members were the same age at a particular historical moment and findings that apply to those who were, say, ten years old in 1956, may have no validity for those who were the same age in 1966 or 1976. For example, the NSHD data linking educational achievement with other variables, important as it was in the policy debates of its time, may not be relevant in a changed educational system. Again, any study retrospectively linking health characteristics of adults today with birth conditions may not represent the life chances of infants now being born because of secular change in services and in the environment.

For this reason, combined cross-sectional and longitudinal studies are often advocated, with cohorts of overlapping age-groups studied for shorter times. The productive series of family and child health studies at the Institute of Psychiatry (of which 18 is an example) has always stressed a combination of prospective, cross-sectional, and follow-up approaches. The longitudinal studies have usually been limited to a restricted time period, chosen to focus sharply on a particular process or stage of development. From a different unit, the Derbyshire Schoolchildren Smoking Study (11) is an example of a particularly careful design (though, of course, on a restricted topic) that answers criticisms about the intervention of possible social change: to compare with a cohort of children studied at various ages, 'secular trend' groups of children who are of *different* ages at the same historical time are studied.

The NSHG (7) is an example of an even more complex design, of overlapping yearly cohorts, which demonstrates secular change particularly well. Each cohort can be shown to differ from the last, not only in cross-sectional characteristics but also in patterns of growth and development (and their relationship to a limited number of social variables) over the years that individual children are included in the study. This has produced some particularly interesting results of direct relevance to inequality. For instance, it has been suggested, from the examination of the associations over time between various social and biological factors and height, that sibship size is associated with height through economic hardship; if this has disappeared, the differences apparently attributable to sibship size are partially eliminated. Again, in each social class, unemployment of father has been shown to be associated (together with father's height) with the height of children. In Scotland, this association was stronger than that with social class. Of particular interest in the context of secular trends is the finding that this association is getting less, as unemployment becomes more 'normal' (Rona, Swan, and Altman 1978). The study of growth in pre-school children (8) is also of mixed longitudinal and cross-sectional design.

In cohort studies that continue over generations, secular trends are, of course, an opportunity and a challenge, not simply a problem in analysis. It is not only changes in the environment, in services, or in economic structures that are relevant, although inter-cohort studies can demonstrate the extent or effects of these. Osborn, Butler, and Morris (1984), for instance, included in a volume from the CHES study (6) an analysis of social change, as it has affected the lives of young children, between the three national birth cohorts. Health is not considered but comparisons of social-class differences in housing tenure, amenities, and parental education suggested reductions in inequality in some ways but not in others. Some specific topics related to health have also been considered in inter-cohort studies (see Stark *et al.* 1981 and Peckham *et al.* 1982 for discussions of the prevalence of childhood obesity and the effects of changing economic circumstances and diets between 1946 and 1958; or Taylor *et al.* 1984, on changing relationships between breastfeeding and eczema).

Perhaps only very recently, the effects of secular change in social norms, societal expectations, patterns of individual response, and lifestyle management are beginning to be examined. These represent what may be the most truly sociological approaches to the explanation of inequalities. Wadsworth (1981), for instance, notes that two hypotheses are possible concerning the firm findings from the NSHD (3) (and, of course, elsewhere) that delinquency, especially violent and sexual offences committed by the age of twenty-one, is associated with family disruption, particularly with the divorce or separation of parents during the child's first five years. It may be that there is a direct effect, through early experience of handling stress, or the association may be through societal expectations, which affect the way in which children from broken homes are identified or treated at any given period. Wadsworth points out that in the NSHD there is evidence for both. Those children were also more likely to suffer some psychosomatic and psychiatric illnesses, which suggests the internalized effects of family disruption; teachers' assessments, on the other hand, demonstrated that they were applying different expectations to these children. Wadsworth notes that the assigning of weights to each sort of cause can be done only by comparing populations in different social environments, as ideas and attitudes change over time, as well as comparing populations who do and do not suffer from broken homes. The intention is stated of examining the 1970 CHES (6) cohort, born in a very different climate of social attitudes to marriage and the family, specifically to attempt a disentangling of the effects of social expectations from those of personal predispositions in the field of delinquency.

Other work is directed at aspects of health and their associations with lifetime experiences, asking who the vulnerable are, how vulnerability is maintained, and what is its timing, form, and outcome. The cultural effects of the group of origin and the group within which the individual lives will be examined, suggesting that the form of outcome is, to an extent, determined by the behaviour culturally appropriate to the individual's age. Factors indicating the earliest vulnerability to mental and physical illness, and to stress, will be analysed and use will be made of the data on social class, religion, and political affiliation in families of origin and at various times in the survey member's life, in order to investigate 'cultural float'. The degree and constancy of movement away from parental views will be examined and the management of life crises compared amongst those who move very little from parents, those who move away and return, and those who move and stay away (Wadsworth *et al.* 1984; Wadsworth and Freeman 1983).

Intergenerational analysis

Some comparisons between successive generations of the same families are part of, or beginning to be part of, studies 2, 3, 5, 9, 18, and 20. Intergenerational analysis presents problems, however, especially for the study of health relationships. It may seem obvious to define the units of study as the individual and his/her offspring but if *all* children of a second generation are to be included, there will be great practical difficulties. A cohort, all of the same age, will of course produce a second generation of widely differing ages. Thus the Second Generation Study (4) focuses on only the first-born children of cohort members, at the time when they are four years old; even so, the picking-up of the sample is complex.

A second generation will, of course, have two parents and in cohort studies detailed data are available on only one. Consideration of the simplest measures relating to the development of the children—height, say—necessitates the collection of data on the other spouse. If the unit of study has been the family, on the other hand, it will be important—and perhaps difficult—to follow up all the children of the family.

For these reasons, intergenerational study has so far tended to focus on restricted areas, notably the parenting behaviour of mothers. Intergenerational effects were a particular feature of the whole DHSS/SSRC programme on Transmitted Deprivation but continuities or discontinuities in *health* disadvantage, or in the social effects of health disadvantage, were not a major part of the programme. There was, however, clear evidence that the disadvantage of parents (including poor physical or mental health) could be reflected in the youthful development and later stability of their children, though it was emphasized that there was no inevitability that social problems, as either the cause or the consequence of disadvantage, would run in families (Madge 1983).

The major longitudinal studies do present an opportunity—for which, of course, extra resources would usually be required—to follow up two, or even three, generations simultaneously. The parental generation of the oldest cohorts is now in middle age, rates of survival are known, and they could be contacted relatively easily through their children. This would provide cohorts in later years, about whom there are contemporary data throughout the years when their children were dependent, who could be followed prospectively. Besides offering the possibility of the study of health variables as people age, there is the potential for examining, in a different way from that which is possible in the data banks, the important mobility effects suggested by Illsley.

Cohort studies and social policy

The traditional emphasis in cohort studies upon internal processes within families, individual development, and specific causes/effects of medical/ social variables as they impinge upon the individual, has meant not only some difficulty in allowing for the intervening variables of secular change but also some neglect of variables in the larger social environment (service provision, geographical differences in the environment, particular structures of occupational opportunities, and soon). Social policy is perhaps only one element in this larger environment but it is a particularly important one. As Douglas has noted:

> 'The point at issue is whether we wish to know to what extent new medical, education and social services fulfill our intentions. If we do, cohort studies can provide the opportunity to show causal relationships between the establishment of new services and later changes in health, growth and behaviour.'

(1976: 11)

Policy-makers may see longitudinal or mixed studies as one method of monitoring the results of policy changes, in the shorter term. Effects may, however, be long term and though the results of longitudinal research may be of no more than historic interest many years afterwards, when policies and structures may have changed, nevertheless it seems important that these long-term effects should be monitored.

The NSHG (7) is an example of a study designed to answer policy questions; its purpose was specifically 'to develop an anthropometric system of surveillance to assess the influence of changes in social circumstances or social policy on growth in primary school children'. It was initially designed to monitor any effects of the change in provision of free school milk in 1971 (concluding that the availability of milk had no real effect on *group* well-being, though particularly deprived children might benefit) and has more recently been examining the take-up of school meals and their possible importance for the growth and development of children. The pre-school child survey (8) has similarly had interests in nutritional policy, examining breastfeeding and the provision and take-up of welfare milk.

The NSHD (3) is perhaps the best example of a longitudinal study that was extremely important in examining the mechanisms and effects of changes in policy, in this case educational policy (Douglas 1964; Cherry 1974). Since its findings are well known and are in the field of education rather than health they will not be discussed here but it can be noted that as well as being influential at the relevant time, monitoring of the long-term effects has continued. Local variation in education provision was equally a topic of the study. The NCDS (5) has also been important in the educational field. Similarly, the Aberdeen Data Bank (2) has continuously produced information of importance for maternity services and for policy in the area of contraception, antenatal care, abortion, and sterilization.

Changes in the provision or use of medical and social services can also be examined, though the potential for this has so far been little used. Certain aspects of the use of medical services have been compared in the cohorts 3, 4, 5, and 6, demonstrating, for instance, changes over time in the use of immunization, dental care, tonsillectomy, circumcision, hospitalization rates in childhood, and lengths of stay. The point at issue is, of course, not simply whether the supply or the use of any particular service has increased or decreased but whether changes in service have altered the *differential* use, according to social variables, over time. Inter-cohort comparisons can show the extent to which services have achieved equality of care or positive discrimination according to need. It may be added that, at the level of *broad* social groupings, the evidence is that there has, in fact, been considerable progress towards 'equality' in aspects of service use. The social-class gradient in such things as immunization rates or clinic attendance still exists but it is not nearly as steep as it was twenty or thirty years ago.

ISSUES RELATING TO THE NATURE OF THE DATA AND THE CATEGORIZATIONS USED

The tabular material, while indicating the range of topics covered by each study, cannot show how much detail is available. It should be noted that—even though it may never be used in its entirety—all the cohort studies, and of course the small intensive studies, have a wealth of detailed data which can be analysed with great finesse. Most have different types of data to be analysed against each other—interview material, not only about events but also covering attitudes; results of medical examinations and developmental, behavioural, psychological, and educational tests; factual data from health service, school, employment, etc. sources. Different considerations apply to the very large studies of mixed design (e.g. 7 and 8), where the focus is on obtaining relatively simple information about large numbers of subjects. The emphasis here is not upon the individual and interview schedules or questionnaires are intended to produce only basic variables against which the dependent variable of principal interest—in both these cases, growth—can be analysed. The attractive schedule produced for completion by parents in a recent sweep of the NSHG (7), for instance, contained some forty-six pre-coded questions, and the pre-school growth survey (8) schedule some thirty-seven pre-coded questions, applied by interviewers.

Indices of social stratification

Most of the large-scale longitudinal studies have, of course, used the category of 'social class' in order to demonstrate inequalities between social groups, whether the classification used has been the usual one of RG occupational class, the now old-fashioned-sounding 'black-coated', 'agricultural', etc. categories used originally in the NSHD (3), or the sevenfold Goldthorpe classification (6). For the analysis of *cross-sectional* inequalities, these have in the past been powerful. They are less obviously meaningful for categorizing individuals over long periods of time or for intergenerational analyses.

Even at a cross-sectional level there are well-known difficulties, which are thought to be increasingly salient. The classification of occupations has been found to be unreliable, especially at the lower end of the scale, in part because of job mobility (Kahan, Butler, and Stokes 1966; Leete and Fox 1977). More important difficulties are the categorization of women or the taking into account of the background variables of mothers as well as fathers, the classification of female single parents, and the conventions that may be used to classify the retired, the unemployed, or the long-term sick and disabled. At the 1971 census, less than 50 per cent of all couples where the woman was economically active had man and wife in the same occupational classsification. Britten and Heath (1983) demonstrated from CHES (6) data that a classification that took into account the occupations of both wives and husbands affected differences in such family characteristics as size, income, and educational qualifications. Associations with health variables remain unexplored.

With regard to the retired and long-term sick, however, Fox and Goldblatt (1982), in their analysis of the OPCS Longitudinal Study (1), show that whether or not the 'permanently sick' are allocated to an occupational classification according to a job that they had previously held substantially affects class gradients in mortality. Similarly, 'last occupation at death' (from death certificates) and 'occupation some years before death' (from census records) will produce differing results.

The identification of one-parent families as a special 'class'—and one that is, of course, increasing in number—for which RG occupational classifications do not provide an obvious place, is stressed by many of the longitudinal studies. The importance of this 'class' in current thought about hypotheses relating disadvantage and inequality to childhood circumstances is attested to by the number of smaller studies, or special samples from national cohorts, that have selected children of single parents for special study.

In the context of longitudinal studies, the difficulties of social class categories over time are particularly relevant. The major problem is the question of change. The 'unskilled' of the first 1946 cohort were a much larger proportion of the population, and perhaps a different sort of category, when compared with their adult children in 'social class V'. These are questions that are being considered in the two data bank studies. In cohort studies, it has been suggested that the seven Goldthorpe classes are more useful than RG social class for the study of general intergenerational mobility. In an important paper deriving from the NSHD (3), Britten (1981) used this to investigate the relationship of the occupations of sons, at the age of thirty-one, to those of their fathers when the sons were fifteen. The model found to fit best provided a simple description of mobility where the main impediment to movement was the distance involved, with particular barriers to medium- and long-range downward movement. Barriers were found at either end of the class structure and between the service class and the intermediate classes.

Occupational social class—however categorized—is, of course, a compressed indicator, concealing wide differences (including regional differences) and it is unlikely to be sufficiently sensitive or specific for the demonstration of what may well be quite small effects or causes of *health* variables upon mobility or unequal life-chances. At the individual level, social class—as an index of many different factors—is lacking in predictive or explanatory power: it is not known what aspect of economic advantage, education, culture, norms, power, etc., is most significant for any given outcome. The same is true for any other indicator chosen as a surrogate: Fox and Goldblatt (1982) have, for instance, demonstrated that household tenure or access to cars are as good as social class in their ability to discriminate the 'inequalities' represented by mortality rates but are obviously not suggesting an explanatory relationship.

Other composite indicators of advantage or disadvantage that could be used in the exploration of inequalities might be found within the 'social area analysis' movement. Though almost as complex an indicator as social class, and little more discriminating at the individual level, 'area' has the possible advantage of pointing more clearly to the *elements* of deprivation in the social and geographical environment that may have consequences for health. The only one of the longitudinal studies reviewed in which area analysis is being used is the pre-school growth study (8), in which Webber and Craig classifications (Webber 1979) of local authority areas are being used as a sampling frame. In the primary-school age growth study (7), an analysis has been provided by ACORN neighbourhood groups, which were shown to differentiate at least as well as social class.

At a much broader level, analysis of (cross-sectional) results by geographical area has been an important and illuminating feature in several of the larger cohorts, notably the NCDS (5), for the demonstration of inequalities in child health. In the NCDS, for instance, the variation by region for, e.g., the incidence of accidents or the state of dental health has been shown to be greater than the variation by social class.

It is notable that *income* is a variable on which few studies have much data, and some none. This seems to be a consequence of the use of health visitors as interviewers in many birth cohorts or childhood studies, or in other studies the reliance for 'social' data on questionnaires filled in by parents. Income, while of course broadly associated with occupation, can by no means be assumed by it, as Townsend (1979) has shown. It could be argued that money deprivation (related properly to family size, housing tenure, geographical location, and so on) might be one of the more important variables in relation to health. Particular areas that might be of interest include health, income, movement in and out of the labour market, and the health of women as associated with the dissolution or reconstitution of marriage.

Composite indices of disadvantage

In an attempt to specify the *components* of social class—including income, to a limited extent—that are the causes (or effect) of health disadvantage, most of the cohort studies have supplemented the use of social class as a category by selecting-out special groups. The 'disadvantaged' have been identified on more detailed composite criteria related to family circumstances, housing, and so forth.

In an important paper deriving from the CHES study (6), Osborn and Morris (1979) offer a rationale for the use of an alternative social stratification index, based on father's occupation, parental education, tenure of accommodation, type of neighbourhood, and domestic crowding. They demonstrate that, in the CHES data, this index (a) can provide a social measure in situations where there is no economically active head of household; (b) emphasizes the specific aspects of inequality under consideration, by referring to the child's environment in the home; (c) shows more and greater differences for young children than occupational social class alone, particularly in language and general developmental indices. This was less true for behavioural indices, which the authors suggest may be better explained by other factors, such as family size, age of mother, etc.

Categorizing families, by this social index, into a collapsed three-class division of 'advantaged' (18.2 per cent of sample), 'neutral' (72.4 per cent of sample) and 'disadvantaged' (9.4 per cent of sample), it was shown in the CHES subsample in SW England and S Wales, at three and a half years, that this was a more efficient classification than occupational class for examining inequalities in service use. There was, for instance, no social-class gradient for attendance at child health clinics but the children in the 'disadvantaged' group attended significantly less often than those in the 'advantaged' or 'neutral' groups. Immunization rates similarly showed much greater differences by social index than by social class. A particularly clear finding was that there was no difference between social classes in the proportion of families who reported difficulty in attending at child clinics, family doctors, or dentists, but for each service 15–20 per cent of families in the 'disadvantaged' group reported difficulty.

In the NCDS (5), a group was selected out at eleven years as 'disadvantaged' on the criteria of (a) large family or one-parent family *and* (b) low income *and* (c) poor housing (6.2 per cent of total cohort). Throughout their childhood, these children were shown to be distinguished in every way (including physical development and ill-health) from the majority 'non-disadvantaged'. The analyses were of particular interest in demonstrating the relationship between the three separate dimensions of disadvantage and in examining any differences between those who were in adverse circumstances at eleven but not at sixteen, or vice versa, and those who were disadvantaged throughout childhood (Wedge and Prosser 1973; Wedge and Essen 1982).

Composite indices of disadvantage have, of course, been used for other cohorts. An early attempt for focus on family functioning, rather than simply material circumstances, was the development in the Newcastle cohort (9) of three broad indicators. The first, called 'deprivation', was defined as a lack of parental care or supervision. The second, called 'deficiency', was a judgement made about the use of resources available, singling out such things as defective cleanliness or diet. The third, called 'dependence', described family malfunctioning or breakdown. 'Deficiency', in particular, was shown to be associated with several indicators of health (Miller *et al.* 1960).

The use (particularly in the early cohorts) of judgemental opinions of this sort, has, of course, been criticized. These are hardly 'scientific' or validated measures. Yet it has been claimed (Douglas 1976) that health visitors' assessments of 'standards of maternal care' were proved to be among the best single predictors in the NSHD (3) of later ill-health, accidents, and educational achievement, and that teachers' similar assessments of parental attitudes and the children's behaviour were also among the best predictors of academic and occupational achievement. It seems probable that such judgements are simply an equivalent of a composite indicator of general disadvantage, less explicit than carefully scored indices but based on the experience that enables practitioners to know disadvantage when they see it and perhaps no more or less valid than other aggregated measures of general disadvantage.

Health disadvantage and risk factors

All these methods of selecting out disadvantaged groups have been very successful in demonstrating just how 'unequal' they are in health and in life-chances. This was, of course, their objective: to illustrate inequality rather than to explain it. It may be suggested that the arguments are somewhat circular: it would be surprising if the disadvantaged, defined in these all-embracing ways, were *not* found to be less fortunate than others. None of the population cohort studies has, perhaps, published adequate analyses of the precise components of *health* disadvantage that may be associated with social disadvantage. The antecedents of some particular conditions have been studied: for instance, when the NSHD (3) children reached the age of twenty, the relationship was examined between the frequency of respiratory symptoms and social class, air pollution, smoking habits, and record of lower respiratory tract disease before two years of age (Colley, Douglas, and Reid 1973). Particular groups of children have also been specially analysed in, for instance, the NCDS (5): those with convulsions (Ross 1973), hearing difficulties (Sheridan 1972; Peckham, Sheridan, and Butler 1972), speech defects (Sheridan 1973; Peckham 1973a), among others.

The recent papers by Wadsworth and others from the NSHD, investigating long-term sources of vulnerability to later stressful circumstances (discussed earlier), are perhaps the first fruits of more sociologically sophisticated longitudinal analyses. Until now, the longitudinal studies have been looking, prospectively, for predictive factors—what are the ranges and probabilities of outcomes of a given infancy or childhood health event, in what circumstances—and because self-righting influences are powerful forces towards normal human development (Sameroff and Chandler 1975), the results have often been disappointing. Extreme composite indicators of disadvantage of the sort discussed are excellent predictors but not very illuminating; but on the whole the predictive power of single factors in childhood is low. Wadsworth and Morris (1978) looked at four sets of risk factors in the NSHD (3) as predictors of 'preventible' admissions to hospital up to the age of five, for a range of conditions susceptible to early intervention. These were family structure and home circumstances, health visitors' assessments of maternal care, use of immunization and ante- and post-natal services, and birthweight of child. None was found particularly helpful and it was suggested that more refined definitions of adverse social and environmental influences were required.

The selection of single 'risk factors' for particular examination is the basis for the method of most of the smaller, focused, longitudinal studies. Where children are concerned, certain factors are generally agreed— adverse birth conditions, single parents, families under stress (ethnic origin is perhaps only very recently beginning to be included). In going beyond childhood, what risk factors would be chosen? Obviously, different indicators, of outcome as well as of risk, are needed in childhood, adulthood, or in middle or old age. For older people, the Aberdeen survey (12) is providing one interesting examination of the concept of risk factors. Eleven potential 'risk-groups' were identified from the literature and each group within the sample was examined in order to produce a 'risk profile' in terms of the presence or absence of personal resources of various kinds, material and psychological, that are relevant to adjustment and well-being in old age. The groups at greatest risk were found to be the 'recently moved', 'recently discharged' (from hospital), 'divorced/separated', and 'very old'. However, it was concluded that the risk-group approach was not an efficient method of case-finding, since the proportion of all cases (of, for instance, disadvantage in 'health and psychological functioning') accounted for by any one group was small. At the level of *individual* 'careers', single risk factors are of limited use for this group, as for children (Taylor, Ford, and Barber 1983).

The nature of the health data available

In general, it is probably true that the social variables have usually been better dealt with than the health variables, except perhaps in infancy. In part, this is due to the fact that health data may be relatively neglected after childhood, in favour of educational achievement or employment interests, and in part it is probably due to a lack of development of appropriate indicators of health generally. Throughout childhood, *growth* is often substituted.

Douglas (1976) has expressed the opinion that the NSHD sample (of over 5,000 children) was too small to give an adequate range of data about any but the most common illnesses and pointed out the practical problem of the demands on local resources if health information is to be checked with hospitals or other services. Wadsworth (1981) notes the inadequacy of gross indicators—such as height, weight, birthweight, the prevalence of common diseases—as individual predictors and suggests that better descriptions or definitions of illnesses or diagnoses are required, since in retrospect a diagnosis represented by a single word is insufficient to allow for, for instance, the grading of severity.

A criticism often levelled at longitudinal studies is that the measures and assessments originally used, perhaps many years before, may be seen as technically out of date, or based on outmoded norms or concepts of possible cause and effect, as time goes on. In fact, this does not appear to be a serious limitation. What is usually being criticized is derived *aggregate* indicators, especially where value judgements (about the 'good' mother, the well-adjusted schoolchild, and so on) are involved. It is, however, a reason for the retention of detailed, raw data, rather than only complex derived indices.

It is also suggested that errors in measurement are inherent where there is, inevitably, a large number of observers. Many studies make very particular efforts to reduce these by interviewer training and reliability studies (e.g. the programme of family studies of the Institute of Psychiatry). In really large and geographically dispersed studies, this may not be possible and assessments may be required from many different people who are not specifically trained. Despite this, Douglas (1976) notes that in the NSHD observer error did not appear to obscure general relationships that may later become clearer—as the measures of 'parental attitudes' and of 'teachers' assessments of parental attitudes' did when considering early school-leaving in the children of the cohort.

It could be argued that as the subjects of the oldest national cohorts grow older, it will be particularly important to collect detailed health data. The interaction of health and social variables in infancy and childhood is now relatively well documented (though secular trends will always introduce new relationships). The effect of health status upon life-patterns and life-chances in adulthood and old age is the next major area.

Perhaps the major development in the assessment of health as a general characteristic in adult life is occurring in the NSHD. When the cohort members were aged thirty-six, they were visited by specially trained nurses who measured blood pressure, respiratory function, height, weight, and girth, collected data on health histories, and applied a mental health assessment. The predictive value of data from early life can thus be tested (see Wadsworth, this volume, and Wadsworth, Peckham, and Taylor 1984).

At the later stages of life, individual attitudes and behaviour, voluntary life-styles, and life events enter more clearly as important possible determinants of health. Many studies associate these things at a cross-sectional level. The importance of a longitudinal approach, now exemplified in the Aberdeen Styles of Ageing Study (12) and the planned Glasgow Cohort Studies (13), cannot be overemphasized.

Area data

Wadsworth has also suggested that, in order to allow for inter-vening variables and examine geographical differences, it would always be advantageous to collect contemporary parameters of the social and physical environment, such as area details of the extent of pollution, or the availability of pre-school facilities. This is also relevant to the problem of temporal change and the evaluation of social policy discussed earlier. It is, of course, to some extent a counsel of perfection, since all the information that might be appropriate can never be collected. It also assumes that it is known in advance which environmental or service-provision variables will be most salient. However, use can be made of information routinely available (e.g. air pollution levels, as in Colley, Douglas, and Reid 1973; Kiernan *et al.* 1976) and it appears to be true that this sort of environmental or administrative data is relatively neglected in the discussion of regional variation in the national cohorts. It can be noted that area data are another important component of the proposed Glasgow Cohort Studies (13).

PRACTICAL PROBLEMS OF ORGANIZATION OF LONGITUDINAL STUDIES: ATTRITION AND BIAS

One of the problems of long-term follow-up that is commonly suggested as a constraint on their usefulness is the attrition that, over many years, is inevitable. While life-long studies may be an ideal from some points of view, their value may depend on questions of fall-out and the possibility of increasing bias in the sample which remains as time goes on.

An examination of the exact nature of the sample at each stage of follow-up in the studies reviewed (not always an easy task) suggests that, in fact, this problem may be exaggerated, as far as the existing birth cohorts are concerned.

Deaths and emigrations, representing inevitable loss, can be estimated from national figures. Deaths will be higher in infancy, fewer in childhood and young adulthood. By the age of thirty, 5.6 per cent of the earliest of the cohorts, the NSHD (3), had died; these children were born in 1946 and the equivalent predicted loss of a cohort born in 1980 would be little over 2 per cent by thirty years.

If cohorts begin in middle or later life, or are followed until then, losses will obviously accelerate and the sample increasingly become rep-resentative only of survivors. This is another reason why several workers in the field have suggested that overlapping, shorter-term cohorts are a preferable design for the study of health/life-style/environmental associations in later years. This does not detract, however, from the importance of *also* following birth cohorts for as long as possible, since the life-long determinants of survival itself may be the issue of interest.

Emigration varies even more by secular (or regional, for local studies) trends. By the age of thirty (in 1976), 10.4 per cent of the NSHD (3) cohort had emigrated; by the age of sixteen (in 1974), 4.3 per cent of the NCDS (5) cohort had emigrated. The loss of emigrants necessarily produces some small bias. Both emigration and immigration are, however, more serious only if the cohort is being viewed cross-sectionally, since the sample can be representative only of the population as it was constituted at the time when the study began; for birth cohorts, perhaps many years before. In those studies that explicitly aim to offer representative, cross-sectional descriptions of an age-cohort at any given time, immigrants of the relevant age can, of course, be added to the sample: this has been done, for instance, in the NCDS (5) and in the CHES study (6), and automatically occurs in any sample defined as, e.g., a school population (7).

National cohort studies have, of course, the great advantage that internal migrants are not necessarily lost, as they may be in local cohorts. (They may, however, be disproportionately represented in 'no contact' losses.) Moving of area of residence also depends on temporal and local trends and may bias a residual cohort greatly if it is geographically defined. In the Newcastle survey (9) only 56 per cent of the children were in the same house at five years and at birth and the drop-out rate through movement was very much greater in SC I/II (53 per cent of a small number) than in SC IV/V (23 per cent). This, it was reported, represented families, especially the more prosperous, moving out of the city 'in the unsettled years following the war'. Very similar findings were reported from the NSHD (3), where 55 per cent of the families were found to be in the same dwelling between 1946 and 1950. Douglas and Blomfield (1958), analysing the difference between local and non-local movers, noted that a third of the professional and salaried families moved across local boundaries.

Exclusion of emigrants and deaths leave a potential total population, which will be further reduced by losses due to refusal or inability to trace. Rates of these have, in fact, been remarkably similar in all the larger national cohorts. At birth or in infancy, there is to some extent an easy-to-trace and captive population (especially where health visitors are being used as interviewers) and response rates are commonly excellent. While children are at school, they are still relatively easily traced and, if information is being collected at or in collaboration with schools, again are captive. At school-leaving age, and again at the young family-building age, there is inevitable movement and difficulty in tracing. Women, changing their names at marriage, present special difficulties. In the NCDS (5) an 'untraced plus refusal' rate of 1.8 per cent at birth rose to 11.5 per cent at age sixteen. Workers have pointed out that these difficult periods need to be planned for, and steps taken in advance to retain contact. This is not always easy if the long-term future of a study is in any doubt, or if adequate staffing and funding are not available in the periods between sweeps. In one at least of the smaller studies (14), the value was stressed, at periods of typical mobility such as the early years of marriage, of retaining the addresses of relatives through whom the subjects might be re-contacted.

Many different methods have been used to retain the interest and collaboration of cohorts, or to retrace those who move—the sending of birthday cards (3), the tagging of child welfare or health records (9), circularizing with feed-back reports and requests for change of name or address (5), the use of national and local media (5, 9), the use of GP and housing records (in the retracing for study 9, 37 per cent of the subjects were traced through GPs and 30 per cent through a local media appeal).

In the larger cohorts, refusal rates appear to be very similar, at 5–7 per cent at any one contact. Refusal (or non-tracing, or even emigration) at one stage does not necessarily mean that the subject is lost to the survey, for some may be picked up again afterwards. It was noted in the NCDS (5) that a proportion of refusals when the child was sixteen, sometimes because of examination pressures at that age, rejoined the sample at twenty-three. Refusal rates are also similar in most of the smaller, focused studies. The result is a generalization that, whatever the size or form of the study, and however long it continues, the achieved response rate is commonly about 80–85 per cent of the potential total. This is true even of those studies retracing their samples after thirty-six years (3) or twenty-three years (5).

Over such lengths of time, however, the potential total inevitably decreases through permanent losses at each stage. There are thus two ways of presenting achievement in follow-up. On the one hand, tracing plus response rates of 80–85 per cent of a potential total, after long periods, seem very satisfactory. On the other, numbers will always be much reduced, e.g.:

(3) 5,362 soon after birth, approximately 3,500 at thirty-six years
(5) 16,883 at birth, approximately 12,500 at twenty-three years
(6) 12,743 at birth, approximately 8,200 at ten years (plus new immigrants)

Looked at in this way, attrition may seem large. It should be emphasized, however, that fall-out of this order—common in small as well as large-scale studies—seems to be what should be expected.

The bias that is represented by refusal and non-tracing, which might be expected to exclude disproportionately the most troubled families, can be checked to some extent. Most of the larger 'representative population' cohorts have done this and have found only very small deficits in, for example, institutionalized children or illegitimate children. It is an advantage of longitudinal studies, as distinct from cross-sectional ones, that any non-response bias can be checked against variables ascertained at an earlier stage; in most cross-sectional studies, nothing is known about the people who have been missed.

Different considerations concerning attrition apply to the larger surveys of mixed cross-sectional and longitudinal design (e.g. 7, 8, 10, 11). Since the production of a cross-sectional analysis is a major objective and numbers are large, the linking of data on individuals is not the only priority and individuals are apt to enter or leave the cross-sectional population. In the NSHG (7), for instance, over 29,000 children had taken part at least once by 1981 but uninterrupted yearly measurements for the maximum number of seven years are available for only a proportion, e.g. about a quarter of one 'completed' cohort. Similarly, in the Derbyshire Smoking Study (11), 4,270 of the original children (numbering 6,617) remained from 1974 to 1978. In studies such as these, where the children may be measured or surveyed at school and other data may be required from parents or teachers, there is commonly a high response rate among the children but responses from others can be relatively low. In the NSHG (7), for instance, there is a rather high proportion of children with social class, or occupational status of father, that is not known.

One issue that has concerned those engaged in cohort studies is whether the study itself, with the attention focused on the children (especially on their health), may not bias outcomes. In local studies, it seems possible that this may be true: in the Newcastle survey (9), for instance, everybody involved in the care of the children knew that they were part of the cohort and a specific service, with special availability of advice and instant medical help, was offered to the families. It was reported, however, that this did not appear to bias the *incidence* of illness. In the NSHD (3), a control sample of 2,000 children was examined during school years, through school health and clinic records, to check for any bias created by the research programme itself. Control groups are, of course, common in studies of selected groups (14, 15, 17, 18, 19). Some have included, as well as control groups without the characteristic under scrutiny, 'Hawthorne' control groups who have not been subjected to repeated investigation.

CONCLUSIONS AND RECOMMENDATIONS

Organization and funding of longitudinal studies

A preliminary issue that must be addressed is the common criticism that longitudinal studies, especially cradle-to-grave cohort studies, represent undue expense, especially since smaller, more focused, hypothesis-testing studies might equally well provide the information. The issue of focus has already been considered. It should perhaps be noted here, however, that the longer-established British cohort studies have been extremely productive. From the two longest-running cohorts, at least 150 (3) and 250 (5) books and other publications have so far been produced. It seems doubtful whether the same resources, put into a plurality of smaller studies, could have achieved equal results. Moreover, the publications have been in many different areas—not only social aspects of child health and development but also epidemiology and clinical medicine, psychology and education, criminology, family studies and service studies, and also (only now, perhaps) important areas of general and theoretical sociology. Data banks, long-term cohorts, and programmes of overlapping studies represent an investment with increasing returns: it would seem foolish to allow the investment to languish.

The experience of workers engaged in longitudinal studies tends to stress two or three particular points concerning organization and funding. The first, relevant to all types of study, is the relative ease with which funding can be obtained for the collection of new data and the inadequate staffing, time, and funding for analysis. In part (especially for shorter, focused studies) the responsibility must lie with researchers, who may not have planned or timed studies in a way that provided adequate resources for analysis. It is sometimes felt, however, that funding bodies do not readily appreciate the proper division of labour between data-collection and analysis. Even funding for the most efficient storage of large-scale data for use in the future (e.g. on microfilm) may not be easy to obtain. Also, studies inevitably uncover areas of interest that were not anticipated or allowed for. Whatever the cause, it is common in both large-scale and intensive studies for the full potential of data not to be realized.

Long-term cohort studies obviously present problems of sponsorship and funding. As already noted, there has been some tendency to use them as cross-sectional studies and this seems in part to be a consequence of having different sponsors, with different interests. To use them in this way may not be the best use of their potential. A fundamental difficulty is that the large cohort studies, potentially interested in all areas of health, development, education, life-chances and life-styles, employment, new family building, mobility, and so on, are essentially multi-disciplinary. Expertise involved in the long-term planning ought ideally to come from many disciplines. By the same token, sponsorship is ambiguous. Almost all the major studies have begun very firmly within the area of 'health', though educational or employment interests may have become prominent later. Ideally, the multi-disciplinary nature of the research needs to be acknowledged and planned for from the beginning.

It may be that full use of the potential of larger longitudinal studies will always depend on the accessibility of the data for secondary analysis and the encouragement of its use by a wide variety of researchers (Wedge 1974). The readiness of teams to make their data available varies but few are willing to contemplate anything but collaborative work under their own auspices. Two things that should probably be encouraged are the depositing of data in the archive after a certain lapse of time and the wider dissemination of information about what data exist.

Technical data handling is not a topic dealt with in this review. However, questions of data handling, linkage, and the statistical methods appropriate to life-history or other longitudinal data are important constraints that must be mentioned (Goldstein 1968, 1969; Samphier and Thompson 1981; Strauss, Barbigian, and Roff 1977). It may be, in part, the difficulties of the linking of multiple assessments from different time-periods that has fostered the tendency to report large-scale longitudinal studies in a cross-sectional way or at best to confine analyses to cor-relations between outcomes and some initial variable. There are, however, new conceptual and methodological approaches available (Sorbom 1981; Carr-Hill and Macdonald 1973; Robins 1977; Carr-Hill 1983) and it can be suggested that methodological and statistical development ought to receive special attention and support. A 'critical mass' of expertise may be needed, gathered together in one unit.

Selected areas of potential research

The summary that follows, considering the areas in which longitudinal studies might, or might not, best contribute to future research on inequality, refers principally to the larger population cohorts. There is some temptation to point out that if a smaller, special group is needed for a study that focuses particularly on certain characteristics or outcomes, then it can almost always be found within these larger cohorts. To use a subsample in this way, with the collection of extra data if necessary, might always be considered as a more economical method than starting afresh. However, it has to be recognized that smaller longitudinal studies are usually designed to test very specific hypotheses, based on special interests and knowledge and often requiring local populations or samples chosen in particular ways. Such studies will always be valuable. Consideration of the different purposes that they and the national cohorts serve may, however, emphasize that studies of selected groups are likely to complement population cohorts best if they have a tight design and a clear focus.

Health and mobility: trends over time in the extent of inequality

At the broadest level, one of the most important debates concerns the relationship of health to mobility; i.e., the extent to which health is a sorting mechanism. The role of social mobility in generating, through selection, the observed mortality differences by social class at various periods of time has, of course, long been recognized but the debate has been given impetus by the Black Report (DHSS 1980) and subsequent critiques. It has been argued that conventional mortality differentials by achieved social class are a poor measure of trends in health inequalities over time, since rates of inter-class mobility vary historically. It is essential to analyse mortality differentials by class of origin as well as achieved social class. On the other hand, this approach has been criticized as resting upon a distributional model of social class, as opposed to a model that emphasizes the formative impact of social and economic structure.

The OPCS Longitudinal Study (1) will, eventually, be able to offer information about mortality by class of origin and class at death. The relationships between class of origin, class of marriage, child-bearing efficiency, and characteristics such as height, are one important focus of the Aberdeen Maternity and Neonatal Data Bank (2). The potential of the larger cohort studies for examining assocations between health status (especially in childhood) and subsequent upward or downward mobility has not, however, yet been utilized. By retrospectively categorizing the health of the cohort members—preferably in various stages: infancy, childhood, adolescence—and examining class of origin and achieved class in young adulthood, it ought to be relatively easy to answer the question, do those with particularly good/poor health show upward/downward mobility, compared with the average experience of cohort members in their class of origin? (It is important to emphasize that experience will always be relative, if secular trends in mobility are not to obscure the results.)

There are also parental generations, now in middle age, who would be relatively easy to contact. There is not, typically, much data on the health of the mother except at child-bearing (though the NSHD has self-assessments during the child's infancy) but detailed social data are available throughout the period of the child's dependency. The opportunity exists, at future contacts with the younger generation, for at least enquiring about mortality and broad occupational/social histories in later years of the parental generation. If an actual return to the survivors of the older generation were possible, this would be a relatively economical way of studying mobility and health both retrospectively and prospectively.

Geographical mobility
The association of geographical mobility and health will be complicated by the fact that it is likely to be related to social mobility. It would seem

important, however, to use the cohort studies also to distinguish those who move between 'worse' and 'better' environments, who are also socially mobile, from those who are geographically mobile *without* social mobility. Again, it must be borne in mind that secular trends—in this case, area trends—must be taken into account. Areas, too, have a 'health history', some improving—as judged by the average experience of their inhabitants—and some deteriorating. Moreover, selective migration into and out of them is part of this history: interpretation of the *effect* of area is therefore complicated. Nonetheless, some attempt could be made to characterize the health of areas by those variables most clearly associated with environment (e.g. housing conditions, pollution) rather than with the population who live in it. It might then be productive to look particularly at the stayers/movers only in selected 'worst' areas.

The mechanisms of association between health and mobility

It must be emphasized that those who have argued that a distributional model explains many features of the apparent trends over time in mortality differentials by social class have in no way sought to dispose of the *fact* of inequality in health. Rather, it is suggested that only when these processes are clearer will it be possible to consider more productively what the real causes, nature, and extent of health differentials are. The arguments about whether these differentials are widening or lessening is, in any case, probably a sterile one: the more useful questions are likely to be *in what respects* are there inequalities and *by what mechanisms* are they widened or lessened. Even the largest of the longitudinal cohorts (as distinct from the data banks) is likely to prove too small, when broken down by social class/sex/social mobility/health status (and, possibly, area or geographical mobility), to offer 'proof' of the relative importance of the distributional or structural effects. The cohort studies do, however, offer the opportunity to look in detail at the mechanisms by which health may affect life-chances. In relation, for instance, to the demonstration by the Aberdeen data bank that the 'most healthy' women tend to marry upwards, is there sufficiently detailed information in the cohort studies to indicate what the specific associated events or characteristics may be— e.g. better educational achievement? Different sorts of jobs held by the young women before marriage? Parents who are also more likely to be upwardly mobile while the woman is still a child or higher aspirations for the child on the part of the parents? Higher social class of origin of the parents themselves (perhaps particularly the mother)? Different attitudes or ambitions on the part of the girl herself?

The effects of health status

It is, in fact, in the examination of the effects of health status upon

life-chances and behaviour, in a wider sense than simply testing distributional effects, that some of the greatest untapped potential of the cohort
studies lies. In their analysis, health has commonly been used as a
dependent variable, e.g. in demonstrations that groups with particular
social characteristics (social class, area, etc.) have particular health
characteristics. The need now is for the analysis to be turned round so that
health is used as the independent variable, e.g. by selection of a group
with particular health characteristics (say, children with chronic conditions), about whom one would ask: What are their educational
achievements, marriage patterns, early occupational patterns?

An obvious corollary is the study of the 'deviant' individuals who have
overcome a health disadvantage and prospered socially. What, within
socio-economic groups, have proved to be protective factors? What
factors have reinforced vulnerability? The variety of retrospective data
available—including attitudinal measures from parents, teachers, and the
cohort members themselves and behavioural, personality, and attainment
measures of the children, as well as histories of family circumstances—
offers many candidates for the testing of hypotheses.

These analyses could be accomplished from existing data. Special
investigations of relevant groups—with re-contract, if necessary—could
explore processes more precisely: given, say, two groups with equally
poor health in childhood, one of which appears to have overcome this
handicap while the other has been affected by it, at what precise point in
the life history, and in what way, did the individual's health status have
an effect? Educational achievement? First job-seeking? Through an effect
on parental attitudes? Are stable social networks or communities
protective?

The natural history of health states

So far, it is the effects of the social environment on health or the effects of
health upon social status that have been considered (i.e. cross-pathways
in *Figure 8.1*). The straight pathway of associations between health states
at different periods of life (with social variables always intervening) is
another important, and very neglected, area in which the cohort studies
have much to offer. What is the relationship between health in childhood
and health in adulthood? This is a simple question to which even a
descriptive answer is lacking, whether it is some concept of general health
status, or vulnerability to specific forms of ill-health, that is being
considered.

The only type of health disorder that has been closely examined is
respiratory disfunction and its association with childhood repiratory disease,
with pollution and smoking as intervening variables. The association in
the NSHD of peptic ulcer and other disorders with family disruption in

childhood is one early, and probably crude, example of the much wider potential for the investigation of the natural history of specific disorders. Which adult conditions should be selected, and which retrospective variables should be examined, will depend on socio-medical theories or 'hunches' about possible associations. Some (perhaps fanciful) candidates might include, for instance, the 'Type-A' personality (and upward mobility) and heart disease; infant nutrition and later-life obesity; the 'cancer-prone' effect of certain personality traits or life events. These examples are offered to make the point that the *breadth* of the data available, combined with the fact that they were inevitably selected for a wide variety of purposes and not to explore a particular hypothesis, means that it would be inappropriate to suggest that precise questions of an epidemiological nature can be answered. This is not data to be used for the testing of scientific hypotheses about aetiology, for which other methods are obviously more appropriate. Rather, the material is suitable for exploring very wide aspects of the natural history of common forms of ill-health.

An individual's health 'biography' is, of course, rarely a steady, even curve. Life-long influences are superimposed upon short-term factors: exposure to environmental insult may be brief or lengthy; the distribution of illness overt the life history has been observed to be related to stress and to take the form of clusters of apparently unrelated disorders. The advantage of using the adult cohorts of the longitudinal studies, or even their parents, to examine these relationsips is that good retrospective data exist on the social environment, and on patterns of stressors, at previous periods of life. It is obvious that as the cohorts grow older, the potential will become greater.

Indicators of health and of social inequality

If the longitudinal cohorts—and, indeed, the data banks—are to be used for these fundamentally important purposes (for which, it must be noted, they were not originally intended), and particularly for intragenerational and intergenerational comparisons, then it is probably necessary to develop new indicators both of social inequality and of health status. It seems likely that occupational classifications, enshrined in the existing data and in official statistics, will continue to be used but they must certainly be refined in the way suggested by Illsley and their changing relationships to socio-economic status, rewards, and life-styles established.

Again, age at death (as in the OPCS study) and child-bearing efficiency (as in the Aberdeen Data Bank) will obviously continue to be used as 'ultimate' indicators. Mortality is not, however, a very satisfactory indicator of health and to use the potential of the cohort studies for examination of health more widely defined will inevitably mean the development, from existing and future data, of other indices. The derivation of simple summary measures of 'better' and 'worse' health in childhood should not be difficult, given the wealth of data available in the major studies. Items that might be used include: birth conditions, congenital handicaps, incidence in infancy of those medical conditions known to have significance; incidence of specific chronic conditions of the sort that have commonly been selected out for special recording (convulsions, asthma, eczema, etc.); number and length of hospitalizations, measures from clinical examinations. Each study may have different data available but each certainly has enough to distinguish arbitrarily-defined 'better' and 'worse' health histories.

The development of an indicator of health status in adulthood may be more difficult, given that the data on health are often less complete. It is certainly possible in the NSHD, however, where the subjects were examined at thirty-six years old. In the NCDS, some categorization could be made from the questions about self-rated health, chronic conditions, limitations on functioning, etc., asked at twenty-three years.

Secular change: social policy: effects of medical care
These, finally, are areas in which the potential contribution of the longitudinal cohorts is more problematic. Mention has already been made of some preliminary approaches to the examination of the effects of secular change on different cohorts: the collaborative work involved in the comparison of the three or four cohorts now available, spanning some twenty-five years in their birth dates, must obviously be applauded and encouraged. Ideally, of course, new cohorts are necessary if secular change is to continue to be monitored; the most economical procedure would be to regard the first-born children of the NSHD (Second Generation Study) as a cohort representing births in the late 1960s and throughout the 1970s, and the first-born children of the NCDS (on whom little information is available without an additional 'sweep') as a cohort representing births throughout the 1980s. It is possible, however, that these 'children of survivors' might prove to be a selected group.

It seems probable that, for the study of secular change and the short-term effects of social policy, overlapping cross-sectional studies such as the NSHG (7) and the pre-school growth surveillance study (8) will be favoured. It might be suggested, however, that the interpretation of their results has not always been sociologically informed. The current interest of both studies in *area* variables, and of the NSHG in inner-city areas and in immigrant populations, is to be applauded.

It is unlikely that the longitudinal studies can help to answer the question of the relative importance of health-care or health-service supply as an influence on health status. While they did, in certain areas of child health, offer valuable cross-sectional evidence about social and geographical variations in the use of services, the available variables are ambiguous for any more ambitious study of the effect of health-care on continuing health status. Area of residence may be taken as surrogate for health-service supply factors but it also, of course, implies environmental factors; rates and patterns of health-service use, which are available for the cohorts throughout childhood, confound 'need' and supply. It might be useful, as the cohort members grow older, to attempt to relate self-declared symptoms and health assessments to patterns of health-service use and eventually to outcomes such as hospitalization, disability, or death. This might, eventually, demonstrate socially patterned variations in the readiness to seek help or illustrate the effects of delay in reaching treatment (or, indeed, of over-enthusiasm for treatment). The cohorts are too small, however, and the service-provision variables too numerous, for much to be achieved in this area.

This review was originally commissioned by the Economic and Social Research Council. Thanks are due to a large number of people, including especially the researchers involved in the studies described, for assistance in providing access to the material.

REFERENCES

Acheson, E. D. (1967) *Medical Record Linkage*. Oxford: Oxford University Press for the Nufield Provincial Hospitals Trust.

Britten, N. (1981) Models of Intergenerational Class Mobility: Findings from the National Survey of Health and Development. *British Journal of Sociology* 32: 224–38.

Britten, N. and Heath, A. (1983) Women, Men and Social Class. In E. Gamarnikow, D. Morgan, J. Purvis, and D. Taylorson (eds) *Gender, Class and Work*. London: Heinemann.

Carr-Hill, R. A. (1983) *Characterising Pregnancy Histories*. (Unpublished paper.)

Carr-Hill, R. A. and Macdonald, J. I. (1973) Problems in the Analysis of Life Histories. *Sociology Review Monograph* 19.

Cherry, N. (1974) Components of Occupational Interest. *British Journal of Educational Psychology* 44: 22–30.

Colley, J. R. T., Douglas, J. W. B., and Reid, D. D. (1973) Respiratory Disease in Young Adults: Influence of Early Childhood Lower Respiratory Tract Illness, Social Class, Air Pollution, and Smoking. *British Medical Journal* 2: 195–98.

Douglas, J. W. B. (1964) *The Home and the School*. London: MacGibbon & Kee.

—— (1976) The Use and Abuse of National Cohorts. In M. Shipman (ed.) *The Organisation and Impact of Social Research*. London: Routledge and Kegan Paul.

Douglas, J. W. B. and Blomfield, J. M. (1958) *Children Under Five: The Results of a National Survey Made by a Joint Committee of the Institute of Child Health, the Society of Medical Officers of Health and the Population Investigation Committee.* London: Allen and Unwin.

Fox, A. J. and Goldblatt, P. O. (1982) *Socio-demographic Mortality Differentials: Longitudinal Study 1971–75.* OPCS Series LS No. 1. London: HMSO.

Goldstein, H. (1968) Longitudinal Studies and the Measurement of Change. *Statistician* 18, 2: 93–117.

—— (1969) *The Design and Analysis of Longitudinal Studies.* London: Academic Press.

Illsley, R. (1980) *Professional or Public Health: Sociology in Health and Medicine.* London: Nuffield Provincial Hospitals Trust.

Kahan, M., Butler, D., and Stokes, D. (1966) On the Analytic Division of Social Class. *British Journal of Sociology* 17: 127.

Kiernan, K. E., Colley, J. R. T., Douglas, J. W. B., and Reid, D. D. (1976) Chronic Cough in Young Adults in Relation to Smoking Habits, Childhood Environment and Chest Illness. *Respiration* 33: 236–44.

Lancet (1983) Editorial. 26 March.

Leete, R. and Fox, A. J. (1977) Registrar General's Social Classes, Origins and Uses. *Population Trends* 4: 1–7.

Madge, N. (ed.) (1983) *Families at Risk.* London: Heinemann Educational.

Miller, F. J. W., Court, S. D. M., Walton, W. S., and Knox, E. G. (1960) *Growing Up in Newcastle-upon-Tyne.* London: Oxford University Press.

Osborn, A. F. and Morris, A. C. (1979) The Rationale for a Composite Index of Social Class and its Evaluation. *British Journal of Sociology* 30, 1: 39–60.

Osborn, A. F., Butler, N. R., and Morris, A. C. (1984) *The Social Life of Britain's Five-year-olds.* London: Routledge and Kegan Paul.

Peckham, C. S., Stark, O., Simonite, V., and Wolff, O. H. (1982) Prevalence of Obesity in British Children Born in 1946 and 1958. *British Medical Journal* 286: 1237–242.

Robins, L. N. (1977) Problems in Follow-up Studies. *American Journal of Psychiatry* 134: 904–07.

Rona, R. J., Swan, A. V., and Altman, D. G. (1978) Social Factors and Height of Primary Schoolchildren in England and Scotland. *Journal of Epidemiology and Community Medicine* 7: 115–24.

Ross, E. (1973) Convulsive Disorders in British Children. *Proceedings of the Royal Society of Medicine* 66, 7: 703–70.

Rutter, M. (1977) Prospective Studies to Investigate Behavioural Change. In J. S. Strauss, H. M. Barbigian, and M. Roff (eds) *The Origins and Course of Psychopathology.* New York: Plenum.

—— (1981) Longitudinal Studies: A Psychiatric Perspective. In S. A. Mednick and A. E. Baert (eds) *Prospective Longitudinal Studies.* Oxford: Oxford University Press.

Sameroff, J. and Chandler, M. J. (1975) Reproductive Risk and the Continuum of Caretaking Casualty. In F. D. Horowitz (ed.) *Review of Child Development Research, Volume IV.* Chicago, Ill.: University of Chicago Press.

Samphier, M. L. and Thompson, B. (1981) The Aberdeen Maternity and Neonatal Data Bank. In S. A. Mednick and A. E. Baert (eds) *Prospective Longitudinal Research*. Oxford: Oxford University Press.

Sheridan, M. D. (1972) Reported Incidence of Hearing Loss in Children of Seven Years. *Developmental Medicine and Child Neurology* 14, 3: 296–303.

—— (1973) Children of Seven Years with Marked Speech Defects. *British Journal of Disordered Communication* 8, 1: 9–16.

Sorbom, D. (1981) A Statistical Model for the Analysis of Longitudinal Data: LISREL. In S. A. Mednick and A. E. Baert (eds) *Prospective Longitudinal Research*. Oxford: Oxford University Press.

Stark, O., Atkins, E., Wolff, O., and Douglas, J. W. B. (1981) A Longitudinal Study of Obesity in the National Survey of Health and Development. *British Medical Journal* 283: 13–17.

Strauss, J. S., Barbigian, H. M., and Roff, M. (eds) (1977) *The Origins and Course of Psychopathology*. New York: Plenum.

Taylor, B., Wadsworth, J., Wadsworth, M. E. J., and Peckham, C. (1984) Change in the Reported Prevalence of Childhood Eczema since the 1939–45 War. *Lancet* 2: 1255–257.

Taylor, R., Ford, G., and Barber, H. (1983) *The Elderly at Risk*. Age Concern Research Monograph No. 6. London.

Townsend, P. (1979) *Poverty in the United Kingdom*. London: Penguin.

Townsend, P. and Davidson, N. (1982) *Inequalities in Health: The Black Report*. London: Penguin.

Wadsworth, M. E. J. (1976) Delinquency, Pulse Rates and Early Emotional Deprivation. *British Journal of Criminology* 16: 245–56.

—— (1981) Social Change and the Interpretation of Research. *Criminology* 19: 53–75.

Wadsworth, M. E. J. and Freeman, S. R. (1983) Generation Differences in Beliefs: A Study of Stability and Change in Religious Beliefs. *British Journal of Sociology* 34: 416–37.

Wadsworth, M. E. J. and Morris, S. (1978) Assessing Chances of Hospital Admission in Pre-school Children: A Critical Evaluation. *Archives of Disease in Childhood* 53: 159–63.

Wadsworth, M. E. J., Peckham, C. S., and Taylor, B. (1984) The Role of National Longitudinal Studies in the Prediction of Health, Development and Behaviour. In D. B. Walker and J. B. Richmond (eds) *Monitoring the Health of American Children*. Cambridge, Mass.: Harvard University Press.

Webber, R. (1979) *Census Enumeration Districts: A Socio-economic Classification*. OPCS Occasional Paper No. 14. London: HMSO.

Wedge, P. (1974) Access to Data in the NCDS. *SSRC Newsletter* 23: 4–5.

Wedge, P. and Essen, J. (1982) *Children in Adversity*. London: Pan.

Wedge, P. and Prosser, H. (1973) *Born to Fail?* London: Arrow Books and the National Children's Bureau.

BIBLIOGRAPHY

Study 1: OPCS Longitudinal Study

Brown, A. and Fox, A. J. (1984) OPCS Longitudinal Study—10 Years On. *Population Trends* 37: 20–2.

Fox, A. J. (1981a) Mortality Statistics and the Assessment of Risk. *Proceedings of the Royal Society of London* A, 376: 65–78.

—————— (1981b) Linkage Methods in Occupational Mortality. In J. Corbett McDonald (ed.) *Recent Advances in Occupational Health*: 107–118. Edinburgh: Churchill-Livingstone.

—————— (1984a) Design Problems and Data Collection Strategies in Studies of Mortality Differentials in Developed Countries 1981. In Seminar on Methodology and Data Collection in Mortality Studies, 1981, Dakar *Proceedings*. Liège: International Union for Scientific Study of Population.

—————— (1984b) Selection and Mortality Differentials. In J. Baldwin (ed.) *Textbook of Medical Record Linkage*. Oxford: Oxford University Press.

—————— (1985) *Social Mobility Around the Time One Has Children*. OPCS Longitudinal Study No. 2. London: HMSO.

Fox, A. J. and Goldblatt, P. O. (1982a) Socio-demographic Differences in Mortality. *Population Trends* 27: 8–13.

—————— (1982b) *Socio-demographic Mortality Differentials: Longitudinal Study 1971–75*. OPCS Series LS No. 1. London: HMSO.

Fox, A. J., Bulusu, L., and Kinlen, L. J. (1979) Mortality and Age Differences in Marriage. *Journal of Biosocial Science* 11: 117–31.

Fox, A J., Goldblatt, P. O., and Adelstein, A. M. (1982) Selection and Mortality Differentials. *Journal of Epidemiology and Community Health* 36: 69–79.

Fox, A. J., Goldblatt, P. O., and Jones, D. R. (1985) Social Class Mortality Differentials: Artefact, Selection or Life Circumstances? *Journal of Epidemiology and Community Health* 39, 1: 1–8.

Fox, A. J., McDowall, M., and Goldblatt, P. O. (1981) Employment During Pregnancy and Infant Mortality. *Population Trends* 26: 12–15.

Fox, A. J., Jones, D. R., Moser, K. A., and Goldblatt, P. O. (1985) Male Socio-demographic Mortality Differentials from the OPCS Longitudinal Study 1971–81. *Population Trends* 140: 10–16.

Goldblatt, P. O. and Fox, A. J. (1979) Household Mortality: An Example from the OPCS Longitudinal Study. *Population Trends* 14: 20–7.

Grundy, E. M. D. (in press) Divorce, Widowhood, Remarriage and Geographic Mobility. *Journal of Biosocial Science*.

Grundy, E. M. D. and Fox, A. J. (1985) Migration in Early Married Life. *European Journal of Population* 1: 237–63.

Jones, D. R., Goldblatt, P. O., and Leon, D. A. (1984) Bereavement and Cancer: Some Results Using Data from the LS. *British Medical Journal* 289: 461–64.

Moser, K. A., Fox, A. J., Jones, D. R., and Goldblatt, P. O. (1984) Unemployment and Mortality in the OPCS Longitudinal Study. *Lancet* December: 1324–329.

Office of Population Censuses and Surveys (1973) *Cohort Studies: New Developments*. Studies in Medical and Population Subjects No. 23. London: HMSO.

Selected Social Statistics Research Unit Working Papers

2. Housing Tenure: an Example of Using Record Linkage to Study Differentials in Cancer Incidence, Survival and Mortality (D. A. Leon) 1983.

5. Cause of Death amongst People Registered with Cancer in 1971–75 (D. A. Leon and A. Adelstein) 1983.

7. From Official Health Statistics to Interactive Epidemiological Data. (A. J. Fox, D. R. Jones, and D. A. Leon) 1983.

8. LS, Mortality 1971–81 in Regional Heart Study Areas: Some preliminary Notes on the Relationship with Region and Water Hardness (D. R. Jones) 1984.

9. Water Nitrates and Stomach Cancer: The role of Socio-economic Factors (P. O. Goldblatt and D. R. Jones) 1984.

14. Mortality of Women in Private and Non-private Households Using Data from the OPCS Longitudinal Study (K. A. Moser) 1984.

17. Was Ciocco Right? A Study of Mortality Following Widow(er)hood, with Particular Reference to Causes of Death in the Widow(er)ed and Their Spouses, Using Data from the OPCS Longitudinal Study (D. R. Jones *et al.*) 1984.

22. Mortality Following Widow(er)hood: Some Evidence Relating to the Role of Social Support and Other Socio-demographic Factors, from the OPCS Longitudinal Study (E. M. D. Grundy) 1984.

28. Migration and Fertility Behaviour in England and Wales: A Record Linkage Study (E. M. D. Grundy) 1985.

29. A Longitudinal Perspective on Recent Socio-demographic Change (A. J. Fox and E. M. D. Grundy) 1985.

Study 2: Aberdeen Maternity and Neonatal Data Bank

Adams, E. M. and Finlayson, A. (1961) Familial Aspects of Pre-eclampsia and Hypertension in Pregnancy. *Lancet* 2: 1373.

Horobin, G. W. (ed.) (1973) *Experience with Abortion: A Case Study of NE Scotland.* Cambridge: Cambridge University Press,

Illsley, R. (1955) Social Class Selection and Class Differences in Relation to Stillbirths and Infant Deaths. *British Medical Journal* 2: 1520–524.

——— (1956) The Social Context of Childbirth. *Nursing Mirror* 14 and 21 September.

——— (1967a) The Sociological Study of Reproduction and its Outcome. In S. A. Richardson and A. F. Guttmacher (eds) *Childbearing — Its Social and Psychological Aspects*. Baltimore, Md: Williams and Wilkins.

——— (1967b) Family Growth and its Effect on the Relationship between Obstetric Factors and Child Functioning. In R. Platt and A. S. Parkes (eds) *Social and Genetic Influences on Life and Death*. Edinburgh: Oliver and Boyd.

Illsley, R. and Gill, D. (1968a) Changing Trends in Illegitimacy. *Social Science and Medicine* 2: 415–33.

——— (1968b) New Fashions in Illegitimacy. *New Society* 14 November: 709–11.

Illsley, R. and Taylor, R. (1974) *Sociological Aspects of Teenage Pregnancy.* Occasional Paper No. 1. Aberdeen: Institute of Medical Sociology.

McKinley, J. (1970) The New Late Comers for Antenatal Care. *British Journal of Preventive and Social Medicine* 24, 1: 52–7.

Samphier, M. L. and Thompson, B. (1981) The Aberdeen Maternity and Neonatal Data Bank. In S. A. Mednick and A. E. Baert (eds) *Prospective Longitudinal Research*. Oxford: Oxford University Press.

Thompson, B. and Aitken-Swan, J. (1973) Pregnancy Outcome and Fertility Control in Aberdeen. *British Journal of Preventive and Social Medicine* 27, 3: 137–45.

Thompson, B. and Illsley, R. (1969) Family Growth in Aberdeen. *Journal of Biosocial Science* 1: 23–9.

Study 3: National Survey of Health and Development

Atkins, E., Cherry, N. M., Douglas, J. W. B., Kiernan, K. E., and Wadsworth, M.E. J. (1981) The 1946 British Birth Cohort Survey: An Account of the Origins, Progress and Results of the National Survey of Health and Development. In S. A. Mednick and A. E. Baert (eds) *Prospective Longitudinal Research in Europe: An Empirical Basis for Primary Prevention*. Oxford: Oxford University Press.

Blomfield, J. M. (1955) *An Account of Hospital Admissions in the Pre-school Period*. University of Bristol (Paper).

Blomfield, J. M. and Douglas, J. W. B. (1956) Bed-wetting: Prevalence among Children aged 4–5 years. *Lancet* 1: 850.

Braddon, F. E. M. (1985) Exercise and Obesity in a National Birth Cohort. *Proceedings of the Nutrition Society* 44: 25A.

Bransby, E. R., Blomfield, J. M., and Douglas, J. W. B. (1955) The Prevalence of Bed-wetting. *Medical Officer* 94: 5.

Britten, N. (1981) Models of Intergenerational Class Mobility: Findings from the National Survey of Health and Development. *British Journal of Sociology* 32: 224–38.

———— (1984) Class Imagery in a National Sample of Women and Men. *British Journal of Sociology* 35: 406–34.

Britten, N., Wadsworth, M. E. J., and Fenwick, P. B. C. (1984) Stigma in Patients with Early Epilepsy: A National Longitudinal Study. *Journal of Epidemiology and Community Health* 38: 291–95.

Calnan, M., Douglas, J. W. B., and Goldstein, H. (1978) Tonsillectomy and Circumcision—A Comparison of Two Cohorts. *International Journal of Epidemiology* 7: 79–85.

Cherry, N. (1974) Components of Occupational Interest. *British Journal of Educational Psychology* 44: 22–30.

———— (1976). Persistent Job-changing—Is It a Problem? *Journal of Occupational Psychology* 49: 203–21.

———— (1978) Stress, Anxiety and Work: A Longitudinal Study. *Journal of Occupational Psychology* 51:259–70.

———— (1984a) Women and Work Stress: Evidence from the 1946 Birth Cohort. *Ergonomics* 27: 519–26.

———— (1984b) Nervous Strain, Anxiety and Symptoms amongst 32-year-old Men at Work in Britain. *Journal of Occupational Psychology* 57: 95–105.

Cherry, N. and Kiernan, K. (1976) Personality Scores and Smoking Behaviour. *British Journal of Preventive and Social Medicine* 30: 123–31.

Cherry, N. and Kiernan, K. (1978) A Longitudinal Study of Smoking and Personality. In R. E. Thornton (ed.) *Smoking Behaviour: Physiological and Psychological Differences*. Edinburgh: Churchill-Livingstone. Pages 12–18.

Chilvers, C., Pike, M. C., Forman, D., Fogelman, K., and Wadsworth, M. E. J. (1984) Apparent Doubling of Frequency of Undescended Testis in England and Wales in 1962–81. *Lancet* 2: 330–32.

Colley, J. R. T. (1984) Relationships between Respiratory Disorders in Infancy and in Early Adult Life. In N. R. Butler and B. D. Corner (eds) *Stress and Disability in Childhood*. Bristol: John Wright.

Colley, J. R. T., Douglas, J. W. B., and Reid, D. D. (1973) Respiratory Disease in Young Adults: Influence of Early Childhood Lower Respiratory Tract Illness, Social Class, Air Pollution, and Smoking. *British Medical Journal* 2: 195–98.

Cooper, J. E. (1965) Epilepsy in a Longitudinal Survey of 5,000 Children. *British Medical Journal* 1: 1020–022.

Crisp, A. H., Douglas, J. W. B., Ross, J. M., and Stonehill, E. (1970) Some Development Aspects of Disorders of Weight. *Journal of Psychosomatic Research* 14: 313–20.

Douglas, J. W. B. (1950a). Some Factors Associated with Prematurity. *Journal of Obstetrics and Gynaecology in the British Empire* 57: 625.

———— (1950b) The Extent of Breast-feeding in Great Britain in 1946, with Special Reference to the Health and Survival of Children. *Journal of Obstetrics and Gynaecology in the British Empire* 57: 336.

———— (1951a) The Health and Survival of Children in Different Social Classes: The Results of a National Survey. *Lancet* 2: 440.

———— (1951b) Social Class Differences in Health and Survival during the First Two Years of Life: The Results of a National Survey. *Population Studies* 5: 35–58.

———— (1956a) Birthweight and the History of Breastfeeding. *Lancet* 2: 685–88.

———— (1956b) The Age at which Premature Children Walk. *Medical Officer* 95: 33–5.

———— (1956c) The Mental Ability of Premature Children. *British Medical Journal* 1: 1210.

———— (1960) Premature Children at Primary Schools. *British Medical Journal* 1: 1008–013.

———— (1962a) Reproductive Loss. In A. T. Welford, M. Argyle, D. V. Glass, and J. N. Morris (eds) *Society, Problems and Methods of Study*. London: Routledge and Kegan Paul.

———— (1962b) The Height of Boys and Girls and their Home Environment. In Hottinger and Berger (eds) *Modern Problems in Paediatrics, Volume VII*.

———— (1964a) Ability and Adjustment of Children who have had Measles. *British Medical Journal* 2: 1301–303.

———— (1964b) The Environmental Challenge in Early Childhood. *Public Health* 78: 195–202.

———— (1964c) *The Home and the School*. London: MacGibbon and Kee.

———— (1969) Effects of Early Environment on Later Development. *Journal of the Royal College of Physicians* 3: 359–64.

———— (1970) Broken Families and Child Behaviour. *Journal of the Royal College of Physicians* 4: 203–10.

Douglas, J. W. B. (1973a) The 1946 National Survey of Health and Development in Britain: Some Early Findings and Later Developments. *Sociological Micro-Journal* 7: 35–6.

—— (1973a) The 1946 National Survey of Health and Development in Britain: Some Early Findings and Later Developments. *Sociological Micro-Journal* 7: 35–6.

—— (1973b) Early Disturbing Events and Later Enuresis. In I. Kilvin, R. C. MacKeith, and S. R. Meadow (eds) *Bladder Control and Enuresis*. London: Spastics International Medical Publications.

—— (1975) Early Hospital Admissions and Later Disturbances of Behaviour and Learning. *Developmental Medicine and Child Neurology* 17: 456–80.

—— (1976) The Use and Abuse of National Cohorts. In M. Shipman (ed.) *The Organisation and Impact of Social Research*. London: Routledge and Kegan Paul.

—— (1981a) The Value of Birth Cohort Studies. In G. Schulsinger, S. A. Mednick, and J. Knop (eds) *Longitudinal Research: Methods and Uses in Behavioral Science*. Boston, Mass.: Martinus Nijhoff.

—— (1981b) The Contribution of Long-term Research to Social Medicine. In G. Schulsinger, S. A. Mednick, and J. Knop (eds) *Longitudinal Research: Methods and Uses in Behavioral Science*. Boston, Mass.: Martinus Nijhoff.

—— (1984) Illness, Handicap and Ultimate Educational Achievement. In N. R. Butler and B. D. Corner (eds) *Stress and Disability in Childhood*. Bristol: John Wright.

Douglas, J. W. B. and Blomfield, J. M. (1956) The Reliability of Longitudinal Surveys. *Milbank Memorial Fund Quarterly* 34: 227–52.

—— (1957) Maternal Employment and the Welfare of Children—An Account of a Survey in Progress. *Eugenics Review* 49: 69.

—— (1958) *Children under Five: The Results of a National Survey Made by a Joint Committee of the Institute of Child Health, the Society of Medical Officers of Health and the Population Investigation Committee*. London: Allen and Unwin.

Douglas, J. W. B. and Gear, R. (1976) Children of Low Birthweight in the 1946 National Cohort. *Archives of Disease in Childhood* 51: 820–27.

Douglas, J. W. B. and Mogford, C. (1953a) The Health of Premature Children, during the First Four Years of Life. *British Medical Journal* 1: 748.

—— (1953b) The Growth of Premature Children. *Archives of Disease in Childhood* 28: 436–45.

Douglas, J. W. B. and Mulligan, D. G. (1961) Emotional Adjustment and Educational Achievement—The Preliminary Results of a Longitudinal Study of a National Sample of Children. *Proceedings of the Royal Society of Medicine* 54: 585–91.

Douglas, J. W. B. and Ross, J. M. (1964) Age of Puberty Related to Educational Ability, Attainment and School Leaving Age. *Journal of Child Psychology and Psychiatry* 5: 185.

Douglas, J. W. B. and Rowntree, G. (1949) Supplementary Maternal and Child Health Services: Part I: Postnatal Care; Part II: Nurseries. *Population Studies* 3: 205–26.

Douglas, J. W. B. and Simpson, H. R. (1964) Height in Relation to Puberty, Family Size and Social Class: A Longitudinal Study. *Milbank Memorial Fund Quarterly* 42: 20–35.

Douglas, J. W. B. and Waller, R. E. (1966) Air Pollution and Respiratory Infection in Children. *British Journal of Preventive and Social Medicine* 20: 1–8.

Douglas, J. W. B., Kiernan, K., and Wadsworth, M. E. J. (1977) Illness and Behaviour. *Proceedings of the Royal Society of Medicine* 70: 530–32.

Douglas, J. W. B., Ross, J. M., and Simpson, H.R. (1956) Some Observations on the Relationship between Heights and Measured Ability among School Children. *Human Biology* 37: 178–86.

—— (1967) The Ability and Attainment of Short-sighted Pupils. *Journal of the Royal Statistical Society* Series A (General) 130: 479–503.

—— (1968) *All our Future: A Longitudinal Study of Secondary Education*. London: Peter Davies.

Douglas, J. W. B., Lawson, A., Cooper, J. E., and Cooper, E. (1968) Family Interaction and the Activities of Young Children. *Journal of Child Psychology and Psychiatry* 9: 157–71.

Hobcraft, J. N. (1980) Forecasting the Components of Population Change with Special Reference to Migration. In J. N. Hobcraft and P. Rees (eds) *Regional Demographic Development*. London: Croom Helm.

Kiernan, K. E. (1977) Age of Puberty in Relation to Age at Marriage and Parenthood: A National Longitudinal Study. *Annals of Human Biology* 4: 301–08.

—— (1980a) Teenage Motherhood—Associated Factors and Consequences: The Experience of a British Birth Cohort. *Journal of Biosocial Science* 12: 393–405.

—— (1980b) Characteristics of Young People who Move Inter-regionally. In J. N. Hobcraft and P. Rees (eds) *Regional Demographic Development*. London: Croom Helm.

Kiernan, K. E. and Diamond, I. (1983) The Age at which Childbearing Starts: A Longitudinal Study. *Population Studies* 37: 363–80.

Kiernan, K. E., Colley, J. R. T., Douglas, J. W. B., and Reid, D. D. (1976) Chronic Cough in Young Adults in Relation to Smoking Habits, Childhood Environment and Chest Illness. *Respiration* 33: 236–44.

MacCarthy, D., Douglas, J. W. B., and Mogford, C. (1952) Circumcision in a National Sample of Four-year-old Children. *British Medical Journal* 2: 755.

McCord, J. and Wadsworth, M. E. J. (1984) The Importance of Time in Stress and Stigma Paradigms. In U. E. Gerhardt and M. E. J. Wadsworth (eds) *Stress and Stigma: Explanation and the Use of Evidence*. Frankfurt: Campus Press; London: Macmillan; New York: St Martin's Press.

McDowell, L. M. (1982) Housing Deprivation: A Longitudinal Analysis. *Area* 14: 144–50.

—— (1983) Housing Deprivation: An Intergenerational Approach. In M. Brown (ed.) *The Structure of Disadvantage*. London: Heinemann. Pages 172–91.

Marmot, M. G., Page, C. M., Atkins, E., and Douglas, J. W. B. (1980) Effect of Breast-feeding on Plasma Cholesterol and Weight in Young Adults. *Journal of Epidemiology and Community Health* 34: 164–67.

Mulligan, D. G., Douglas, J. W. B., Hammond, W. A., and Tizard, J. (1963) Delinquency and Symptoms of Maladjustment: The Findings of a Longitudinal Study. *Proceedings of the Royal Society of Medicine* 56: 1083–086.

National Survey of Health and Development (1947) A Survey of Childbearing in Britain. *Population Studies* 1: 99–136.

—— (1948) *Maternity in Great Britain.* Oxford: Oxford University Press.

Nelson, D. M. (1964) Studying the Employment and Training of a National Sample of 17-year-olds. *Occupational Psychology*: 38.

Peckham, C. S., Stark, O., Simonite, V., and Wolff, O. H. (1982) Prevalence of Obesity in British Children Born in 1946 and 1958. *British Medical Journal* 286: 1237–242.

Pless, I. B. and Douglas, J. W. B. (1971) Chronic Illness in Childhood, Part I: Epidemiological and Clinical Characteristics. *Paediatrics* 47: 405–14.

Rodgers, B. (1978) Feeding in Infancy and Later Ability and Attainment. *Developmental Medicine and Child Neurology* 20: 421–26.

—— (1979) Future Prospects for ESN (M) School-leavers. *Special Education: Forward Trends* 6, 1: 43–5.

Rowntree, G. (1950a) Diphtheria Immunization in a National Sample of Children Aged Two Years in March 1948. *Monthly Bulletin of the Ministry of Health* 9: 134.

—— (1950b) Supplementary Child Health Services, Part III: Infant Welfare Centres. *Population Studies* 3: 375.

—— (1950c) Accidents among Children Under Two Years of Age in Great Britain. *Journal of Hygiene* 48: 323–37.

—— (1951) Accidents among Children. *Monthly Bulletin of the Ministry of Health* 10: 150–54.

—— (1955) Early Childhood in Broken Families. *Population Studies* 8: 247.

Stark, O., Atkins, E., Wolff, O., and Douglas, J. W. B. (1981) A Longitudinal Study of Obesity in the National Survey of Health and Development. *British Medical Journal* 283: 13–17.

Taylor, B., Wadsworth, J., Wadsworth, M. E. J., and Peckham, C. (1984) Changes in the Reported Prevalence of Childhood Eczema since the 1939–45 War. *Lancet* 2 1255–257.

Wadsworth, M. E. J. (1969) The National Survey of Health and Development. *Health Visitors Journal* 42: 143–44.

—— (1975) Delinquency in a National Sample of Children. *British Journal of Criminology* 15: 167–70.

—— (1976) Delinquency, Pulse Rates and Early Emotional Deprivation. *British Journal of Criminology* 16: 245–56.

—— (1979a) Delinquency Prediction and its Uses: The Experience of a Twenty-one-year Follow-up Study. *International Journal of Mental Health* 7: 43–62.

—— (1979b) *Roots of Delinquency: Infancy, Adolescence and Crime.* Oxford: Martin Robinson.

—— (1979c) Early Life Events and Later Behavioural Outcomes in a British Longitudinal Study. In S. B. Sells, R. Crandall, M. Roff, J. S. Strauss, and W. Pollin (eds) *Human Functioning in Longitudinal Perspective.* Baltimore, Md: Williams and Wilkins.

—— (1984a) Early Stress and Associations with Adult Health, Behaviour and Parenting. In N. R. Butler and B. D. Corner (eds) *Stress and Disability in Childhood.* Bristol: John Wright.

—— (1984b) A Lifetime Prospective Study of Human Adaptation and Health. In J. Cullen and J. Siegrist (eds) *Breakdown in Human Adaptation to 'Stress'—Towards a Multidisciplinary Approach. Volume I, Part 1.* Boston, Mass.: Martinus Nijhoff.

———— (forthcoming) Cross-generation Differences in Health. In H. B. Miles and E. Still (eds) *The Health and Development of Children*. London: The Eugenics Society.

Wadsworth, M. E. J. and Jarrett, R. J. (1974) Incidence of Diabetes in the First 26 Years of Life. *Lancet* 2: 1172–174.

Wadsworth, M. E. J. and Maclean, M. (forthcoming) Parents' Divorce and Children's Life Chances. *Children and Youth Services Review*.

Wadsworth, M. E. J. and Morris, S. (1978) Assessing Chances of Hospital Admission in Pre-school Children: A Critical Evaluation. *Archives of Disease in Childhood* 53: 159–63.

Wadsworth, M. E. J., Peckham, C. S., and Taylor, B. (1984) The Role of National Longitudinal Studies in the Prediction of Health, Development and Behaviour. In D. B. Walker and J. B. Richmond (eds) *Monitoring the Health of American Children*. Cambridge, Mass.: Harvard University Press.

Wadsworth, M. E. J., Cripps, H. A., Midwinter, R. E., and Colley, J. R. T. (1985) Blood Pressure in a National Birth Cohort at Age 36, Related to Social and Familial Factors, Smoking and Body Mass. *British Medical Journal* 2, 291: 1534–538.

Study 4: Second Generation Study

Wadsworth, M. E. J. (1981) Social Class and Generation Differences in Pre-school Education. *British Journal of Sociology* 32: 560–82.

———— (1985a) Inter-generational Differennces in Child Health. In *Measuring Socio-demographic Change*, IOCS Occasional Paper No. 34. London: HMSO.

———— (1985b) Parenting Skills and their Transmission through Generations. *Adoption and Fostering* 9: 28–32.

Wadsworth, M. E. J. and Freeman, S. R. (1983) Generation Differences in Beliefs: A Study of Stability and Change in Religious Beliefs. *British Journal of Sociology* 34: 416–37.

Study 5: National Child Development Survey

Adams, B. (1972) Adoption and After. *New Society* 19: 495, 590–92.

Alberman, E. D. (1969) The Prevalence of Congenital Defects in the Children of the 1958 Cohort. *Concern* 3: 29–33.

Alberman, E. D. and Goldstein, H. (1970) The 'At Risk' Register: A Statistical Evaluation. *British Journal of Preventive and Social Medicine* 24, 3: 129–35.

Alberman, E. D., Butler, N., and Sheridan, M. (1971) Visual Acuity of a National Sample (1958 Cohort) at Seven Years. *Developmental Medicine and Child Neurology* 13: 1, 9–14.

Alberman, E. D., Fedrick, J. M., and Schutt, W. H. (1967) The Hypoplastic Left Heart Complex. *Journal of Medical Genetics* 4: 83–7.

Butler, N. R. (1961a) National Survey of Perinatal Mortality: First Results. *British Medical Journal* 1: 1313–315.

———— (1961b) Perinatal Mortality Survey under Auspices of the National Birthday Trust Fund. *Proceedings of the Royal Society of Medicine* 54, 12: 1089–092.

———— (1962a) Perinatal Mortality Survey. *British Medical Journal* 2: 1463–465.

Butler, N. R. (1962b) Fatal Coxachie B Myocarditis in a Newborn Infant. *British Medical Journal* 2: 1463–465.

—— (1963) Complications of Birth Asphyxia with Special Reference to Resuscitation. In T. Barnett and J. Joyce (eds) *The Obstetrician Anaesthetist and the Paediatrician in the Management of Obstetrical Problems*. Oxford: Pergamon.

—— (1965a) The Problems of Low Birthweight and Early Delivery. *Journal of Obstetrics and Gynaecology of the British Commonwealth* 72: 6.

—— (1965b) Perinatal Death. In M. Dawkins and W. G. MacGregor (eds) *Gestational Age, Size and Maturity*, Clinics in Developmental Medicine No. 19. London: Spastics Society in association with Heinemann Medical.

—— (1965c) An Analysis of Data on 'High Risk' Mothers in Relation to Perinatal Mortality. In *Report on Symposium on the Role of Obstetricians in Maternal and Child Health Programmes*. Geneva: WHO.

—— (1969) Children at Risk. *Concern* 3: 8–16.

Butler, N. R. and Alberman, E. D. (eds) (1969) *Perinatal Problems: The Second Report of the 1958 British Perinatal Mortality Survey*. Edinburgh: Churchill-Livingstone.

Butler, N. R. and Bonham, D. G. (1963) *Perinatal Mortality: The First Report of the 1958 British Perinatal Mortality Survey*. Edinburgh: Churchill-Livingstone.

Butler, N. R. and Claireaux, A. E. (1962) Congenital Diaphragmatic Hernia as a Cause of Perinatal Mortality. *Lancet* 2: 1187.

Butler, N. R. and Goldstein, H. (1973) Smoking in Pregnancy and Subsequent Child Development. *British Medical Journal* 4: 573.

Butler, N. R. and Pringle, M. K. (1966) Prevention of Handicaps in Children. *Maternal and Child Care* 2, 17: 237–42.

Butler, N. R., Goldstein, H., and Ross, E. M. (1971) Cigarette Smoking in Pregnancy: Influence on Birth and Perinatal Mortality. *British Medical Journal* 1: 127–30.

Butler, N. R., Peckham, C., and Sheridan, M. D. (1973) Speech Defects in Children Aged Seven Years: A National Study. *British Medical Journal* 1: 253–57.

Calnan, M. and Peckham, C. (1977) Incidence of Insulin-dependent Diabetes in the First Sixteen Years of Life. *Lancet* 1: 89–90.

Calnan, M. and Richardson, K. (1976a) Speech Problems in a National Sample, Part I: Associations with Hearing, Handedness and Therapy. *Community Health* 8: 101–05.

—— (1976b) Developmental Correlates of Handedness. *Journal of Human Biology* 3, 4: 329–42.

—— (1976c) Speech Problems in a National Survey: Assessment and Prevalence. *Child: Care, Health and Development* 2, 4: 181–202.

—— (1977) Speech Problems among Children in a National Survey—Associations with Reading, General Ability, Mathematics and Syntactic Maturity. *Educational Studies* 3, 1: 55–66.

Calnan, M., Douglas, J. W. B., and Goldstein, H. (1978) Tonsillectomy and Circumcision—A Comparison of Two Cohorts. *International Journal of Epidemiology* 7: 79–85.

Crellin, E., Kellmer Pringle, M. L., and West, P. J. (1971) *Born Illegitimate: Social and Educational Implications*. London: National Foundation for Educational Research in England and Wales, for the National Children's Bureau.

Davie, R. (1966) *Summary of the National Child Development Study.* London: National Bureau for Co-operation in Child Care.

────── (1967) Summary of the First Report of the National Child Development Study. Special Education: *Forward Trends* 2, 1: 5–13.

────── (1969) The First Follow-up of the Children Born in the Control Week. In N. Butler and E. Alberman (eds) *Perinatal Problems.* Edinburgh: Churchill-Livingstone.

────── (1970) Children at Risk. *Froebel Journal:* 16.

────── (1971) Size of Class, Educational Attainment and Adjustment. *Concern* 7: 8–14.

────── (1972) Socio-biological Influences on Children's Development. In F. J. Monks (ed.) *Determinants of Behavioural Development.* London: Academic Press.

────── (1973) Eleven Years of Childhood. *Statistical News* 22: 14–18.

Davie, R., Butler, N., and Goldstein, H. (1972) *From Birth to Seven: The Second Report of the National Child Development Study (1958 Cohort).* London: Longman.

Donnison, D. (ed.) (1972) *A Pattern of Disadvantage.* Windsor: National Foundation for Educational Research.

Essen, J. (1978) Living in One-parent Families: Income and Expenditure. *Poverty* 40: 23–8.

────── (1979) Living in One-parent Families: Attainment at School. *Child: Care, Health and Development* 5, 3: 189–200.

Essen, J. and Fogelman, K. R. (1979) Childhood Housing Experiences. *Concern* 32: 5–10.

Essen, J. and Ghodsian, M. (1977) Sixteen-year-olds in Households in Receipt of Supplementary Benefits and Family Income Supplement. *Appendix to Supplementary Benefits Commission Annual Report 1976.* London: HMSO.

────── (1980) Children of Immigrants: School Performance. *New Community* 7, 3: 1–8.

Essen, J. and Lambert, L. (1977) Living in One-parent Families: Relationships and Attitudes of Sixteen-year-olds. *Child: Care, Health and Development* 3, 5: 301–18.

Essen, J. and Peckham, C. (1976) Nocturnal Enuresis in Childhood. *Developmental Medicine and Child Neurology* 18, 5: 577–89.

Essen, J. and Wedge, P. (1982) *Continuities in Childhood Disadvantage.* London: Heinemann Educational.

Essen, J., Fogelman, K. R., and Ghodsian, M. (1978) Long-term Changes in the School Attainment of a National Sample of Children. *Educational Research* 20: 2.

Essen, J., Fogelman, K. R., and Head, J. (1978a) Children's Housing and their Health and Physical Development. *Child: Care, Health and Development* 4, 6: 357–69.

────── 1978b) Childhood Housing Experiences and School Attainment. *Child: Care, Health and Development* 4, 1: 41–58.

Essen, J. Ghodsian, M. and Head, J. (1978) Psychological Cost-benefit as an Intervening Construct in Career Choice Models. *Journal of Vocational Behaviour* 12: 279–89.

Essen, J., Head, J., and Tibbenham, A. (1979) Non-academic Correlates of Ability-grouping in the Secondary School. *Educational Studies* 5, 1: 8–23.

Essen, J., Lambert, L., and Head, J. (1976) School Attainment of Children who have been in Care. *Child: Care, Health and Development* 2, 6: 339–51.

Fedrick, J. (1969) Comparison of Birth Weight/Gestation Distribution in Cases of Stillbirth and Neo-natal Death According to Lesions Found at Necropsy. *British Medical Journal* 3: 745–48.

——— (1971) Neonatal Deaths—Time of Death, Maturity and Lesion. *Biology of the Neonate* 18: 369–78.

Fedrick, J. and Alberman, E. (1972) Reported Influenza in Pregnancy and Subsequent Cancer in the Child. *British Medical Journal* 2: 485–88.

Fedrick, J. and Butler, N. R. (1970a) Certain Causes of Neonatal Death, Part I: Hyaline Membranes. *Biology of the Neonate* 15: 3–4, 229–55.

——— (1970b) Certain Causes of Neonatal Death, Part II: Intraventricular Haemorrhage. *Biology of the Neonate* 15: 5–6, 257–90.

——— (1970c) Certain Causes of Neonatal Death, Part III: Pulmonary Infection (a) Clinical Factors. *Biology of the Neonate* 17: 1–2, 458–71.

——— (1971a) Certain Causes of Neonatal Death, Part III: Pulmonary Infection (b) Pregnancy and Delivery. *Biology of the Neonate* 17: 1–2, 45–7.

——— (1971b) Certain Causes of Neonatal Death, Part IV: Massive Pulmonary Haemorrhage. *Biology of the Neonate* 18: 243–62.

——— (1971c) Certain Causes of Neonatal Death, Part V: Cerebral Birth Trauma. *Biology of the Neonate* 18: 321–29.

——— (1972) Accuracy of Registered Causes of Neonatal Deaths in 1958. *British Journal of Preventive and Social Medicine* 26, 2: 101–05.

Fedrick, J., Alberman, E., and Goldstein, H. (1971) Possible Teratogenic Effects of Cigarette Smoking. *Nature* 231, 5304: 529–30.

Ferri, E. (1972) Children in One-parent Families. In *The Parental Role*. London: National Children's Bureau.

——— (1973) Characteristics of Motherless Families. *British Journal of Social Work* 3, 1: 91–100.

——— (1974) One-parent, Single or Unmarried? *Concern* 14: 5–6.

——— (1975a) The Single-parent Family: Aspects of Children's Welfare. *Papers of the Royal Society of Health Annual Congress*: 168–70.

——— (1975b) Background and Behaviour of Children in One-parent Families. *Therapeutic Education* 3, 2: 6–10.

——— (1976a) Growing Up in a One-parent Family. *Concern* 20: 7–10.

——— (1976b) *Growing Up in a One-parent Family*. London: National Foundation for Educational Research.

——— (1976c) One-parent Families. *Journal of the Association of Workers for Maladjusted Children* 4: 1–4.

——— (1984) *Step Children: A National Study*. London: National Foundation for Educational Research in association with Nelson.

Ferri, E. and Robinson, H. (1976) *Coping Alone*. London: National Foundation for Educational Research in England and Wales, for National Children's Bureau.

Fogelman, K. R. (1975) Developmental Correlates of Family Size. *British Journal of Social Work* 5, 1: 43–57.

Fogelman, K. R. (1976a) Research Feedback—Britain's Sixteen-year-olds. *Concern* 21: 28–31.

—————— (1976b) *Britain's Sixteen-year-olds: Preliminary Findings from the Third Follow-up of the National Child Development Survey*. London: National Children's Bureau.

—————— (1978a) The Effectiveness of Schooling—Some Recent Results from the National Child Development Study. In W. H. G. Armytage and J. Peel (eds) *Perimeters of Social Repair*. London: Academic Press.

—————— (1978b) Drinking among Sixteen-year-olds. *Concern* 29: 19–25.

—————— (1978c) School Attendance, Attainment and Behaviour. *British Journal of Educational Psychology* 68, 2: 148–58.

—————— (1979) Educational and Career Aspirations—Findings from a National Sample of Sixteen-year-olds. *British Journal of Guidance Counselling* 7: 1.

—————— (1980a) Smoking and Health. *Concern* 37: 25–9.

—————— (1980b) Smoking in Pregnancy and Subsequent Development of the Child. *Child Care, Health and Development* 6, 4: 233–51.

—————— (ed.) (1983) *Growing Up in Great Britain: Collected Papers from the National Child Development Study*. London: Macmillan.

—————— (1984a) Exploiting Longitudinal Data: Examples from the National Child Development Study. In A. R. Nicol (ed.) *Longitudinal Studies in Child Psychology and Psychiatry*. Chichester: John Wiley.

—————— (1984b) Progress and Employment of Handicapped Children. In N. R. Butler and B. D. Corner. *Stress and Disability in Childhood*. Bristol: John Wright.

Fogelman, K. R. and Goldstein, H. (1976) Social Factors Associated with Changes in Educational Attainment between 7 and 11 Years of Age. *Educational Studies* 2, 2: 95–109.

Fogelman, K. R., Essen, J., and Tibbenham, A. (1978) Ability Grouping in Secondary Schools and Attainment. *Educational Studies* 4, 3: 201–12.

Fogelman, K. R., Goldstein, H., Essen, J., and Ghodsian, M. (1978) Pattern of Attainment. *Educational Studies* 4, 2: 12–30.

Goldstein, H. and Peckham, C. (1976) Birthweight, Gestation, Neonatal Mortality and Child Development. In D. F. Roberts and A. M. Thomas (eds) *The Biology of Human Fetal Growth*. London: Taylor and Francis.

Goldstein, H. and Wedge, P. (1975) The British National Child Development Study. *World Health Statistics Report* 28, 5: 202–11.

Hitchfield, E. (1974) *In Search of Promise*. London: Longman, in association with National Children's Bureau.

Hutchison, D., Prosser, H., and Wedge, P. J. (1979) Prediction of Educational Failure. *Educational Studies* 5, 1: 56–65.

Kellmer Pringle, M., Butler, N. R., and Davie, R. (1966) *11,000 Seven-year-olds. First Report of the National Child Development Study*. London: Longmans.

Kurtz, Z. (1984) Migraine in Children: Results from the National Child Development Study. In F. C. Rose (ed.) *Progress in Migraine Research*. London: Pitman Medical.

Lambert, L. (1977) Sex and Parenthood: Sources of Information for Teenagers. *Health and Social Services Journal* 77: 4536.

—————— (1978a) Living in One-parent Families: Leaving School and Future Plans for Work. *Concern*: 29–33.

—————— (1978b) Careers Guidance and Choosing a Job. *British Journal of Guidance*

Counselling 6: 2–7.

—— (1978c) Living in One-parent Families: School Leavers and their Future. *Concern* 29: 26–30.

—— (1980) Children in Changing Families. *Concern* 37: 12–15.

—— (1981) Adopted from Care by the Age of Seven. *Adoption and Fostering* 105: 28–36.

Lambert, L. and Hart, S. (1976) Who Needs a Father? *New Society* 37, 718: 80.

Lambert, L., Essen, J., and Head, J. (1977) Variations in Behaviour Ratings of Children who have been in Care. *Journal of Child Psychology and Psychiatry* 18: 335–46.

Lambert, L. and Pearson, R. (1977a) Sex Education, Preparation for Parenthood and the Adolescent. *Community Health* 9, 2: 84–90.

—— (1977b) Sex Education in Schools. *Journal of the Institute of Health Education* 5: 4–8.

Lambert, L. and Streather, J. (1980) *Children in Changing Families*. London: Macmillan.

Mapstone, E. (1969) Children in Care. *Concern* 3: 23–8.

Newens, E. and Goldstein, H. (1972) Height, Weight and the Assessment of Obesity in Children. *British Journal of Preventive and Social Medicine* 26, 1: 33–9.

Pearson, J. S. and Peckham, C. (1972) Preliminary Findings at the age of Eleven Years on Children in the National Child Development Study (1958 Cohort). *Community Medicine* 27: 113–16.

Pearson, R. and Peckham, C. (1977) Handicapped Children in Secondary Schools from the National Child Development Study (1958 Cohort). *Public Health* 91: 296–304.

Pearson, R. and Richardson, K. (1978) Smoking Habits of 16-Year-Olds in the National Child Development Study. *Public Health* 92: 3–10.

Peckham, C. (1973a) Speech Defects in a National Sample of Children Aged Seven Years. *British Journal of Disorders of Communication* 8: 1–8.

—— (1973b) A National Study of Child Development. Preliminary Findings in a National Sample of 11 Year Old Children. *Proceedings of the Royal Society of Medicine* 1, 2: 93–106.

Peckham, C. and Adams, B. (1975) Vision Screening in a Sample of 11 Year Old Children. *Child: Care Health and Development* 11, 2: 93–106.

Peckham, C. and Butler, N. (1978) A National Study of Asthma in Childhood. *Journal of Epidemiology and Community Health* 32, 2: 79–85.

Peckham, C. and Gardiner, P. (1977) Acquired Myopia in 11-Year-Old Children. *British Medical Journal* 1, 6060: 542–45.

Peckham, C. and Pearson, R. (1976a) Handicapped Eleven-year-olds. *Concern* 19: 27–9.

—— (1976b) The Prevalence and Nature of Ascertained Handicap in the National Child Development Study (1958 Cohort). *Public Health* 90: 111–21.

—— (1976c) Preliminary Findings at the Age of 16 Years on Children in the National Child Development Study (1958 Cohort). *Public Health* 91: 286–90.

—— (1977) Handicapped Children in Secondary Schools. *Public Health* 91: 296–304.

Peckham, C. S. and Sheridan, M. (1976) Follow Up at 11 Years of 46 Children with

Severe Unilateral Hearing Loss at 7 Years. *Child: Care, Health and Development* 2, 2: 107–11.

Peckham, C., Gardiner, P., and Tibbenham, A. (1979) Vision Screening of Adolescents and their Use of Glasses. *British Medical Journal* 1, 6171: 1111–113.

Peckham, C., Marshall, W., and Dudgeon, D. (1977) Rubella Vaccination of School-Girls: Factors Affecting Vaccine Uptake. *British Medical Journal* 1, 6063: 760–61.

Peckham, C. S., Sheridan, M. D., and Butler, N. R. (1972) School Attainment of Seven-Year-Old Children with Hearing Difficulties. *Developmental Medicine and Child Neurology* 14, 5: 592–602.

Peckham, C., Stark, O., Simonite, V., and Wolff, O. H. (1983) Prevalence of Obesity in British Children Born in 1946 and 1958. *British Medical Journal* 286: 1237–242.

Pringle, M. K. (1967) Follow-up of Adopted Children. *Journal of the Medical Women's Federation* 43, 3: 146–48.

———— (1970) Scotland for Good Parents and Happy Children. *Times Educational Supplement* Jan. 9: 4.

———— (1972) Born Illegitimate. *Concern* 8: 7–13.

Prosser, H. (1973) Family Size and Children's Development. *Health and Social Services Journal* 432: 11–12.

Richardson, K. (1977a) The Writing Productivity and Syntactic Maturity of Eleven-year-olds in Relation to their Reading Habits. *Reading* 11: 46–53.

———— (1977b) Reading Attainment and Family Size: an Anomaly. *British Journal of Educational Psychology* 47, 1: 71–5.

Richardson, K., Peckham, C., and Goldstein, H. (1976) Hearing Levels of Children Tested at Seven and Eleven: a National Study. *British Journal of Audiology* 10, 4: 117–23.

Richardson, K., Calnan, M., Essen, J., and Lambert, L. (1976) The Linguistic Maturity of Eleven Year Olds. *Journal of Child Language* 3.1: 99–115.

Richardson, K., Hutchison, D., Peckham, C., and Tibbenham, A. (1977) Audiometric Thresholds of a National Sample of British Sixteen-year-olds: A Longitudinal Study. *Developmental Medicine and Child Neurology* 19, 6: 797–802.

Robinson, H. (1975) Lone Parenthood. *Concern* 18: 26–31.

Ross, E. M. (1969) 16,000 Home Visits. *Nursing Times* 27 November: 1511–513.

———— (1973a) Convulsive Disorders in British Children. *Proceedings of the Royal Society of Medicine* 66, 7: 703–70.

———— (1973b) Some Nutritional Aspects of Large-scale Prospective Studies in Child Development. In D. Hollingsworth and M. Russell (eds) *Nutritional Problems in a Changing World*. Barking: Applied Science Publications.

Ross, E. M., Peckham, C., West, P., and Butler, N. (1980) Epilepsy in Childhood: Findings from the National Child Development Study. *British Medical Journal* 280, 6209: 207.

Seglow, J., Kellmer Pringle, M. L., and Wedge, P. (1972) *Growing Up Adopted*. London: National Foundation for Educational Research in England and Wales with National Children's Bureau.

Shepherd, P. (1980) The National Child Development Study (1958 Cohort) at Twenty. *Concern* 37: 20–4.

Sheridan, M. D. (1972) Reported Incidence of Hearing Loss in Children of Seven Years. *Developmental Medicine and Child Neurology* 14, 3: 296–303.

——— (1973) Children of Seven Years with Marked Speech Defects. *British Journal of Disorders of Communication* 8, 1: 9–16.

Sheridan, M. D. and Peckham, C. S. (1975) Follow-up at Eleven Years of Children who had Marked Speech Defects at Seven Years. *Child: Care, Health and Development* 1, 3: 157–66.

——— (1978) A Follow-up to 16 Years of School Children who had Marked Speech Defects at 7 years. *Child: Care, Health and Development* 4, 3: 145–57.

Steedman, J. (1980) *Progress in Secondary Schools*. London: National Children's Bureau.

——— (1983) *Examination Results in Selective and Non-Selective Secondary Schools*. London: National Children's Bureau.

Tibbenham, A., Essen, J., and Fogelman, K. (1978) Ability Grouping and School Characteristics. *British Journal of Educational Studies* 26, 1: 8–23.

Tibbenham, A., Peckham, C., and Gardiner, P. (1978) Vision Screening in Children Tested at 7, 11 and 16 Years. *British Medical Journal* 1, 6123: 1312–314.

Walker, A. (1980) The Handicapped School-leaver and the Transition to Work. *British Journal of Guidance Counselling* 8, 2: 212–23.

——— (1982a) The Handicap Stakes. *New Society* 60, 1020: 383–84.

——— (1982b) *Unqualified and Underemployed: Handicapped Young People and the Labour Market*. London: Macmillan.

Walker, A. and Lewis, P. (1977) Career Advice and Employment Experiences of a Small Group of Handicapped School-leavers. *Careers Quarterly* 29: 5–14.

Wedge, P. (1969) The Second Follow-up of the National Child Development Study. *Concern* 3: 34–9.

——— (1973) Children and the Cycle of Deprivation. *Family Services Unit Quarterly* 4: 8.

——— (1974) Social Disadvantage—The Facts and the Practitioner. *Concern* 13: 6–7.

——— (1977) Children at Risk—A Pattern of Disadvantage. In *CARE Planning for our Children: Report of a CARE Conference*. Dublin.

Wedge, P. and Essen, J. (1982) *Children in Adversity*. London: Pan.

Wedge, P. and Prosser, H. (1973) *Born to Fail?* London: Arrow Books and the National Children's Bureau.

Wedge, P., Alberman, E., and Goldstein, H. (1970) Health and Height in Children. *New Society* 16, 428: 1044–045.

Whitehead, L. (1977) Research Feedback—Early Parenthood. *Concern* 24: 28–30.

——— (1979) Sex Differences in Children's Responses to Family Stress: A Re-evaluation. *Journal of Child Psychology and Psychiatry* 20, 3: 247–54.

Study 6: Child Health and Education Study

Atkinson, S., and Butler, N. R. (1985) Vision Problems in Under-fives. In S. Harel and N. J. Anastasion (eds) *The At-Risk Infant: Psycho/Socio/Medical Aspects*. London: Paul Brookes.

Britten, N. and Heath, A. (1983) Women, Men and Social Class. In E. Gamarnikow,

D. Morgan, J. Purvis, and D. Taylorson (eds) *Gender, Class and Work*. London: Heinemann.

Butler, N. R. (1977) Family and Community Influences on 0–5s: Utilisation of Preschool Day-care and Preventive Health care. 0–5s: A Changing Population; Implications for Parents, the Public and Policymakers. In *Papers from a Seminar of the Institute of Child Health, University of London, 20 May 1977*. London: Voluntary Organisations' Liaison Council for Under Fives. Pages 30–62.

—— (1980) Child Health and Education in the Seventies: Some Results on the Five-year Follow-up of the 1970 British Birth Cohort. *Health Visitor* 53: 81–2.

Butler, N. R., Golding, J., and Howlett, B. C. (eds) (1985) *From Birth to Five: A Study of the Health and Behaviour of a National Cohort*. Oxford: Pergamon.

Butler, N.R., Taylor, B., and Wadsworth, J. (1981) *Teenage Mothering*. Report to the Department of Health and Social Security. Bristol: Department of Child Health, University of Bristol.

Butler, N. R., Golding, J., Haslum, M., and Stewart-Brown, S. (1982a) Recent findings from the 1970 Child Health and Education Study (Section of Epidemiology and Community Medicine, meeting held 11 February 1982). *Journal of the Royal Society of Medicine* 75: 781–84.

Butler, N. R., Haslum, M. N., Barker, W., and Morris, A. C. (1982b) *Child Health and Education Study*. First report to the Department of Education and Science on the Ten-year Follow-up. Bristol: Department of Child Health, University of Bristol.

Butler, N. R., Haslum, M. N., Howlett, B. C., Stewart-Brown, S. (1983) *Child Health and Education Study: A Collection of Papers from the Ten-year Follow-up*. Report to the Department of Health and Social Security. Bristol: Department of Child Health, University of Bristol.

Butler, N. R., Haslum, M. N., Stewart-Brown, S., Howlett, B. C., Prosser, H., Brewer, R., Porter, C. M., and Lyons, P. J. (1982c) *Child Health and Education Study*. First report to the Department of Health and Social Security on the Ten-year Follow-up. Bristol: Department of Child Health, University of Bristol.

Chamberlain, G. V. P., Phillip, E., Howlett, B. C., and Masters, K. (1978) *British Births 1970, Volume II: Obstetric Care*. London: Heinemann.

Chamberlain, R. and Davey, A. (1975) Physical Growth in Twins, Postmature and Small-for-dates Children. *Archives of Disease in Childhood* 50: 437–42.

—— (1976) Cross-sectional Study of Developmental Test Items in Children Aged 94 to 97 Weeks: Report of the British Births Child Study. *Developmental Medicine and Child Neurology* 18: 54–70.

Chamberlain, R. and Simpson, R. N. (1979) *The Prevalence of Illness in Childhood*. Tunbridge Wells: Pitman Medical.

Chamberlain, R., Chamberlain, G., Howlett, B. C., and Claireaux, A. (1975) *British Births 1970, Volume I: The First Week of Life*. London: Heinemann.

Cook, K. and Lawton, D. (1985) Housing Circumstances and Standards of Families with Disabled Children. *Child: Care, Health and Development* 11: 71–9.

Dowling, S. F. O. (1977) The Interrelationship of Children's Use of Child Health Clinics and Day-care Facilities in the Preschool Years. In *Papers from a Seminar of The Institute of Child Health, University of London, 20 May 1977*. London: Voluntary Organisations' Liaison Council for Under Fives. Pages 63–7.

Golding, J. (1983) Accidents in the Under-fives. *Health Visitor* 56: 203–04.

———— (1984) Britain's National Cohort Studies. In J. A. Macfarlane (ed.) *Progress in Child Health Number 1*. Edinburgh: Churchill-Livingstone.

———— (in press) Cross-cultural Correlates of Ill-health in Childhood. *Society and Biology*.

Golding, J. and Butler, N. R. (1983) Convulsive Disorders in the Child Health and Education Study. In F. Clifford Rose (ed.) *Epilepsy*. London: Pitman.

———— (1984a) The Socioeconomic Factor. In F. Falkner (ed.) *Prevention of Perinatal Mortality and Morbidity*. Basel: Karger.

———— (1984b) Wheezing and Stress. In N. R. Butler and B. D. Corner (eds) *Stress and Disability in Childhood: The Long-term Problems*. Bristol: John Wright.

Golding, J. and Porter, C. (1982) The National Cohort Studies. *Health Visitor* 55, 12: 639–43.

Golding, J., Hicks, P., and Butler, N.R. (1982) *Eczema in the First Five Years*. Bristol: Department of Child Health, University of Bristol.

———— (1984) Blood Groups and Socioeconomic Class. *Nature* 31 May: 309.

Golding, J., Howlett, B. C., and Butler, N. R. (1981) *Immunisation Reactions and Long-term Follow-up*. Report to the Department of Health and Social Security. Bristol: Department of Child Health, University of Bristol.

Haslum, M. N. (1978) *Some Origins of Handicap and Disadvantage in Young Children*. Report to Action Research for the Crippled Child. (Unpublished.)

Haslum, M. N., Morris, A. C., and Golding, J. (1984) What Do Our Ten-year-old Children Eat? *Health Visitor* 57: 178–79.

Osborn, A. F. (1984) Maternal Employment, Depression and Child Behaviour. *Equal Opportunities Commission Research Bulletin* 8: 48–67.

Osborn, A. F. and Butler, N. R. (1985) *Ethnic Minority Children: A Comparative Study from Birth to Five Years*. London: Commission for Racial Equality.

Osborn, A. F. and Milbank, J. E. (1985) *The Association of Preschool Educational Experience with Subsequent Ability, Attainment and Behaviour*. Report to the Department of Education and Science. Bristol: Department of Child Health, University of Bristol.

Osborn, A. F. and Morris, A. C. (1979) The Rationale for a Composite Index of Social Class and its Evaluation. *British Journal of Sociology* 30, 1: 39–60.

———— (1982) Fathers and Child Care. *Early Child Development and Care* 8: 279–307.

Osborn, A. F., Morris, A. C., and Butler, N. R. (1979) *Regional Study of Children Born 5–11 April, 1970*. Report to the Social Science Research Council.

Osborn, A. F., Wadsworth, J., and Butler, N. R. (1983) *Ethnic Minority Children—A Comparative Study from Birth to Five Years, Volumes I and II*. Report to the Commission for Racial Equality. Bristol: Department of Child Health, University of Bristol.

Peters, T. J., Golding, J., and Butler, N. R. (1985) Breastfeeding and Childhood Eczema. *Lancet* 5 January: 49–50.

Peters, T. J., Golding, J., Butler, N. R., Fryer, J. G., Lawrence, C. J., and Chamberlain, G. V. P. (1983) Plus ça Change: Predictors of Birthweight in Two National Studies. *British Journal of Obstetrics and Gynaecology* 90: 1040–045.

Peters, T. J., Golding, J., Lawrence, C. J., Fryer, J. G., Chamberlain, G. V. P., and Butler, N. R. (1984) Factors Associated with Delayed Onset of Regular Respiration. *Early Human Development* 9: 209–23.

———— (1984) Delayed Onset of Regular Respiration and Subsequent Development. *Early Human Development* 9: 225–39.

Rush, D. and Cassano, P. (1983) Relationship of Cigarette Smoking and Social Class to Birthweight and Perinatal Mortality Among All Births in Britain, 5–11 April 1970. *Journal of Epidemiology and Community Health* 37: 249–55.

St Claire, L. and Osborn, A. F. (1985) *Ability and Behaviour of Children in Care or Separated from Parents.* Report to the Economic and Social Research Council. Bristol: Department of Child Health, University of Bristol.

Stewart-Brown, S., Haslum, M. N., and Butler, N. R. (1983) Evidence for an Increasing Prevalence of Diabetes Mellitus in Childhood. *British Medical Journal* 286: 1855–857.

Taylor, B. (1983) Social Factors and Related Influences on Lower Respiratory Illness of Early Childhood. *Respiratory Disease in Practice* 1: 30–5.

Taylor, B. and Wadsworth, J. (1984) Breastfeeding and Child Development at Five Years. *Developmental Medicine and Child Neurology* 26: 73–80.

Taylor, B., Wadsworth, J. and Butler, N. R. (1983) Teenage Mothering, Admission to Hospital, and Accidents during the First Five Years. *Archives of Disease in Childhood* 58: 6–11.

Taylor, B., Wadsworth, J., Golding, J., and Butler, N. R. (1982) Breastfeeding, Bronchitis and Admissions for Lower Respiratory Illness and Gastroenteritis during the First Five Years. *Lancet* 1: 1227–229.

———— (1983) Breastfeeding, Eczema, Asthma and Hayfever. *Journal of Epidemiology and Community Health* 37: 95–9.

Taylor, B., Wadsworth, J., Wadsworth, M. E. J., and Peckham, C. (1984) Changes in the Reported Prevalence of Childhood Eczema since the 1939–45 War. *Lancet* 2: 1255–257.

Tissier, G. (1983) Bedwetting at Five Years of Age. *Health Visitor* 56: 333–35.

Verity, C. M., Butler, N. R., and Golding, J. (1985) Febrile Conclusions in a National Cohort Followed Up from Birth, 1: Prevalence and Recurrence in the First Five Years of Life. *British Medical Journal* 290: 1307–315.

Wadsworth, M. E. J., Burnell, I., Taylor, B., and Butler, N. R. (1983) Family Type and Accidents in Preschool Children. *Journal of Epidemiology and Community Health* 37: 100–04.

Wadsworth, M. E. J., Taylor, B., Osborn, A., and Butler, N. R. (1984) Teenage Mothering: Child Development at Five Years. *Journal of Child Psychology and Psychiatry* 25: 305–14.

Study 7: National Study of Health and Growth

Altman, D. G. and Cook, J. (1973) A Nutritional Surveillance Study. *Proceedings of the Royal Society of Medicine* 66: 646–47.

Altman, D. G. and Irwig, I. M. (1975) Men, Women and Obesity (letter to the Editor). *British Medical Journal* 1: 573–74.

Chinn, S. and Morris, R. W. (1980) Standard of Weight-for-height for English Children 5–11 Years. *Annals of Human Biology* 7: 457–71.

Chinn, S. and Rona, R. J. (1984) The Secular Trend in the Height of Primary School Children in England and Scotland 1972–1980. *Annals of Human Biology* 11: 1–16.

Cook, J., Irwig, L. M., Chinn, S., Altman, D. G., and Florey, C. du V. (1979) The Influence of Availability of Free School Milk on the Height of Children in England and Scotland. *Journal of Epidemiology and Community Health* 33: 171–76.

Foster, J. M., Chinn, S., and Rona, R. J. (1983) The Relation of the Height of Primary School Children to Population Density. *International Journal of Epidemiology* 12: 199–204.

Garman, A. R., Chinn, S., and Rona, R. J. (1982) The Comparative Growth of Primary School Children from One and Two Parent Families. *Archives of Disease in Childhood* 57: 453–58.

Holland, W. W., Chinn, S., and Rona, R. J. (1980) The Effect of Cessation of Free School Milk. In S. H. Davies (ed.) *Symposium on Nutrition 1979 in the Royal College of Physicians of Edinburgh*. Edinburgh: Royal College of Physicians.

Holland, W. W., Chinn, S., and Wainwright, A. (1980) Weight and Blood Pressure in Children. In R. M. Lauer and P. B. Shekelle (eds) *Childhood Prevention of Atherosclerosis and Hypertension*. New York: Raven.

Holland, W. W., Beresford, S. A. A., Bewley, B. R., Florey, C. du V., and Rona, R. J. (1978) The Very Early Recognition of Coronary Heart Disease—Epidemiology of Risk Factors in Early Life. In L. McDonald, J. Goodwin, and L. Resuckov (eds) *Very Early Recognition of Coronary Disease*. Amsterdam: Excerpta Medica.

Holland, W. W., Rona, R. J., Chinn, S., Altman, D. G., Irwig, L. M., Cook, J., and Florey, C. du V. (1981) The National Study of Health and Growth, Surveillance of Primary School Children (1972–1976). In Department of Health and Social Security, *Report on Health and Social Subjects, No. 21: Sub-committee on Nutritional Surveillance; Second Report*. London: HMSO.

Irwig, L. M. (1976) Surveillance in Developed Countries with Particular Reference to Child Growth. *International Journal of Epidemiology* 5: 57–61.

Morris, R. W. and Chinn, S. (1981) Weight-for-height as a Measure of Obesity in English Children 5 to 11 Years Old. *International Journal of Obesity* 5: 359–66.

Rona, R. J. (1980) The Nutritional Study of Health and Growth (NSHG): Surveillance on Nutritional Status of Primary Schoolchildren. *Health Visitor* 53: 309–12.

——— (1981) Genetic and Environmental Factors in the Control of Growth in Childhood. *British Medical Bulletin* 37: 265–72.

——— (1984) Ecological Environment: Environmental and Physical Growth; Random Comments on Ferr-Luzzi's Overview. In *Proceedings of the Symposium 'Genetical and Environmental Factors during the Growth Period'*. Brussels: Plenum.

Rona, R. J. and Altman, D. G. (1977) National Study of Health and Growth: Standards of Attained Height, Weight and Triceps Skinfold in English Children 5–11 Years Old. *Annals of Human Biology* 4: 501–23.

Rona, R. J. and Chinn, S. (1982a) National Study of Health and Growth: Social and Family Factors and Obesity in Primary Schoolchildren. *Annals of Human Biology* 9: 137–45.

——— (1982b) Nutritional and Social Circumstances of Primary Schoolchildren: Proceedings of the British Nutrition Foundation 3rd Annual Conference. In M. R. Turner (ed.) *Nutrition and Health: A Perspective*. Pages 147–56. Lancaster: MTP Press.

——— (1984a) The National Study of Health and Growth: Nutritional Surveillance of Primary Schoolchildren 1972–81 with Special Reference to Unemployment and Social Class. *Annals of Human Biology* 11: 17–28.

—— (1984b) Parents' Attitudes Towards School Meals for Primary Schoolchildren in 1981. *Human Nutrition: Applied Nutrition* 38A: 187–98.

Rona, R. J. and Florey, C. du V. (1980) National Study of Health and Growth: Respiratory Symptoms and Height in Primary Schoolchildren. *International Journal of Epidemiology* 9: 35–43.

Rona, R. J. and Morris, R. W. (1982) National Study of Health and Growth: Social and Family Factors and Overweight in English and Scottish Parents. *Annals of Human Biology* 9: 147–56.

Rona, R. J., Chinn, S., and Florey, C. du V. (1985) Exposure to Cigarette Smoking and Child's Growth. *International Journal of Epidemiology* 14: 402–09.

Rona, R. J., Chinn, S., and Smith, A. M. (1979) Height of Children Receiving Free School Meals (letter to the Editor). *Lancet* 11: 534.

—— (1983) School Meals and the Rate of Growth of Primary Schoolchildren. *Journal of Epidemiology and Community Health* 37: 8–15.

Rona, R. J., Swan, A. V., and Altman, D. G. (1978) Social Factors and Height of Primary Schoolchildren in England and Scotland. *Journal of Epidemiology and Community Medicine* 7: 115–24.

Rona, R. J., Chinn, S., Marshall, B. S. M., and Eames, M. (1983) Growth Status and the Risk of Contracting Primary Tuberculosis. *Archives of Disease in Childhood* 58: 359–61.

Rona, R. J., Florey, C. du V., Clarke, G. C., and Chinn, S. (1981) Parental Smoking at Home and Height of Children. *British Medical Journal* 283: 1363.

Rona, R. J., Barney, A., Altman, D., Irwig, L., and Florey, C. du V. (1979) Surveillance of Growth as an Index of Health in the Community. In W. W. Holland, J. Iper, and J. Kostrewski (eds) *Measurement of Levels of Health*. Copenhagen: WHO Regional Office for Europe.

Smith, A. M., Chinn, S., and Rona, R. (1980) Social Factors and Height Gain of Primary Schoolchildren in England and Scotland. *Annals of Human Biology* 7: 115–24.

Somerville, S. M., Rona, R. J., and Chinn, S. (1984) Obesity and Respiratory Symptoms in Primary School. *Archives of Disease in Childhood* 59: 940–44.

Study 8: National Surveillance of Growth in Pre-school Children

Fox, P. T., Elston, M. D., and Waterlow, J. W. (1981) *DHSS Report on Health and Social Subjects, No. 21. Second Report by the Sub-Committee on Nutritional Surveillance*. London: HMSO.

Study 9: Newcastle Thousand Families Survey

Kolvin, I., Miller, F. J. W., Garside, R. F., and Gatzanis, S. R. M. (1983a) One Thousand Families over Three Generations: Method and Some Preliminary Findings. In N. Madge (ed.) *Families at Risk*. London: Heinemann Educational.

Kolvin, I., Miller, F. J. W., Garside, R. F., Wolstenholme, F., and Gatzanis, S. R. M. (1983b) A Longitudinal Study of Deprivation: Life Cycle Changes in One Generation—Implications for the Next Generation. In M. H. Schmidt and H. Remschmidt (eds) *Epidemiology Approaches in Child Psychiatry II*. Stuttgart and New York: G. Thieme.

Kolvin, I., Miller, F. J. W., Garside, R. F., Gatzanis, S. R. M., and McI. Scott, D. (1985) Parent, Child, Grandchild: The Transmission of Disadvantage. In J. Anthony (ed.) *The Child in his Family: Volume 8 of the International Year Book*. New York: Wiley.

Miller, F. J. W., Billewicz, W. Z., and Thomson, A. M. (1972) Growth from Birth to Adult Life of 442 Newcastle-upon-Tyne Schoolchildren. *British Journal of Preventive and Social Medicine* 26: 224–30.

Miller, F. J. W., Kolvin, I., and Fells, H. (1985) Becoming Deprived: A Cross-generation Study Based on the Newcastle-upon-Tyne 1000 Family Survey. In A. R. Nicol (ed.) *Longitudinal Studies in Child Psychology and Child Psychiatry: Practical Lessons from Research Experiences*. Chichester: John Wiley.

Miller, F. J. W., Court, S. D. M., Knox, E. G., and Brandon, S. (1974) *The School Years in Newcastle-upon-Tyne*. London: Oxford University Press.

Miller, F. J. W., Court, S. D. M., Walton, W. S., and Knox, E. G. (1960) *Growing Up in Newcastle-upon-Tyne*. London: Oxford University Press.

Spence, J., Walton, W. A., Miller, F. J. W., and Court, S. D. M. (1954) *A Thousand Families in Newcastle-upon-Tyne: An Approach to the Study of Health and Illness in Children*. London: Oxford University Press.

Study 10: Aberdeen Child Development Survey

Illsley, R. (1967) The Sociological Study of Reproduction and its Outcome. In S. A. Richardson and A. F. Guttmacher (eds) *Childbearing—Its Social and Psychological Aspects*. Baltimore, Md: Williams and Wilkins.

Illsley, R. and Wilson, F. (1981) The Aberdeen Child Development Survey. In S. A. Mednick and A. E. Baert (eds) *Prospective Longitudinal Research*. Oxford: Oxford University Press.

Oldman, D., Bytheway, W., and Horobin, G. (1971) Family Structure and Educational Achievement. *Journal of Biosocial Science* 3: 81–91.

Study 11: MRC Derbyshire Schoolchildren Smoking Study

Banks, M. H., Bewley, B. R., and Bland, J. M. (1981) Adolescent Attitudes to Smoking: Their Influence on Behaviour. *International Journal of Health Education* 24, 1: 39–44.

Banks, M. H., Bewley, B. R., Bland, J. M., Dean, J. R., and Pollard, V. (1978) Long-term Study of Smoking by Secondary Schoolchildren. *Archives of Disease in Childhood* 53, 1: 12–19.

Bewley, B. R. (1978) Smoking in Childhood. *Postgraduate Medical Journal* 54: 197–99.

Bewley, B. R. and Bland, J. M. (1976) Smoking and Respiratory Symptoms in Two Groups of Schoolchildren. *Preventive Medicine* 5: 63–9.

——— (1977) Academic Performance and Social Factors Related to Cigarette Smoking by Schoolchildren. *British Journal of Preventive and Social Medicine* 31: 18–24.

——— (1978) The Child's Image of a Young Smoker. *Health Education Journal* 37: 236–41.

Bewley, B. R., Johnson, M. R. D., and Banks, M. H. (1979) Teacher's Smoking. *Journal of Epidemiology and Community Health* 33: 219–22.

Bland, J. M., Bewley, B. R., Pollard, V., and Banks, M. H. (1978) Effect of Children's and Parents' Smoking on Respiratory Symptoms. *Archives of Disease in Childhood* 53, 2: 100–05.

Holland, W. W. and Elliott, A. (1968) Cigarette Smoking, Respiratory Symptoms and Anti-smoking Propaganda. *Lancet* 1: 41–3.

Holland, W. W., Halil, T., Benett, A. E., and Elliott, A. (1969) Indications for Measures to be Taken in Childhood to Prevent Chronic Respiratory Disease. *Milbank Memorial Fund Quarterly* XLVII, 3, 2: 215–27.

Johnson, M. R. D., Murray, M., Bewley, B. R., Clyde, D. C., Banks, M. H., and Swan, A. V. (1982) Social Class, Parents, Children and Smoking. *Bulletin of the International Union against Tuberculosis* 57: 3–4, 258–62.

Murray, M., Kiryluk, S., and Swan, A. V. (1984) School Characteristics and Adolescent Smoking: Results from the MRC/Derbyshire Smoking Study 197408 and from a Follow-up in 1981. *Journal of Epidemiology and Community Health* 38: 167–72.

Murray, M., Swan, A. V., Bewley, B. R., and Johnson, M. R. D. (1983) The Development of Smoking during Adolescence—the MRC/Derbyshire Smoking Study. *International Journal of Epidemiology* 12: 185–92.

Murray, M., Swan, A.V., Johnson, M. R. D., and Bewley, B.R. (1983) Some Factors Associated with Increased Risk of Smoking by Children. *Journal of Child Psychology and Psychiatry* 24: 223–32.

Study 12: Aberdeen Styles of Ageing Study

Ford, G. (1984) Illness Behaviour in the Elderly. In K. Dean and B. Holstein (eds) *Self-care in Old Age*. Cambridge: Cambridge University Press.

Ford, G. and Taylor, R. (1983) Risk Groups and Selective Case Findings in an Elderly Population. *Social Science and Medicine* 17: 10–17.

——— (1984) Differential Ageing: An Exploratory Approach Using Cluster Analysis. *International Journal of Ageing and Human Development* 18, 2: 144–56.

——— (1985) The Elderly as Underconsulters: A Critical Reappraisal. *Journal of the Royal College of General Practitioners* 35: 244–47.

Taylor, R. and Ford, G. (1979) A Coping Model for a Longitudinal Study of the Elderly. In M. Johnson (ed.) *Transitions in Middle and Later Life*. London: British Society of Gerontology.

——— (1981) Life-style and Ageing. *Ageing and Society* 1, 3: 329–45.

——— (1983a) Inequalities in Old Age: An Examination of Age, Sex and Class Differences in a Sample of Community Elderly. *Ageing and Society* 3, 2: 183–208.

——— (1983b) The Elderly at Risk: A Critical Examination of Commonly Identified Risk Groups. *Journal of the Royal College of General Practitioners* 33: 669–705.

Taylor, R. and Ford, G. (1983c) *Arthritis/Rheumatism in the Community*. Report to Scottish Home and Health Dept, Edinburgh.

———— (1984) Arthritis/Rheumatism in an Elderly Population: Prevalence and Service Use. *Health Bulletin* 42: 5–8.

Taylor, R., Ford, G., and Barber, H. (1983) *The Elderly at Risk*. Age Concern Research Monograph No. 6. London.

———— (1984) *Approaches to Screening and Case Finding in Elderly Populations*. Report to WHO (Europe).

Study 14: Mothers at Risk

Ghodsian, M., Zajicek, E., and Wolkind, S. N. (1984) A Longitudinal Study of Maternal Deprivation and Child Behaviour Problems. *Journal of Child Psychology and Psychiatry* 25: 97–109.

Hall, F. and Pawlby, S. J. (1981) Continuity and Discontinuity in the Behaviour of British Working-class Mothers and their First-born Children. *International Journal of Behaviour and Development* 4: 13–36.

Holt, G. and Wolkind, S. N. (1983) Failure to Continue Breast-feeding. *Child: Care, Health and Development* 9: 349–55.

Kruk, S. and Wolkind, S. N. (1983) A Longitudinal Study of Single Mothers and their Children. In N. Madge (ed.) *Families at Risk*. London: Heinemann Educational.

Pawlby, S. J. and Hall, F. (1979) Evidence from an Observational Study of Transmitted Deprivation among Women from Broken Homes. *Child Abuse and Neglect* 3: 844–50.

Wolkind, S. N. (1985) The First Years: Pre-school Children and their Families in the Inner City. In J. Stevenson (ed.) *Aspects of Current Child Psychiatry Research*. JCPP Book Supplement No. 4. Oxford: Pergamon.

Wolkind, S. N. and Kruk, S. (1985a) From Child to Parent: Early Separation and the Transition to Parenthood. In R. Nichol (ed.) *Practical Lessons from Longitudinal Studies*.

———— (1985b) Teenage Pregnancy and Motherhood: Findings from a Longitudinal Study. *Journal of the Royal Society of Medicine* 78: 112–16.

Wolkind, S. N., Hall, F., and Pawlby, S. J. (1978) Individual Differences in Mothering Behaviour: A Combined Epidemiological and Observational Approach. In P. J. Graham (ed.) *Epidemiological Approaches in Child Psychiatry*. London: Academic Press.

Wolkind, S. N., Kruk, S., and Hall, F. (1983) The Family Research Unit Study of Women from Broken Homes. In A. White Franklin (ed.) *Family Matters: Perspectives on the Family and Social Policy*. Oxford: Pergamon.

Study 17: Pre-school Language and Behaviour Study

Graham, P., Stevenson, J., and Richman, N. (1980) Epidemiology of Language Delay in Childhood. In F A. C. Rose (ed.) *Clinical Neuroepidemiology*. Tunbridge Wells: Pitman Medical.

Richman, N. (1977) Behaviour Problems in Pre-school Children: Family and Social Factors. *British Journal of Psychiatry* 131: 523–27.

—— (1978a) Is a Behaviour Checklist for Pre-school Children Useful? In P. Graham (ed.) *Epidemiological Approaches in Child Psychiatry*. London: Academic.

—— (1978b) Short-Term Outcome of Behaviour Problems in Three-year-old Children. In P. Graham (ed.) *Epidemiological Approaches in Child Psychiatry*. London: Academic.

—— (1978c) Depression in Mothers of Young Children. *Journal of the Royal Society of Medicine* 71: 489–93.

Richman, N. and Graham, P. (1971) A Behavioural Screening Questionnaire for Use with Three-year-old Children: Preliminary Findings. *Journal of Child Psychology and Psychiatry* 12: 5–33.

Richman, N. and Stevenson, J. (1977) Language Delay: Family and Social Factors. *Acta Paediatrica Belgica* 30: 213–19.

Richman, N. and Tupling, H. (1974) A Computerized Register of Families with Children Under Five in a London Borough. *Health Trends* 6: 9–13.

Richman, N., Stevenson, J., and Graham, P. (1975) Prevalence of Behaviour Problems in Three-year-old Children: An Epidemiological Study in a London Borough. *Journal of Child Psychology and Psychiatry* 16: 222–87.

—— (1982) *Pre-school to School: A Behavioural Study*. London: Academic.

—— (1983) The Relationship between Language Development and Behaviour. In M. H. Schmidt and H. Remschmidt. (eds) *Epidemiological Approaches in Child Psychiatry II*. Stuttgart: Thieme.

—— (1985) Sex Differences in Outcome of Pre-school Behaviour Problems. In R. Nicol (ed.) *Practical Lessons from Longitudinal Studies*. London: John Wiley.

Stevenson, J. E. (1974) The Test Re-test Reliability of a Battery of Developmental Tests and a Rating Scale of Test Behaviour for Use with Three-year-old Children. (Mimeo.)

Stevenson, J. E. and Graham, P. (1982) Processes of Transmission of Deprivation in Families of Pre-school Children. In N. Madge (ed.) *Families at Risk*. London: Heinemann Educational.

Stevenson, J. E. and Richman, N. (1976) The Prevalence of Language Delay in a Population of Three-year-old Children and Its Association with General Retardation. *Developmental Medicine and Child Neurology* 18: 431–41.

Study 18: Children in Care

King, R. D., Raynes, N. V., and Tizard, J. (1971) *Patterns of Residential Care: Sociological Studies in Institutions for Handicapped Children*. London: Routledge and Kegan Paul.

Quinton, D. and Rutter, M. (1984a) Parents with Children in Care, I: Current Circumstances and Parenting Skills. *Journal of Child Psychology and Psychiatry* 25: 211–29.

—— (1984b) Parents with Children in Care, II: Intergenerational Continuities. *Journal of Child Psychology and Psychiatry* 25: 231–50.

—————— (1985a) Family Pathology and Child Disorder: A Four-year Prospective Study. In A. R. Nicol (ed.) *Longitudinal Studies in Child Psychology and Psychiatry: Practical Lessons from Research Experience.* Chichester: John Wiley.

—————— (1985b) Parenting Behaviour of Mothers Raised 'In Care'. In A. R. Nicol (ed.) *Longitudinal Studies in Child Psychology: Practical Lessons from Research Experience.* Chichester: John Wiley.

Quinton, D., Rutter, M., and Liddle, C. (1984) Institutional Rearing, Parenting Difficulties and Marital Support. *Psychological Medicine* 14: 107–204.

Rutter, M. and Quinton, D. (1981) Longitudinal Studies of Institutional Children and Children of Mentally Ill Parents (United Kingdom). In S. A. Mednick and A. E. Baert (eds) *Prospective Longitudinal Research: An Empirical Basis for the Primary Prevention of Psychosocial Disorders.* Oxford: Oxford University Press.

—————— (1984) Long-term Follow-up of Women Institutionalized in Childhood: Factors Promoting Good Functioning in Adult Life. *British Journal of Developmental Psychology* 2: 191–204.

Rutter, M., Quinton, D., and Liddle, C. (1983) Parenting in Two Generations: Looking Backwards and Looking Forwards. In N. Madge (ed.) *Families at Risk.* London: SSRC/DHSS/Heinemann Educational.

Yule, W. and Raynes, N. V. (1972) Behavioural Characteristics of Children in Residential Care in Relation to Indices of Separation. *Journal of Child Psychology and Psychiatry* 13: 249–50.

Study 19: Aberdeen Mental Subnormality Survey

Birch, H. G., Richardson, S. A., Baird, Sir D., Horobin, G., and Illsley, R. (1970) *Mental Subnormality in the Community; A Clinical and Epidemiological Study.* Baltimore, Md: Williams and Wilkins.

Koller, H., Richardson, S. A., Katz, M., and McLaren, J. (1983) Behavior Disturbance Since Childhood in a Five-year Birth Cohort of All Mentally Retarded Young Adults in a City. *American Journal of Mental Deficiency* 87, 4: 306–95.

Richardson, S. A. (1978) Careers of Mentally Retarded Young Persons: Services, Jobs and Interpersonal Relations. *American Journal of Mental Deficiency* 82, 4: 349–58.

—————— (1980) Growing Up as a Mentally Subnormal Young Person: A Follow-up Study. In S. A. Mednick and A. E. Baert (eds) *Empirical Basis for Primary Prevention: a Prospective Longitudinal Research in Europe.* Oxford: Oxford University Press.

—————— (1981) Family Characteristics Associated With Mild Mental Retardation. In M. Begab, H. C. Haywood, and H. Garber (eds) *Psychosocial Influences in Retarded Performance, vol. II: Strategies for Improving Competence.* Baltimore, Md: University Park Press.

Richardson, S. A., Koller, H., Katz, M., and McLaren, J. (1980) Seizures and Epilepsy in a Mentally Retarded Population Over the First 22 Years of Life. *Journal of Applied Research in Mental Retardation* vol. 1: 123–38.

—————— (1981) A Functional Classification of Seizures and its Distribution in a

Mentally Retarded Population. *American Journal of Mental Deficiency* 85, 5: 457–66.

———— (1983) Severity of Intellectual and Associated Functional Impairments of those Placed in Mental Retardation Services Between Ages 16 and 22: Implications for Planning Services. In K. T. Kernan, M. J. Bagab, and R. B. Edgerton (eds) *Environments and Behavior. The Adaptation of Mentally Retarded Persons.* Baltimore, Md: University Park Press.

———— (1984) Patterns of Disability in a Mentally Retarded Population Between Ages 16 and 22 Years. In J. M. Berg (ed.) *Perspectives and Progress in Mental Retardation. Vol. II: Biomedical Aspects.* Baltimore, Md: University Park Press.

Richardson, S. A., Katz, M., Koller, H., McLaren, J., and Rubinstein, B. (1979) Some Characteristics of a Population of Mentally Retarded Young Adults in a British City. *Journal of Mental Deficiency Research* 23: 278–93.

Study 20: Sheffield Problem Families

Parry, W. H., Wright, C. H., and Lunn, J. E. (1967) Sheffield Problem Families—A Follow-up Survey. *Medical Officer* 118: 130–32.

Tonge, W. L., James, D. S., and Hillam, S. M. (1975) Families Without Hope: A Controlled Study of 33 Problem Families. *British Journal of Psychiatry* 11.

Tonge, W. L., Lunn, J. E., Greathead, M., McLaren, S., and Bosanko, C. (1983) Generations of 'Problem Families' in Sheffield. In N. Madge (ed.) *Families at Risk.* London: Heinemann Educational.

Wright, C. H. and Lunn, J. E. (1971) Sheffield Problem Families: A Follow-up Study of their Sons and Daughters. *Community Medicine* 126: 301–07, 315–21.

Name index

Subject index